Acclaim for *Fall River Dreams*

"It's all about a dedicated coach who's consumed by his responsibilities and love for his kids, and driven to win. The pinnacle of many of our athletic lives is high school glory. Savor the memories and passion of Fall River's fame as you reflect on your own past."

—Bill Raftery, CBS Sports

"This book is as much about history, education, the New England economy, sociology, and modern society. It is about people first and sports second. . . . Bill Reynolds has put together a book that should become a New England classic."

—*Providence Phoenix*

"Being a personal friend of Bill Reynolds and of Coach Karam, I felt compelled to read this book as a favor. But it was I who got the treat. This is a marvelously written book about the game I love and its effect on an entire city, which encompasses decades of tradition."

—Rick Pitino, head coach, University of Kentucky basketball

"A marvelous book." — *The Boston Globe*

"Reading *Fall River Dreams* is like taking a long sip of lemonade. Bill Reynolds has given us a written soundtrack of a time and place we'd all like to visit."

—Lesley Visser, ABC and ESPN sportscaster

"Insightful . . . Reynolds is at his best when he focuses on the tempestuous relationship between Durfee's veteran coach and his rebellious star player. It's a classic generational clash. . . ."

—*Los Angeles Times Book Review*

Also by Bill Reynolds

Born to Coach with Rick Pitino
Big Hoops
Lost Summer

Fall River
DREAMS

A Team's Quest for Glory–
A Town's Search for Its Soul

Bill Reynolds

St. Martin's Griffin ✖ New York

Design by Ellen R. Sasahara

Library of Congress Cataloging-in-Publication Data

Reynolds, Bill.
    Fall River dreams : a team's quest for glory, a town's search for
its soul / Bill Reynolds.
        p. cm.
    ISBN 0-312-13491-6
    1. Durfee High School (Fall River, Mass.)—Basketball—History.
2. Fall River (Mass.)—History. I. Title.
GV885.43.D86R49   1995
706.323'62'09744—dc20   95-34017
                                                         CIP

First published by St. Martin's Press

First Griffin Edition: November 1995
10 9 8 7 6 5 4 3 2 1

*To Skippy and the 1992–1993 B.M.C. Durfee
basketball team, with memories and affection.*

Preface

ONE NIGHT in December 1991, I was coerced by a friend into attending a high school basketball game in Fall River, Massachusetts.

At the time I was a sports writer who had grown jaded by sports—worn down by the overt greed of the professional athletes I routinely cover, by the hypocrisy and exploitation that surrounds big-time sports, by the overkill that sucks most of the joy out of sports in America. I was forty-six years old, at one of those personal demarcation lines when I wondered just how much longer I could continue to care and write about sports. The last thing I wanted on a night off was to watch a high school basketball game.

I knew almost nothing about Fall River. Once upon a time there, Lizzie Borden took an axe and gave her mother forty whacks and when she saw what she had done she gave her father forty-one. Or so the nursery rhyme had taught me.

I had grown up in a Rhode Island suburb, about fifteen miles away, but there never had been any occasion to go to Fall River as a child, no reason to even think about it. Fall River was just a place we drove through on the way to Cape Cod, a tired little city with a lot of old gray stone mills that stood like monuments from another time. Fall River was, quite simply, a euphemism for the end of the world. I knew that Fall River's high school, B. M. C. Durfee, always had good basketball teams and that they were coached by a Damon Runyon character named Skip Karam, but they rarely played against Rhode Island schools and I had paid no attention to them.

A few years before 1991, quite by accident, I had gone to a banquet honoring a state championship Durfee team. Over two thousand people had attended, including the Fall River mayor and all the city's politicians. Rick Pitino, then the coach of the New York Knicks, had been the main speaker. There had been an awards ceremony that lasted an hour, complete with endless gifts for the players that ranged from the obligatory jackets, to rings, to tanning salon coupons, to fitness center memberships, to restaurant coupons, to a trip to Disney World. Oh, yeah: The coach also got a new car. It was the kind of attention an NCAA champion doesn't receive, and I remember coming back to the office and telling everyone how bizarre it had been. But I soon forgot about it, once again immersed in writing four sports columns a week for the *Providence Journal-Bulletin*.

But when I walked into the gym in December 1991 it was as if I had stepped into a time warp, thrown back to some lost day thirty years ago, when high school sports were important. Roughly three thousand people were packed in the Durfee gym, an astounding number for a high school basketball game in the Northeast. Most of the fans were adults, many over forty-five. It instantly reminded me of the early sixties, before the Beatles and long hair and the birth of the counterculture and all the other late-sixties events that changed America forever, when I played high school basketball and thought it was the only thing I would ever do. The sense of urgency. The buzz of the crowd. The frenzied passion of the players. Everything.

I was hooked, the perfect antidote to a case of midcareer

crisis, and in the winter of 1992 Durfee basketball games became my secret passion. I would make the half-hour drive on Interstate 195 from Providence to Fall River, cross the Braga Bridge as if leaving my present life behind, and walk into the field house at Durfee. It was 1962 again and the most important thing in my world was whether or not my jump shot went in.

At the time I saw it as my own little obsession, similar to periodically driving down the street where you grew up, but I soon realized how unique Durfee basketball actually is. How their games have been on the radio for fifty years. How they've only had two coaches in over five decades. How the official scorer has been doing their games since 1945. How when Durfee plays neighboring New Bedford the gym seems like kindling just waiting for a match, full of police, frenzy, hostility, wild joy. How Durfee has the best basketball tradition of any high school in New England.

One night, simply making conversation during halftime, I asked an older guy which had been the best all-time Durfee team.

"I can't answer that," he said.

"Why not?" I asked.

"Because I've only seen every team since 1962," he replied.

Some days, before a game, I would simply ride around Fall River, past the closed mills, the most visible symbol of the city's decline. Fall River still has an Old World quality to it, forming a triangle with Cape Cod and Boston, a place that time seems to have forgotten. It's not suburban Boston. It's not the Cape. It's not even New Bedford, the site of *Moby Dick*, which has a fishing industry and a small, gentrified waterfront area.

Fall River has virtually no visible means of support. Twenty years ago it had the highest dropout rate of any school system in America. The unemployment rate hovers at about sixteen percent, over twice the national average. Michael Dukakis's "Massachusetts Miracle" never made it to Fall River. The only waterfront development has essentially been a bust, a grim parody of what it was supposed to be.

"Lizzie sure left her legacy on this place," a Durfee teacher once said to me.

Lizzie.

On a sultry summer day in 1892, Lizzie Borden supposedly took an axe to her parents and became part of American folklore. There are some in Fall River who think it was the city's original sin. Those grisly murders seem to hang over the city even now, one hundred years later. A restaurant in the city is called Lizzie's. In August 1992 there was a four-day "Lizzie Festival," with a symposium that attracted people from around the country, and thousands of people that peered through the windows of the murder house.

"How much do you know about Lizzie Borden?" I asked one of the Durfee players.

He looked at me strangely. "You can't grow up here and not know about Lizzie Borden," he said. "It's the biggest thing that ever happened around here."

It seemed like a strange image for a city.

One night, in that winter of 1992, one of the best players in Fall River's long basketball history had sat in the front row at a game, there to see his brother, who was the latest hero. The older brother was home from college, just three years after he'd starred for Durfee, one of the princes of the city. Now he looked forlorn, a little lost.

"I knew when I looked at him during his last game it would never be as good for him again," his aunt told me. "It couldn't be."

I knew then that I wanted to write about high school basketball and this city. I wanted to get inside a season, inside the cheers and the tradition. To follow someone who has coached high school basketball for over thirty years, and who grew up in Fall River. To find out what it's like to play high school basketball in a town where many adults treat it like some family heirloom. What were the kids' lives like? What did they study? What did they think about such things as race and poverty, Hillary Clinton and problems in the Gulf, the world outside Fall River? What did they dream?

So in November 1992 I set out to chronicle the upcoming season. I went to the practices. I sat in the locker room before games, after games. I rode the school bus to away games. I went to class with some of the kids. I hung out in the corridors and the cafeteria. I stayed around after practice and shot games of HORSE with them. I gave them rides home.

From the beginning I had two advantages. As a sports columnist at a paper read in Fall River, I had a certain status. More importantly, I wasn't their teacher. I wasn't their coach. I certainly wasn't their parent. I didn't judge them, or discipline them, or do much of anything except laugh when they did something funny or roll my eyes when they did something particularly sophomoric. And I was always there, eventually part of the fabric, no longer a novelty, no longer someone they had to behave for.

One day early in the season a kid said something disparaging about a cheerleader, looked over and realized I'd heard it, then quickly shrugged and said, "Hey, if you're going to be around us all the time, you're going to see it all anyhow."

That was my intention: to see it all.

All of us—if we were to be eavesdropped upon for a year—would have days we wouldn't want recorded, moments best forgotten. Still, there was never a time when Durfee's head coach Skip Karam said "Don't write this" or tried to censor me in any way. The players were remarkably candid, rarely attempting to smooth over rough spots or present things in a more favorable light. Some of this candor, of course, came from familiarity; a book is a long process, and as the season wore on, this book to them became a vague thing that would appear in some undetermined future. Yet there is a definite lack of pretense in Fall River, a feeling that this is the way we are, warts and all, take it or leave it.

"You aren't going to make us out to be like jerks, are you?" a kid named Jeff Caron asked me in practice one day.

"I'm going to make you out to be what you are," I quipped.

Caron looked around at his teammates and laughed. "That's what I said."

In the beginning of the project I had envisioned myself as an objective reporter, someone who would look upon all that he saw and write it all down with a cold, professional detachment. That perspective didn't last very long. By the first game I was hoping Durfee would win, and I soon found myself sharing in their triumphs, suffering through the losses, more emotionally involved with a basketball season than I'd been since I last played myself, nearly a quarter of a century earlier.

One night, moments after a big game had ended, a fight broke out right in front of the Durfee bench. The players had just gotten through the traditional postgame handshake when an opposing fan supposedly pushed Skip Karam. At that point Karam's twenty-five-year-old son had jumped on the back of the fan and things quickly erupted, spontaneous combustion, an emotional catharsis full of bodies on the floor, punches, scuffling, cops jumping into crowds of people trying to break it up, a two- or three-minute melee with the potential to escalate into something much larger.

I had been standing on the periphery of it, both trying to protect myself and entranced at how quickly things had gotten out of control, when Al Herren, the father of Durfee's star player and a state representative, looked at me and said with a laugh, "Welcome to Fall River."

Welcome to Fall River.

Acknowledgments

I FEEL EXTREMELY FORTUNATE to have been able to do this book, thus owe a debt to a number of people.

David Vigliano, who has been my agent for four books now, saw the possibilities back in the early beginning. George Witte at St. Martin's Press not only believed in the idea, but throughout the editing process he had the same vision of the book that I did, and always guided it with skill and insight. May all writers be so fortunate.

As always, Wayne Worcester provided both support and another set of eyes that always seem to point me in the right direction. Liz Abbott no doubt heard all the stories too many times, but she was always there, always supportive, and eventually came to realize that when she couldn't locate me I was invariably in Fall River. Dave Bloss, my boss at the *Providence Journal*, is always supportive and understanding and deserves a public thank you.

In a sense my research on this book started thirty years ago when I was in high school in Rhode Island and had a basketball coach named Tom Burns, who had grown up in Fall River and used to tell me about Durfee basketball. Reconnecting with him after so many years was an unexpected pleasure.

Then there were the numerous people in Fall River who always made me feel comfortable and went out of their way to be helpful. In the course of two years I talked to over a hundred people, too numerous to mention, but some of them who helped shape this book in one way or the other are Mitch Lown, Abe White, Fran Desmairas, Paul Connors, Father Jay Maddock, Alex Stylos, Jim Manley, Charley Carey, Mary Carey, Mike Viera, Julie Kitchen, Skippy Karam, Jr., Greg Ford, Nancy Ford, Al Attar, Bernie Sullivan, Ronnie Fahey, Tom Burke, Phil Silvia, Rick Caron, Robert Karam, Joe Callahan, Jerry Reed, Annie Palumbo, Chuckie Moniz, Ronny Berube, "The Hawk," "Fester," "Galv," "Johnny B." and all the old guys who sit in the first row who always made going to the Durfee games such a treat.

Special thanks to Bob Dempsey, whose insight and perspective was always appreciated, and the Herrens, who invited me into their lives.

I also benefitted from several books that deal with Lizzie Borden and Fall River history in various ways, specifically *A Private Disgrace* by Victoria Lincoln, David Kent's *Forty Whacks*, Judith Boss's *Fall River: A Pictorial History*, and *Mortal Remains* by Henry Scammell. And for the definitive word on Fall River history I found no better books than the *Victorian Vistas* series by Phil Silvia.

But this book never could have been written without the kids on the team who included me in a season I'll always treasure. They did not ask to have their lives intruded upon, their ambitions and dreams chronicled, and I was always aware that, as Joan Didion once supposedly said, writers are always ripping someone off. I got to know some more than others, but they all have a piece of my heart.

Most of all, a special mention to Skip Karam. He couldn't have been any better. He was open, honest, and always made me feel a part of things. He has my enduring thanks.

Chapter

1

SKIPPY WAS NOT HAPPY.

Two yellow school buses were waiting in the parking lot when Thomas "Skip" Karam, whom everyone calls "Skippy," came walking toward the front door of the Luke Urban Field House. On his left, high on the mud-brown wall of the adjacent building, big letters said B. M. C. DURFEE HIGH SCHOOL OF FALL RIVER. In front of him was the entrance to the field house, named after his old high school coach, though missing letters made the name incomprehensible.

Karam wore a camel-colored cashmere overcoat, dark slacks, and tasseled loafers. His gray hair, thinning on top, was combed across his head. At five-foot-eight, still in decent shape nearing 58, he was only a few pounds removed from when he had been a great guard for the 1952 Durfee "Hilltoppers," when all he knew about the future was that he didn't want to end up in one of the city's 140 textile mills. He pulled his collar up against the late afternoon chill, his face etched in a frown.

He was frowning because the cheerleaders were milling around one of the buses, and he'd coached long enough to know that cheerleaders and away games are a potential distraction. He was frowning because he didn't see the car of his assistant coach Bob Dempsey in the parking lot, and here it was another year, and it seemed Dempsey always was the last to arrive. He was frowning because he had come to hate the bus rides, all those late-night rides down through the years as the kids' radio music had changed from rock 'n' roll to acid rock to heavy metal to punk to funk to rap, unlistenable noise.

Most of all, he frowned because this was the day of the first game, and on game days the anxiety bloated in his stomach early in the morning. That feeling had started in his first year, 1961, when Kennedy was in the White House and Skippy was the new Durfee basketball coach. He was following Lake Urban, Lukey, a tiny martinet of a man who had coached basketball and football and baseball for twenty years, a man larger than life in Fall River, this tired old textile city in southeastern Massachusetts, a region that had one of the highest unemployment rates in the country. Skippy had been twenty-six in 1961, and those first years were trials. Every time he won, he'd hear that he was winning with Lukey's kids, that he hadn't proved anything yet. It only made the pressure worse. But in those first few years, when the weight of Urban perched on his shoulders, he figured he'd eventually throw it off.

He never did. If anything, it only got heavier. By the time this game actually began, Skippy would be off in some private hell, his insides churning, the fear of losing so powerful that it overshadowed everything else. He had won five state titles, numerous sectional titles, suffered only one losing season in thirty-two years, is one of the most successful high-school coaches in Massachusetts history. In 1991, he had won his six hundredth high school game. He long ago became Durfee basketball, and most of the kids who play for him now grew up going to his summer camp, hearing all the stories about his toughness, his sarcasm, his profanity, his legend that's firmly ingrained in the city.

And local legend he is.

In fact, the Durfee court is named for him, the "Thomas 'Skip' Karam Basketball Court." He has come a long way from his childhood in Fall River in the 1940s, the son of a Lebanese immigrant. His father worked in the mills every day of his adult life, and made Skippy work there summers so the boy could swelter in them, a motivational tool for his oldest son to do something different with his life.

Skippy had grown up watching the great Durfee teams of the late forties, going to games with his father, who loved sports. He had starred as a guard in the 1950s, playing under Urban's firm hand. After graduating, he had used basketball to attend Providence College, and then returned to Fall River as a teacher-coach, perhaps because he had seen the reverence with which Urban was held in the city.

But, in many ways, nothing has changed for Karam since those early years of his coaching career. Losing is still a form of death. Criticism resurrects old hurts, hidden insecurities. He still feels he constantly has to prove himself, even after all these years. Long ago he became a victim of his own success, to the point that any season that doesn't end deep into the state tournament is now viewed by Fall River as a failure. This season would be no different.

Last year Durfee lost in the finals of the sectionals, one game away from going to Boston Garden and the semifinals of the state tournament. It was like most Durfee teams, small, with little depth, full of overachieving kids as tough and gritty as the city that raised them. The team really shouldn't have won as many games as it did, but when it had lost, on a last-second, desperation shot in overtime, all that triumph was forgotten. It was merely another team that didn't win, a team whose failure would be buried beneath the legends of the state championship teams, the large red banners with the black lettering staring down from the gym walls, at once inspiring and accusatory. *We won; why didn't you?*

So, as he walked to the field house on this late afternoon in early December, just a month away from being fifty-eight years old and about to start another season, Skippy Karam displayed his usual pregame face.

"Uh-oh," said Chris Herren, who was standing with the other players in the lobby. "Mr. Karam's in a bad mood."

Herren wore a white cap on his head, turned backward. His baggy dungarees hung so low on his hips it seemed inevitable they would eventually fall down. On his feet were black sneakers, the style of the day. He is six-foot-two, roughly two hundred pounds, with brown hair that he wears slicked back when he plays. He walks with a pronounced slouch, the form of contemporary urban expression known for its exaggerated knee dip, walks with the easy assurance of someone comfortable with his body. He also has the charisma of all great high school athletes; watching him play, with his seventeen-year-old swagger and his young James Dean looks, you understand what it means to be a high school hero, to live your life inside the bubble of fame. He is a star in his own movie and he knows it. Yet there's a self-consciousness about him too, a kid's vulnerability, as if he knows he's always the center of attention and, at times, is uncomfortable with that.

He is only a junior, but already he's one of the top high school players in the East, receiving recruiting letters from many of the major colleges. He spent the summer going to national showcase basketball camps and playing in AAU tournaments, places where the best high school kids are paraded in front of college coaches like show cattle. He is one of the most talented players in decades to come out of southeastern Massachusetts, yet he and Karam have an uneasy love-hate, stern father–rebellious son relationship. In the first week of practice Karam threw him out twice, believing he wasn't working hard enough. The first time, Herren had gone to a phone booth and called his mother. He was crying on the phone, telling his mother he couldn't play for

Mr. Karam anymore, that he wanted to quit the team, leave Durfee, and maybe go to a prep school somewhere. Then he saw that his friend Peter Pavao also had been thrown out and he began feeling better. That episode had blown over, but the tension between the two remained.

One day last week Herren had told me, "He's losing it. I can't play for him anymore. He's driving me crazy."

Minutes later, Karam had come over to me and said, "Chrissie's driving me crazy. He won't listen to me. He's always fighting me."

The past threatened to overwhelm both of them. Chris Herren might just have the best bloodlines of any Durfee basketball player ever, as if he had been created in some science class laboratory deep in the basement of the high school. His father Al had captained the 1970 team, and one uncle also played for that team. Another older uncle was on one of Karam's first Durfee teams, and still another played under Urban in the late fifties. His grandfather had been a Durfee sports star. His mother and grandmother were Durfee cheerleaders, his aunt was a majorette. His older brother Michael is Durfee's all-time scoring leader, and when Michael graduated in 1989 he had won back-to-back state titles, forty-six straight games, and was a dominating presence on and off the court. This is the baggage that Chris Herren carries, and it's heavy. He is not just another high school junior trying to find his own identity. Even without the basketball legacy, being the son of a state representative would be its own form of pressure. There are HERREN signs on cars all over the city, a name that's always visible.

He knows that not only is he compared to his brother, but his team is compared to his brother's team. He knows that the only way his team can measure up is to win two state titles too, that anything less will be viewed as a failure. When Durfee's season had ended last year, on that last-second desperation shot, he had taken his shirt off, walked around the court shirtless, both hands on his head, his eyes glassy.

Later, he had said he didn't remember doing it, that it all had been a daze, a soundless movie that passed before his eyes.

But he had been only a sophomore then, and though he had been the best player, making the Boston *Herald*'s "Dream Team," named "All-Scholastic" by the Boston *Globe*, he never truly felt it had been *his* team. There had been three seniors, and in many ways he had acquiesced to them.

Now it was *his* team.

The players slouched in the lobby, holding their traveling bags. Once upon a time, back in the sixties, the Durfee players had conformed to an unofficial dress code for away games. No more. Now they wear the baggy clothes of high school kids in the early nineties, dungarees, sweatshirts with the names of professional athletic teams, hats.

"Chrissie, nice of you to get dressed up for the trip," Karam said.

Herren wasn't fazed. He knew it was Mr. Karam just being Mr. Karam. It's a lesson he learned early, for he can't remember when he didn't know Mr. Karam. He first attended Karam's summer basketball camp when he was in the third grade. He was afraid of him then. He would hear his voice that seemed it could cut through glass and he would cringe. Even when his brother Michael was playing and Chris would go to the games, he avoided Karam.

Then came the first day of practice in the ninth grade. He knew Karam knew who he was. How could he not? Not only was he Michael's brother, but the word was already out around the city that Chris Herren was going to be the next great Durfee player, and Skippy always knows which players are coming up, even if he no longer watches the young kids' Milliken League games the way he once did. So there was Chris at his first practice and at one point, during a break, he had his hands in the waistband of his shorts, turning to watch the girls' team practice on the adjoining court. Suddenly, without warning, a ball hit him in the back of the head.

"Stop playing with yourself and get over here," Karam had yelled.

Last year, when Herren had been a sophomore, he scored twenty-seven points in the first half against a bad team. Early in the second half he had gotten the ball on a break, with a teammate in front of him for an easy layup. Instead of giving the ball to him, he chose to go in for the crowd-pleasing dunk, because he knew his friends in the stands were waiting for him to dunk the ball, like Michael Jordan or Charles Barkley or Shaquille O'Neal on television of commercials, the only validation of true greatness. But the ball hit the back of the rim and bounced high into the air, as a hush fell over the gym.

"You asshole," yelled Karam, the words reverberating through the quiet arena.

So now Herren said nothing, put a Walkman on his head, and prepared to board the bus.

"Chrissie, you got to play defense tonight," said Karam, not noticing the Walkman.

Herren didn't respond.

"Don't walk away when I talk to you," said Karam.

Suddenly he realized Herren couldn't hear him.

"Jesus Christ," he yelled in disgust. "How can I talk to you with that damn thing on?"

Herren took it off, but Karam walked away. "Do you believe these kids?" Karam asked no one in particular.

Once he would have made an issue out of it. No more. There have been too many battles through the years, too many changes. But it bothers him, for he knows once upon a time he wouldn't have allowed it. That's what wears on him now in coaching, what seems to make it more difficult the longer he continues. It's not the games. It's not the practices. It's not the pressure. It's not even the bus rides, though Lord knows he's had enough of them to last a lifetime. It's the little things, the way the kids dress, the lack of standards, the lack of fundamentals when it comes to playing basketball, the dissolution of the many details that used to give everything its structure.

It's what bothers him so much about Herren, the feeling that he allows him to get away with rebellions that his players never used to get away with. Little things. Like how Herren will often talk back to him. Not in any overt, dramatic way. But always something, some remark, some need to get the last word in.

He believes Herren is squandering his talent, that he doesn't work hard enough in practice, doesn't try to improve his weaknesses. That he's content to coast on his great natural ability. He thinks he drinks too much on weekends—that all his players drink too much—and that Herren has gained some bad weight, weight that affects his quickness. He wants him to work harder on his jump shot, specifically on the mechanics of it, for he knows that if Herren is ever going to be the big-time college player he has the potential to become, he's going to have to consistently make jump shots, not just continually take the ball to the basket as he does now, overpowering kids not as athletic as he is. Karam wants him to practice his free throws more, for Herren too often struggles af the foul line, is inconsistent at best, downright bad at worst. Karam is forever telling Herren this, but feels the kid doesn't listen to him, doesn't believe it.

"He's only hurting himself," he says, whenever someone mentions Herren to him. "He won't listen to anybody. He's only hurting himself."

Karam also knows he's not as strict as he once was, that both the years and the times have mellowed him. Back when he first began coaching, he used to run a very structured, patterned offense, the kind he had learned playing for Urban. That had changed as basketball changed, so that now the players have much more freedom, especially on offense. And especially Herren, who generally can do whatever he wants. Yet there will be times when a kid will throw up some crazy shot he saw Michael Jordan do on television, or throw some look-away pass he saw Magic Johnson make, and Skippy will throw up his hands in disgust, upset at the basketball sacrilege and at himself for creating the climate that allows this to happen.

But he is still old-school, in the tradition of those coaches who now seem mostly to belong to some other era, dictatorial, authoritative, larger than life, their mystique inviolate. He still measures his players against perfection. It's the way he learned the game, and for all the changes and all the years, it's still his frame of reference.

"I want to see things done right," he had told a reporter last year after he'd won his six hundredth game. "Perfection. I get irritated when that perfection is not there, whether the desire is not there or whether a 100 percent effort is not there. That bothers me. I don't like carelessness."

It is not hyperbole.

Practices are hard, dogmatic. Karam seems to have three eyes. He sees everything, usually prowling the court in a black and red warm-up suit, the school colors, a scowl on his face. Plays are run over and over again. Then over and over again some more. There is a certain tension at practice that's almost palpable. Failure is not tolerated. He berates anyone who makes stupid mistakes, or who he thinks is not playing hard enough, or doesn't care enough. His anger seems always there, just beneath the surface, ready to boil over at a moment's notice, sparing no one. One time, when his son Skip, Jr., played for him, he grabbed the boy by the throat in practice. When his son gave him a dirty look, he said, "Go home and complain to your mother."

And the players take it. Karam yells and they say nothing. He criticizes them. They say nothing. He belittles them. They say nothing. They all have grown up hearing the Skippy stories, so that when it starts happening to them, they've been prepped. But for all their macho posturing and locker room bravado, they are afraid of him. This is just the way it is at Durfee, the way it's always been.

Not that they always like it.

Sometimes Karam yells during practice and Jeff Caron, the other returning starter from last year's team, can feel himself tightening up, feel the anger start to rise. His mother is always reminding him not to talk back to Mr. Karam, to calm down.

"I love Mr. Karam," he said one day during practice. "He's a wicked nice guy. But I hate him out here."

"He's a bitch," said Herren, who was standing nearby. "Why does he have to be such a bitch?"

Karam got on the school bus and sat in the first seat. Several cheerleaders, in their skimpy white uniforms with the red and black trim, were in the middle of the bus. The players lounged in the back. Some indecipherable rap song reverberated through the bus.

"Turn the music off," he yelled.

He settled into his seat. Across the aisle from him was seventy-eight-year-old Abe White, who has been scoring Durfee games for over fifty years, a short, kindly man who looks as if he just stepped off some old *Saturday Evening Post* cover.

Bob Dempsey, his assistant coach, was a seat behind him, eating a tuna grinder. Now forty-four, he had been a great guard for Skippy in the mid-sixties, gifted enough to win a scholarship to the University of Massachusetts, where he had been a teammate of Julius Erving's. He's been the jayvee coach for eight years, long enough to become Karam's coaching alter ego, soothing the bruised feelings and fragile psyches caused by Karam's hard-edged coaching style. The players listen to Dempsey, for they know that he's been there too, has also felt the brunt of Karam's wrath.

"See the difference between the head coach and the assistant?" Karam said, motioning toward Dempsey's sandwich.

It's a standing joke between them, namely that the assistant coach has no pressure on him, thus can sit and eat a tuna grinder with not a care in the world.

The irony is that Dempsey would love to be the head coach, sitting here in the bus with the anxiety building in the pit of his stomach. He began as Skippy's assistant, thinking that it would only be a few years before Skippy would retire and give the team to him. Skippy had hinted about retiring, for he didn't particularly want to coach his son, Skippy, Jr. He had stayed, though, and Dempsey has come to feel that Skippy will always stay, that coaching Durfee is something he will never walk away from easily.

There also are times Dempsey feels that maybe it might be better not to follow Skippy at Durfee, that following Skippy will be like trying to follow John Wooden at UCLA, that it will be impossible for anyone to follow him and survive. He had come close to quitting this year, but now he was here, set to begin another year, the loyal assistant, someone who knows and understands Karam as well as anyone.

It was late afternoon, the sky a thickening gray, the smell of snow in the air. Another bus, with jayvee players and cheerleaders, was behind them.

"I don't believe this shit," Karam said, looking back toward the cheerleaders. "I wanted the cheerleaders on the other bus, but they all started crying when they found out. So here they are."

He shook his head in disgust, one further lament for a changing world.

But he can't keep thinking about cheerleaders. The game tonight is with Duxbury, a suburban town just a few miles from Plymouth Rock, on the rocky coast between Boston and Cape Cod. They are a Division II team, as opposed to Durfee's Division I status, and in most years this would be considered a breather for Durfee. Not tonight. Duxbury is led by the Curley brothers, six-ten Mickey and six-five Matty, and are rated one of the top teams in Massachusetts. They are the younger brothers of Billy Curley, the Boston College star, and their presence makes this a very difficult opener for Durfee.

Karam worries that his team isn't ready.

He's had a few preseason scrimmages with other teams, and the Jamboree four nights earlier, when six Massachusetts high school teams play one half each, but with the exception of Herren and Caron, he doesn't know what to expect from anyone. As usual, he has a team with little height, his two biggest kids—Dan Callahan and John Jones—being only six-four. In his thirty-two years at Durfee he's only had a handful of kids who could be called big, never has coached a great big man.

Peter Pavao is a senior, a five-ten shooter, who played on the varsity in the ninth grade, thanks primarily to his reputation as an outstanding player in the Milliken League. Yet he's never had any success as a varsity player. Last year he functioned as the seventh man, but often seemed to wilt when he came into games, nervous and tentative. There is the consensus among the team that Pavao cannot play for Skippy, that of all the kids on the team, Skippy's yelling bothers him the most. He is of Portuguese ancestry, dark hair, swarthy, with dark, haunted eyes that give him the look of a wounded animal when Skippy yells at him. He will start at one forward.

Dan Callahan is a junior, a thin kid with dark hair and a long, narrow face, and Skippy has been all over him in preseason practice. He has been trying to make the big jump from the jayvees to a starter, and Karam wants him to get tougher, more assertive. "Over there, Callahan. . . . Rebound, Callahan. . . . You'd better get tough, Callahan. . . . What are you doing, Callahan?" This has been the soundtrack to the season so far, all in Karam's loud, piercing voice, a voice that all the players have come to dread, especially when it's directed at them.

Ironically, one of Karam's brothers is married to Callahan's aunt, so Callahan and Karam are almost family. No matter. Callahan is one of the prime whipping boys.

"Callahan," Skippy asked one day, when he thought his young center had been particularly unassertive. "Did your parents have any sons?"

Callahan already is accustomed to Karam's yelling. He had been around it last year on the jayvee team, so he knows that's just the way it is if you play for Durfee. On the first day of varsity practice Karam had run over, put his face in Callahan's, and screamed, "Callahan, I'm going to kill you this year." For an instant Callahan had been afraid, but the fear had quickly subsided, and Karam's anger had quickly turned to someone else. Callahan knows he's going to play, for even though Karam yells at him to be tougher, sometimes calls him "Liz," which is his sister's name, he's always had him on the first team. So Callahan has learned to let the yelling roll off his back, even laughs inwardly sometimes when Karam gets a good one-liner off at someone else's expense.

John Jones had been penciled in to start, mainly because he had been the sixth man last year. But he hadn't played on Durfee's summer league team. Instead, he had spent the summer surfing, growing his blond hair long. Unlike the other players, who were distinctly urban in style, he seemed like some leftover from the early seventies counterculture. His life wasn't centered around basketball. He recently had turned himself into a good student. He talked of one day going to Vermont and maybe being an artist. Many of his teammates don't understand him, calling him a "burnout," questioning his desire.

"It takes balls to play inside," Skippy had said to both Callahan and Jones one day, pointing to his crotch. "Jonesy, you've got one, and Callahan, you've got none."

But Jones had sprained his ankle in practice the day before, and senior Mike Cioe, another jayvee last year, will take his place. Burly and blond, with a skinhead haircut,

Cioe stands only about six-one, has few skills, but is tough and will dive on the floor at a moment's notice. A typical Fall River kid, with one exception. Last year his girlfriend, who is black, got pregnant, and now he has a daughter.

Kevin Mikolazyk will be a reserve guard. He is a senior, only five-seven with short brown hair on top of a long forehead. Last year he played on the junior varsity team. Once, he too had harbored big basketball dreams, but in the ninth grade he began realizing his fate; he would not grow any more. The dreams were stashed in some childhood footlocker, alongside the toys he'd outgrown. In its place he's become the court jester, living for weekend parties, for drinking and hanging out with his friends, his face often stamped in a mischievous smirk, as if he knows some secret you don't. Everyone has taken to calling him "Igor," or "Gore" for short, a nickname that was started by Michael Herren. As Mikolazyk says, "When Michael starts calling you something, it sticks and there's nothing you can do about it."

Yet this season has become vitally important to him, for he knows this is his last chance, that he will never play serious basketball again.

The only other kid with any size is Shawn Thames, a gangly six-three sophomore. He is the only black player on the varsity, part of the first wave of black kids who are moving into the city to live in Fall River's public housing, the first significant number of blacks in a city that's traditionally had almost none. For all of Durfee's great basketball teams over the past fifty years, there only has been one great black player, and he played in the sixties.

Skippy has no idea what to expect of Thames. He had missed the second day of practice and when Karam had inquired why, Thames had said he lived on the other side of the city and wasn't going to come to practice unless he could get a ride home. As Skippy had looked at him in disbelief, the exchange reflected one more example of how Fall River was changing, Durfee basketball was changing, and there wasn't a whole lot Skippy could do about it.

It is not a big team. It's not an experienced team, with only two players who played a lot last year. And Caron hurt his foot two days ago, has been soaking it in ice ever since, is questionable to play.

Yet the perception around the city is it's a team that can compete for the state title, largely because Herren and Caron generally are considered the best backcourt in Massachusetts, and doesn't Skippy always seem to find a way to get kids to play better than they are?

The driver closed the door, the air hissing, then started the engine, its loud drone muffling the conversation. The bus pulled out of the parking lot, took a right on Elsbree Street, went past Papa Gino's and the side entrance to the small shopping mall, then a left onto President Avenue and into the rotary that leads to the entrance to Route 24, the highway to Boston.

The bus traveled up Route 24, heading toward Route 128, the beltway that circles Boston. Past Taunton, a small city with a new shopping mall, its sign high above the highway a contemporary siren song. Past the sign to the Taunton-Raynham Dog Track, where many Fall River residents have gone for years to buy their little cardboard dreams. Past Brockton, the small city once known for making shoes, then for boxing champions Rocky Marciano and Marvelous Marvin Hagler. Despite the cities, however, much of this part of southeastern Massachusetts is surprisingly rural, full of fields and scrub pine, and there are stretches of the highway when you'd never know that you are only half an hour or so from Boston.

Karam leaned back in his seat, eyes closed. There are times like this, on some endless bus ride, worried about the cheerleaders on the bus and the stupid Walkmans on the kids' heads, that he wonders why he keeps coaching.

He wonders whether his relationship with his own son would be better today if he hadn't spent so many years coaching other people's kids. He wonders if he would have been better off if years ago he had left the security blanket of Fall River and gone off to coach in college somewhere, and what would have happened. Wonders about the road not taken.

He tried once. It was in the early seventies, and he'd been coaching at Durfee for roughly ten years. In his mid-thirties, still a young man, he was still at an age when it was possible to dream about being a college coach. He regularly attended coaching clinics then, and he'd see the big-name college coaches, listened to them talk about their philosophies, their strategies, and he wondered how he'd stack up. He already had found success at Durfee, had won a state title, and he looked into the future and couldn't see himself coaching at Durfee forever.

He had spent a couple of summers working the Providence College basketball camp then, a camp run by Dave Gavitt, then the PC coach. An assistant's job to Gavitt was open. One of the top basketball schools in the East, Providence was about to start playing in a new thirteen-thousand-seat downtown civic arena, one of the first of its kind in the Northeast. And since Providence, Rhode Island, was about a half hour from Fall River, Karam wouldn't have needed to move, wouldn't have had to uproot his wife and three young children. He also felt he got along well with Gavitt. So he mulled it over and over, finally decided to apply for the job. He didn't get it. He never applied for another one.

It was quiet inside the bus, the muffled conversations drowned out by the drone of the engine. A procession of rush-hour commuter headlights passed in the other direction as the late afternoon started turning into early evening. The bus went south on 128, then south again on route 3, past the sprawling Braintree Mall and the exits to the suburban towns of the South Shore. Route 3 is the highway from Boston to the Cape, and Duxbury is near Plymouth, and the Sagamore Bridge, the gate way to the mid-Cape. The bus had been going for over an hour now, and Skippy was getting restless.

"I didn't know it was this far," he said. "But I needed the game."

For years Durfee was in the old Bristol County League and played against the neighboring towns, rivalries that had gone on for decades. Then, almost one by one, worn down by too many defeats and controversies, and the fact that Durfee was a much bigger school, many of the schools refused to continue in the same basketball league with Durfee. They would play Durfee in other sports, but not basketball. The result was the formation of the so-called "Big Three," a league comprised of Durfee and schools from the two other biggest cities in the region, New Bedford and Brockton. So now Karam, also Durfee's athletic director, has to scrounge for games, creating a hodgepodge schedule that makes little sense geographically and is a source of continual frustration.

The bus pulled off an exit, wove through the center of a small suburban town with cute little colonial signs on the buildings. Lights glowed from houses that were nestled in picturesquely bare trees, houses that sat on quiet, peaceful streets. Some displayed Christmas lights, the promise of seasonal warmth. It all seemed a long way from Fall River. The bus eventually pulled in front of an elementary school before the driver realized he was lost.

"I shouldn't be surprised," Karam said resignedly. "I've been getting lost for thirty years."

Duxbury has a medium-sized gym for a suburban Massachusetts high school, direct from Central Casting. Wooden bleachers on both sides, plus under one of the baskets. Green banners all over the cinder-blocked walls, symbols of championship seasons.

The team sat in a small locker room, between pale institutional walls. They were dressed in their red uniforms with the black trim, DURFEE stitched on the front of the jerseys and FR in black on both sides of the pants. In the late seventies, when the new high school was built, there had been a move to change the name to Fall River High School, but it had failed. Now the one concession is the "FR" on the side of the uniform.

Herren stood in front of the mirror slicking back his hair with his hands. The more he did it the more determined he looked, his face set. He wore number 24, as both his brother and father had done before him, his red shorts baggy and worn as low on his hips as he could get away with, and when he looked around the locker room at his teammates, he knew, for the first time, that it really was *his* team.

He had grown up with virtually all of them, had played in the Milliken League with them since he was seven years old. They had been on all-star teams together when they were kids, traveling around New England to tournaments, where they had lost one game in four years.

Most of them were his closest friends. Kevin Mikolazyk had virtually grown up in his house, since first grade when Herren used to beat him up in school. Peter Pavao, who had played with him in the Fall River youth leagues, once rivalled him in athletic potential. Danny Callahan he had known all his life, and Peter Suneson lived just up the street in the house where the basement had become a sort of clubhouse where they often hung out.

And Jeff.

Caron had grown up in Westport, a rural resort town on the Atlantic Ocean only a few miles away, but he too had played in all the Fall River youth leagues, and used to sleep at Herren's house when they were kids. They always had appeared on the all-star teams together, had been playing basketball together since they were seven years old. His parents had gone to Durfee with Jeff's mother. Jeff always had been a good player, and Herren believed the Carons had moved back to Fall River so that Jeff could play at Durfee. But in junior high school the boys had had sort of a falling out, had become rivals in a way. Jeff hadn't hung out with Herren and his friends, and there were times in the corridor when they would bump each other, circle each other like alley cats. When they played junior high basketball together, they would rarely pass the ball to each other.

Last year Chris and Jeff had been the only two sophomores to start, and Jeff had had a great year. On virtually any other team he would have been all but lionized as one of the best sophomores in years, yet at Durfee he was overshadowed by Herren. Herren was quicker, flashier, jumped better. Caron was a better shooter. In a sense they had complemented each other well, Herren taking the ball to the basket, Jeff hitting the perimeter shots.

They also respected each other. Herren admired the way Caron never backed down from anyone who tried to give him shit in school, how he would fight if he had to. Caron was continually amazed at what Herren would say to anybody—girls, teachers, Mr. Karam, anyone.

Like the time in November when Karam had taken both Caron and Herren to the University of Connecticut to watch a practice, because UConn had shown interest in recruiting Herren. At one point during the ride Herren had asked, "Mr. Karam, does your wife dye her hair?"

Karam had looked at him, the disbelief all over his face, and said nothing.

"Yeah," he finally said. "She does."

"What's she trying to do?" Herren countered. "Attract younger men?"

Jeff couldn't believe that anyone would talk to Mr. Karam that way, not even Chris. He had been so embarrassed he wanted to disappear. Afterward, he'd asked Chris what he was thinking of. "He's always messing with my head," Chris said. "I wanted to mess with his a little too."

Jeff just shook his head and laughed. It was one more bit

of evidence that Chris really was crazy, he thought. Not just playing around crazy, like a lot of kids. But really crazy.

So he liked Chris, considered him one of his best friends on the team, but he also thought that "everyone kisses his ass. Mr. Karam. Other kids. Everyone," and something about that bothered him.

Even with all their respective success last year, they still hadn't been overly friendly. Over the summer, though, that had started to change, as if they both began realizing they no longer were rivals, that they needed each other if they were going to have the kind of team they both wanted to have.

There also had been an incident at a Burger King in Fall River that Herren believed had brought him and Caron closer. Caron had been at one table, Herren and some of his friends at another. Caron had started to be hassled by some other guys, and Herren and his buddies had gone over to stick up for Caron. That had seemed to change everything.

They still had their moments, though. One day in practice Jeff had hit Chris in the chest with an inadvertent elbow and Chris had thrown the ball at him. Jeff had picked it up and thrown it back at him. The incident had been like spontaneous combustion, only took a few seconds, but it resurrected old memories. But the next day Chris kept passing Jeff the ball, a sure sign that Chris was apologizing, for Jeff had come to know that passing was Chris's way of saying he was sorry, that they were friends again.

But they were different too. Herren was usually comfortable with the attention that came from being a Durfee basketball star, wore it as easily as he wore his T-shirts. Little kids would gather around him after games wanting autographs and he would sign them as if there were nothing more normal than little kids wanting the autograph of a high school junior. Caron was uncomfortable with it. He'd been surprised the year before when older people in the city said hello to him. Had been surprised when teachers in school whom he didn't know said "Good luck" to him on game days.

"Why would anyone want our autographs?" he asked one day. "We haven't done anything yet. We haven't won a state championship or anything."

While Herren was the son and brother of former Durfee stars, Caron's father never had played for Durfee, often said that his time at Durfee had been the worst time in his life. He had been a star in the Catholic Youth Organization (CYO) teams as a kid, but he couldn't shine at Durfee. Jeff had grown up hearing his father say that there were a lot of things about Durfee basketball he didn't like, most notably the spectacle of the players behaving as if they were some form of adolescent royalty. Herren's perspective was completely different.

Now they were both co-captains, so clearly the two best players that Karam had told the team the first day of practice that Herren and Caron were the only two guys who were assured of starting; after that it was all unsettled.

The locker room was full of nervous energy, visible tension, the kids like soldiers going off to their first battle. Outside the door you could hear the cheers from the jayvee game. Players filed back and forth to the bathroom. Caron bounced a ball hard against the cement, the *slap-slap* reverberating through the room.

"All right, listen up," barked Karam, his voice loud, strident. He stood in the front of the room, tightness lining his face.

"We're going to start off in twenty-two, twenty-two defense. Chrissie, make sure you come to the middle when the ball goes to the other wing. Callahan, don't try and block shots on the big Curley. Box him out and keep him off the boards. Don't try and block his shot because you'll only foul. Same goes for you, Cioe. Don't try and block the big Curley's shot because you can't get to it. But we got to box out. If we don't, we can back up the bus now."

"Mr. Karam, we're going to have to get back on defense," Herren piped in.

"No shit, Chris. And Jeff," he said, addressing Caron, "test out your foot. If it's no good, tell me. It's up to you."

Caron nodded. He had his dark hair slicked back, revealing a face that could have been right out of some Dead End Kids' script, pugnacious and tough, yet with a smile that instantly softened everything. There was no way he wasn't going to play. He had worked too hard in the summer lifting weights. He had spent too many years playing for Buddy's, the AAU team in New Bedford. Basketball was too important not to play in this game simply because his foot hurt. Basketball was why he was was at Durfee in the first place. He had gone to elementary school in nearby Westport, but even then, at twelve years old, he knew basketball at Westport was a joke. He played in the Milliken League in Fall River, where basketball was important and everyone knew it. Not like Westport, where basketball was treated like any other activity, no different than the band or the glee club, just something you did after school.

Karam hesitated, pacing back and forth, then looked again at the young faces staring up at him.

"All right, listen up. This is the first game, and yes, we want to win. Shit, I want to win if it's tiddlywinks. But this is only the first game. If we lose, it's not the end of the world. There are a lot of games left. And let's not do anything stupid. No fights. No giving the referees shit. Don't embarrass yourself, and don't embarrass me. Okay, wait for the jayvees to come in."

Dempsey stood nearby holding a clipboard.

"Skippy never uses one," he said in a whisper. "Every year I used to give him one before the first game and every year he'd break it before halftime. I don't even know why I brought one."

Karam came over, took the clipboard with a rueful smile. "At least we'll look like a coaching staff."

* * *

The two teams warmed up, the cheerleaders danced, the Duxbury pep band played, people started filling the wooden bleachers. Underneath the basket, just a few feet from the court, sat many of the Duxbury students. Durfee always attracts Fall River people to away games, even on a Tuesday night in early December nearly an hour and a half away. Most of them sat behind in the bleachers behind the Durfee bench. There are those who go to every game, year after year. Many are Skippy's people, like Rabby Raposa and Ronnie Fahey and Jimmy Taylor, whom everyone calls "Clocker," and Jerry Reed, nicknamed "The Master," although no one seems to know how the nicknames got started. They often sit behind the bench, close enough to hear Skippy during time-outs. He, in turn, often says things to them during games.

Raposa, the captain of Karam's first Durfee team in 1961, first saw a Durfee game with his father in 1955. Excepting a couple of years when he was in the service, he's been going ever since.

"In the last thirty or forty years I've missed maybe two or three games," he said. "Am I a super fan? I'm way past that. I'm a Durfee guy."

Karam's brother "Boo Boo" used to sit behind the bench too, and was sometimes even tougher than Skippy on referees. But his wife, who is Callahan's aunt, doesn't like to hear Skippy yell at her nephew, so "Boo Boo" sits with her in self-imposed exile in some other part of the gym.

Higher up in the bleachers is Michael Herren and a group of guys, all in their early twenties. Many of them are former players, still as devoted as when they were on the team.

"I really got in my brother's face after the Jamboree Friday night," Michael Herren said, the words all but tumbling over themselves. "I rarely ever talk to him about basketball. But he drove me crazy the way he played the other night. I told him he played like a pussy. That he had no heart. That it made me sick to my stomach to watch him play like that. I got over all those kids. I know all of them. They practically grew up in my house. I've coached them. To see them play like that made me sick."

Maybe no one in Durfee's history had ever been as intense as Michael Herren. He had been a case study in determination, one of those kids who had virtually willed himself to be a great Durfee player. It had been his first dream, beginning early in his childhood when his father used to take the rattle out of his right hand and put it in his left, because he wanted his son to grow up with skills in both hands. He always had known that his father had played for Durfee, had worn number 24, and that he would one day do the same thing. He had never doubted it, and by the time he was in junior high school he had acquired a reputation throughout the city. By the time he was a freshman he was starting on the varsity, a rarity in Durfee basketball history.

Michael's intensity was there for all the world to see, from throwing his fist into the air after a key basket to the relentless way he played the game. He was not particularly quick, couldn't jump exceptionally well. But he was six-foot-four and a warrior, fueled by the belief that he and the kids he had grown up with were never going to lose, because when you played for Durfee you weren't supposed to lose. He liked to think of himself and his teammates as contemporary gunslingers, riding into alien gyms and taking on all comers, Shane with a jump shot. There was nothing he enjoyed more than away games, with everyone against him, yelling at him, hating him, and then, finally, losing to him.

When Michael's team won the state title in his junior year, he had T-shirts made and gave them to his teammates. They said WE WILL REPEAT on the front. He liked the fact that it put more pressure on him and his teammates, that many people viewed it as arrogant. When they won the next year too, he put I TOLD YOU SO on the back of the shirts. No one ever said Michael Herren didn't have a flair for the dramatic.

Michael is about to turn twenty-two, already home between semesters from Belmont Abbey College in North Carolina. The small school is a long way from Fall River and from Boston College, where his basketball dreams had turned sour, the result of injuries and the pressure of his expectations. He is burly now, no longer the skinny little freshman who fired up seniors with his exuberance. But the emotion is still there, bubbling to the surface when he speaks, and as he watched Durfee go through its layup drill, one sensed he would have traded a few years of his life for one more high school season, one more chance to be the gunslinger, to go into some gym like this one and turn all the jeers into silence.

Karam stood on the sidelines as the buzzer sounded and his players huddled together in the middle of the court. Before every game he has the same fear, the fear that nothing will go right, that nothing they have worked on in practice will function, that the game will start and his team will be impotent, unable to do anything, and then what's he supposed to do?

"Come on," he yelled to his team. "Let's go."

The players remained huddled together in the middle of the court, their hands joined together high over their heads.

"Come on," Karam yelled, louder now, a look of disgust on his face. He turned and walked back toward the bench, spoke to the people behind the bench. "They're probably figuring out where the party is after the game."

The game started and all of Karam's fears started coming true. Duxbury was too big, got too many second shots. Callahan picked up three quick fouls trying to block Mickey Curley's shot. Pavao couldn't put anything in. Durfee fell behind.

"Callahan, can you get *at least one* rebound tonight? Is that asking too much?" he said in an early time-out, the edge in his voice. "Come on, Pavao, make a shot, for chrissakes."

Karam roamed the sideline in apparent pain, the anguish all over his face. It has long been his trademark. He has kung-fued innumerable chairs. He has stamped his feet and kicked the air. Once, one of his loafers flew off into the crowd. Minutes later, someone threw it back onto the middle of the court. He has been ejected from games. He has thrown many a tantrum on the sidelines, grimacing and holding his head in his hands and giving referees the choke sign. He once described his actions by saying "Once it starts, it's like someone sticks a needle in my arm and off I go." Numerous times through the years he's been told by either the superintendent or the principal to restrain himself on the bench, but now he's outlasted three or four superintendents and six or seven principals, and his behavior on the sidelines is still the same.

Duxbury continually threw the ball over the Durfee press. They also seemed to have little trouble with the Durfee zone, often throwing the ball over the top of it. Only Herren and Caron were not intimidated. Able to penetrate almost at will, Herren played with a confidence gained from the summer AAU tournaments, feeling that no one could stop him one-on-one. He was by far the best athlete in the game and constantly used his quickness and agility to get around defenders in the open floor, then his strength and jumping ability to get the ball to the rim. Caron also picked up where he had left off last year, burying jump shots, playing with poise, though it was apparent his foot was bothering him.

The rest of the players looked overwhelmed, not yet ready for a game of this intensity.

Midway through the second half, Karam put Shawn Thames into the game. Thames was scared. He'd never even played an entire jayvee game, and here he was in a varsity game, against one of the best teams in the state. He was in the game only a couple of minutes when Herren threw him a pass that went through his hands. The next time down the floor Herren maneuvered into the middle of the lane, then gunned another pass to Thames. This one, too, went through his hands, as Herren threw up his own hands in frustration.

"He can't catch the ball," Herren yelled over to the bench.

"Shut up, Chrissie," Karam yelled, before turning to the crowd behind him. "What's he trying to do with that pass, kill Thames?"

With 2:19 left in the game, Durfee trailed by nine, seemed hopelessly out of the game. But the Durfee press and two Herren drives to the basket got them closer, Karam exhorting them from the sidelines, a jockey trying to get his horse to the finish line first, even though he's three lengths back coming down the stretch.

With only a few seconds left to play, Durfee had the ball underneath the Duxbury basket, in front of the screaming Duxbury students, the small gym a cacophony of noise. They were down 78–74. The game appeared over. But the pass went to Herren in the left corner. He caught it behind the three-point line, turned and shot in one motion, colliding with a Duxbury player as he did. Somehow the ball went in, as the Durfee players leaped off the bench in jubilation. The referee blew his whistle signaling a foul. The score was now 78–77. There was no time left on the clock, but Herren could tie the game with a successful foul shot and send the game into overtime. Duxbury quickly called time-out.

Herren rushed to the bench, fists clenched, shouting, as the other players embraced him.

"Calm down, Chrissie," Karam snarled above the noise. "Everyone calm down."

Herren grabbed a water bottle and started squirting water on his face and his hair, then rubbed his hair back with his hand. Intensity seemed to run off him along with the water. He had not shot free throws particularly well in the game, even one time throwing an air ball, but he was confident. He'd always been someone who would come through under pressure, who shot better the higher the stakes. And this was one of those moments he'd always visualized for himself: at the foul line, the game on the line, a personal destiny. So he walked to the foul line confident, self-assured, as the Duxbury students screamed at him, waved their arms. He stared at the rim, trying to focus, to block everything else out. When he finally shot the ball, he felt sure it was in. It was not. It hit the back of the rim and bounced away, as the Duxbury students exploded onto the court in frenzied excitement.

At first Herren just stood there, almost in disbelief, then a wave of emotion surged through him, seemed to overwhelm him, a feeling that he had let everyone down, that he had failed. He saw a mass of Duxbury students swarm the court in joyous celebration as if they'd just won the state title. He felt someone hit him in the back of the head, was spun around, before he started running toward the locker room. He went through the door, tears in his eyes, viciously punched a locker with his right hand, the noise ricocheting through the room. Then he slumped on a bench, his head in his hands, inconsolable. The room was silent, funereal. The other players sat on the benches, as though there were no words, the emotion spent. The season was not supposed to start like this.

Suddenly, into the room strode Michael Herren, along with Mikey Martin and Nick Salmon, both of whom had played on state championship teams. They came over into the middle of where the Durfee players were sitting, loud and aggressive.

"Get your heads up," yelled Michael Herren. "You got nothing to be ashamed of. Stop feeling sorry for yourself. *Get your heads up.* You should be proud of yourselves."

It worked. Michael Herren's career at Boston College may have unraveled, but in this locker room he was still an icon, still the one that led Durfee to two back-to-back state titles. For many of the kids, Michael and Michael's teams were the first Durfee teams they ever knew. He was still the one they all want to emulate, the one who had already lived their own Fall River dreams.

They also are intimidated by him. He had coached them in the city's summer league and when they had lost a game one night, feeling as if they hadn't tried hard enough, he had come into the locker room and started telling them they had no pride, no balls, no nothing. He had slapped Kevin Mikolazyk on the side of the head, Callahan and Pavao too. Nothing infuriated Michael Herren more than the thought of players who don't play hard, who don't want it badly enough. To him, it's the greatest sin.

"Get your heads up," he yelled again, and some of the leaden atmosphere started to lessen just a bit.

"Yeah," echoed Salmon, pounding his fist on a nearby locker for emphasis. "You were nine points down and you came back. You were nine points down and you didn't quit. *You didn't quit.* That's Durfee basketball."

Chapter

2

MOST PEOPLE first see Fall River on Route 195, the interstate from Providence, Rhode Island, to Cape Cod, and it seems to rise out of nowhere. The road out of Providence is nondescript, through the Massachusetts towns of Seekonk, Swansea, and Somerset, past land that once was small farms and now is making the transformation to suburbs. Then the road goes around a slight bend and there is the long pale-green Braga Bridge hovering over Mount Hope Bay, and Fall River on the other side, a city that was built on a series of granite ledges that rise from the bay.

It is best viewed at twilight, with the lights twinkling and the large, foreboding gray stone mills in shadows. It is almost picturesque then, especially from a distance, with the church spheres rising out of the horizon and the city spreading out over the small hills. It is possible then to see it as it once was seventy years ago, back when Fall River was the leading textile city in the world, with 140 mills operating twenty-four hours a day, and the mill owners lived on top of the hill with a view of both the mills and the world they had created.

From a distance you don't see the decay, the remnants of

a city in decline since after World War I, a city with an unemployment rate that's among the highest in the country, a city with all the social problems that plague this country in the last part of the twentieth century.

Fall River rose to industrial prominence in the 1870s, fueled by the burgeoning mills and cheap labor, the succession of immigrants from Ireland, Canada, England, and Portugal that began descending on the city and building their own ethnic enclaves throughout Fall River. Some of those enclaves exist to this day. The South End, parts of which are called the Globe, is overwhelmingly Portuguese. The Flint, largely French-Canadian, is at the eastern end of the city. Then there is "below the hill," long the demarcation line of social standing in Fall River, the line that separates everyone else from the "Highlands," the area north of Main Street where the old Yankee mill owners and lace-curtain Irish once lived. Even now, signs welcome people to the "Historic Highlands," and on some streets, lined by spacious Victorian homes with a sweeping view of the mills and bay below, it's easy to think it's still the late nineteenth century and Fall River is in its heyday, to believe the last hundred years haven't happened.

There was money in Fall River at the end of the nineteenth century, old money belonging to the families that had first brought the mills to Fall River back in the 1840s: the Durfees, the Bordens, the Braytons. The Fall River Line ran opulent steamships daily from Fall River to New York, ships the newspapers described as "floating palaces." There was electricity, telephones, street cars, the amenities of a thriving city. The construction of a public library, an armory, a spacious Boys Club, and several large churches was made possible by money raised by private gifts. Large public parks offered recreation, one in the north end, one in the south.

And in 1883 a new high school was founded. It was the gift of Mrs. Mary Brayton Durfee Young, who donated a prime parcel of land on the hill just west of downtown and paid for the school's construction, the biggest gift in the city's history. It was named after her son, Bradford Mathew Charloner Durfee, who had died at age twenty-nine. A granite building in the Renaissance style, modeled after City Hall in Paris, the school had laboratories, a gym, an auditorium, and a drill area where the male students were supposed to march every day. It also boasted two towers, one an observatory equipped with a telescope, and the other a clock tower that was to be tolled twenty-nine times every morning in memory of B.M.C. Durfee. The cost was $1 million, a huge sum for the times, and it was considered one of the finest public high schools in the United States. It would serve as the city's only public high school until 1976.

At the turn of the century Fall River was one of the most cosmopolitan cities in the United States, with the highest percentage of foreign-born citizens. It already had evolved into a group of ethnic neighborhoods that operated almost like individual duchies, complete with their churches, traditions, customs, and language. They were neighborhoods full of wooden three-decker tenements, many of which had been built virtually in the shadows of the mills.

Yet even by World War I the seeds of the city's decline already were being sown. The growth of labor unions and the increased awareness of the mills' horrible working conditions had politicized much of the workforce. By 1900 nearly 10 percent of the workforce in the mills was under fourteen years old, and four years later there was a strike of nearly twenty-five thousand workers that lasted six months. Many of the mill owners were unwilling to put profits back into new machinery, a decision that would cripple the city's future. Much of the textile industry was shifting to the South, where there was cheaper labor and newer machinery.

After the war the process accelerated, a gradual disintegration until the Crash of '29 and the ensuing Depression stripped away the pretense and brought a grim reality to Fall River. Few American cities were hit any harder. The city declared bankruptcy in 1931, the result of roughly half of the individuals and corporations in the city being unable to pay their taxes, and the city's finances for a decade were controlled by a state finance board.

By the start of World War II roughly 80 percent of the mills that had existed in 1916 were out of business, leaving a plundered industrial ghost town, abandoned mills, high unemployment, and hopelessness. More than 10 percent of the population moved away during the 1950s.

Now, after forty years of benign neglect, Fall River is like many small, formerly industrial American cities, full of disaffected people, weird little cults, and a lot of drugs. About fifteen years ago there was a bizarre string of murders of lesbians, complete with Satanic rituals. Over the past few years southeastern Massachusetts has been the setting for more than a dozen unsolved murders of prostitutes. The celebrated "Big Dan's" rape case, the basis of Jodie Foster's film *The Accused*, took place in New Bedford, just fifteen miles away. Recently, a former Catholic priest in the Diocese of Fall River, James Porter, had been accused of molesting over a hundred boys, a bombshell in this heavily Catholic city.

But there is no better symbol of the city's decline than the huge abandoned gray mills, some as long as a city block. They are everywhere. Along the water on the north end of town, where Mount Hope Bay meets the Taunton River. In the south end of the city. In the Flint. Just off of downtown, in the heart of the city, visible from Route 195, the interstate that was built in the early seventies and bisects the city, allowing tourists to the Cape to zip through Fall River in a matter of minutes, left with only a lingering impression of monolithic factories, urban blight, and billboards advertising mill outlets.

Through much of this sad decline one of the few sources of pride was Durfee basketball.

Its real success began in 1947 when the "Hilltoppers," so

named because the old high school was near the top of the hill, won the Eastern Massachusetts title at the Boston Garden. Sports always had been big in Fall River, part of the immigrant experience, and certain kids had won local notoriety through athletic acheivement.

But the title was the city's triumph, and it came at a time when Fall River was all but wallowing in its own despair. Scores of people made the pilgrimage to the Boston Garden, communicants to a shrine. Even now, so many years later, they remember the route, up the old Route 138 (for there was no Route 24 then), through Somerset, Dighton, Taunton, Raynham, Bridgewater, Stoughton, Canton, then into Mattapan and into downtown Boston. Legend has it that it was the first time the Boston Garden was ever filled to capacity for basketball; back then, the Celtics never filled the Garden. And when the Durfee band played the school's alma mater, the faithful stood up all over the Garden and sang it, many with tears in their eyes. Back home in Fall River people huddled next to their radios, living and dying through the static, even those who had never been to a game, had no interest in basketball. This had transcended sports. This was their kids representing their city, kids who were young, proud, strong, all the qualities people in the city liked to think they had passed on.

So there developed a certain mystique about Durfee basketball, one that's lasted for nearly fifty years. The mills may have closed, the economy might have gone to hell, but there is still something good that comes out of Fall River, something that can't be taken away, regardless of what else happens. Something that makes the rest of the state take notice of Fall River, for there is the strong feeling that Boston doesn't even know Fall River exists, until those years when Durfee makes a strong run at the state tournament.

In 1988, when Durfee was in the state tournament in the Boston Garden, Marjorie Eagan, a columnist for the Boston *Herald*, couldn't resist writing about it. She grew up in Fall

River, graduated from Durfee in 1972, and for her the tournament game in the Garden that year was déjà vu. She expressed it this way:

Basketball made amends for a lot of what was not happening around town, because on Tuesday and Friday nights you could pay 50 cents, go to the Armory with 2,000 sweaty fans packed in, the overflow spilling onto the court. And you were big shots. Durfee fans. When you followed the team to the Boston Garden, people had heard of you. Durfee. A powerhouse. Famous.

When Durfee's '66 state champs rode convertibles down Main Street they may as well have been the astronauts on Fifth Avenue, coming back from the moon. . . . I figure it's pretty basic. Everybody wants to feel proud of the ol' hometown, to be a winner. Durfee basketball made thousands proud, and all of us winners. It was the proudest thing in my hometown for as long as I can remember. It still is, and it's great.

After Durfee won the Eastern Massachusetts title in 1947 the players were given testimonials, jackets, watches, and a trip to New York City. The next year they won the New England championship. The best player was a kid named Andy Farrissey, and to this day he lives in the city's memory, as if frozen in time, still as young and strong as he was in 1948, still regarded by many of the old-timers as the greatest player in the city's history.

Luke Urban was the coach, and legend had it that he once had roomed in the minor leagues with Babe Ruth. He ruled his players with an iron hand, austere, autocratic, imperial, to the point that when he passed one of the players in the hallways at school, he never spoke. The players quickly learned that you did what Lukey wanted, or you didn't play. It was that simple.

"Lukey was Lukey," said Abe White. "He did things his own way and nobody ever questioned him."

Maybe no one understands the Durfee basketball tradition any better than White. Certainly no one's been around it longer.

He grew up in the city's North End, the youngest of fifteen children, the son of a man who had emigrated from Austria, where he had been a cowboy. His father had become a loader at the American Print Works, the large brick factory near the base of the Braga Bridge. It was the era of the sweatshops, the years before the Depression when Fall River's era as a great industrial city was already in decline, and White's family was just one of many that didn't have any money.

He started working when he was seven, a paper route through the Highlands where the rich people lived, shining shoes downtown, delivering dinner pails to the American Print Works on his little red wagon. His father died when he was twelve, and things got worse. His family went on welfare for a couple of years, and White bounced back and forth between relatives in Providence, Attleboro, and Fall River.

He had been an amateur prizefighter in his youth, then started coaching basketball at the Boys Club, where he first met Charley Carey, Chris Herren's grandfather, who played for him. White had been the Durfee jayvee coach in 1937, also the timer for the varsity games. When he returned from the war in 1945, he became the offical scorer.

Fifteen years later, when Luke Urban was about to give up basketball, White had wanted to be the Durfee coach. Urban told him no, that he didn't have a college degree and he was too soft on the kids. So he kept scoring. He's been doing it ever since. Now Abe White keeps all the records. He knows where Chris Herren stands in the all-time Durfee scoring list. He is the official caretaker of the tradiion.

White was there when Durfee won the New England championship in 1948, beating a team from Waterbury, Connecticut, whose star was Jimmy Piersall, the future center fielder for the Boston Red Sox who would be immortalized in the movie *Fear Strikes Out*, which told about his bout with mental illness. White was there in 1952 when Durfee won the Eastern Massachusetts title, led by a little guard named Skippy Karam, a Lebanese kid in a city that was overwhelmingly Portuguese. He was there in 1956 when they won it again, this time led by Al Attar, now the Durfee principal. He was there in 1960 when Karam came back to coach. He was there in 1970 when Herren's father, Al, was the captain. And when after high school Al Herren married Cynthia Carey, the daughter of Charley Carey, Abe White often babysat, first for Michael, then for Chris. To them he was "Uncle Abe," just as he was "Uncle Abe" to generations of Durfee players.

"The only thing that's changed is now it's Grandfather Abe," said White. "I give Chris an allowance. I base it on how he plays. When he was younger I just used to give it to him. Now I base it on his performance. I did the same thing with Michael."

The tradition is everywhere. It's in the Fall River Boys Club, where a guy in his sixties named Charlie Frascatore has played pickup games for years while wearing a Durfee uniform. It's in the program on sale at all Durfee games, a white booklet that starts off with a history of the tradition. It's in the dusty trophy case in the school lobby, where Michael Herren's All-American plaque is displayed. It hangs on the walls of the "Thomas 'Skip' Karam" court, the red banners for all the great teams, the white sign inside the door that lists all the members of the Durfee Hall of Fame, the red banner that lists the eight players in the school's history that have scored at least a thousand points in their careers. Most of all, it's lodged securely in the memory banks of the older men who have followed Durfee teams for generations.

They are a sort of Greek chorus, at the games year after year, hovering over everything, forever arguing over who are the five best players in Durfee history, which was the best team, and so on. Walk into virtually any Fall River bar and the quickest way to get an argument going is to ask who was the best basketball player in the city's history.

The older men were there the night of Durfee's first home game of the season, against St. John's of Danvers, a Catholic school north of Boston. Nearing halftime of the jayvee game, the varsity players were getting ready to go out on the court in their street clothes, a long-standing custom. Herren bounced a ball outside the locker room just off the small coach's office, a black cap turned backward on his head.

"Chrissie, take the hat off when you go out to shoot," said Karam.

"Why?" he asked.

"Because I said so," Karam said. "Do you need another reason?"

Herren shrugged. Then he dropped the ball and threw a fake left hand at Karam, darting in front of him like a boxer, moving in and out, as Karam instinctively threw his hands up in front of his face.

"Chrissie, knock it off," he said.

"One punch." Herren grinned, holding his fist just off his shoulder. "Just one."

Karam pulled his own fist back in mock anger, Ralph Kramden threatening to send Alice to the moon.

"Come on." Herren laughed. "Me and you. Right here."

"Don't tempt me," Karam said.

"Don't tempt *me*," Herren said.

"Chrissie, I already raised my three kids and I thought I was done with babies. Now I got another one."

Herren picked up the ball and began, once again, to bounce it hard against the floor. Karam just rolled his eyes. It's only the second game of the season and sometimes Karam wonders if he can get through the season without

Herren driving him crazy. All of Herren's idiosyncracies have become a high-pitched whine he keeps hearing in his head. It always seems to be something, little inconsequential things that on the surface mean nothing, but seem to build on one another. The other day he'd been informed that Chris already had been tardy to school something like fourteen times, even though he only lives about a jump shot away. When he'd asked him why, Chris had answered that his parents left for work early and he didn't have an alarm clock. Skippy just shook his head, one more example of his theory that Herren lived in his own world, very different than the one Skippy had grown up in. Then there were the recruiting letters that kept piling up in his office, mail that Chris seemingly had no interest in picking up, never mind opening. Now it was the hat.

"And one more thing, Chrissie," said Karam. "No trash-talking out there tonight. You guys did it against Duxbury all night long and I'm sick of it. No more. If you do it tonight, you're coming out. Understand?"

Chris said nothing. He loved to trash-talk. He liked nothing better than to belittle opponents, seeing it was just one more aspect of competition. Sometimes when he scored he'd run back down the court and proclaim in a loud voice, "You guys playing with only four or what?" or "Better put someone on me." When Caron scored, Chris would yell, "Hey, Jeff, anyone playing you?"

He also liked to taunt opponents on the foul line. One of his favorite ploys was to look at Caron when someone was shooting a foul shot and say, "Hey, Jeff, can you believe what an ugly geek this is? I mean, can you fucking believe it?" He also loved it when Caron talked trash, was always urging him to do so, pushing all the right buttons, though Caron rarely did.

But last year, in one of the early games on the schedule against Milton, Chris had goaded Jeff so much that Jeff had started in on one of the Milton players, saying that he shot foul shots like a fucking queer, a remark that later led to a bench-clearing brawl between the two teams.

"Understand, Chrissie?" Karam said.

Herren bounced the ball on the floor through his legs, right hand to left, then back through again, left to right, full of pregame adrenaline and youthful exuberance, as Dempsey walked over.

"That's all right," Herren said. "I'm going to bust them for forty tonight anyway."

Karam shook his head.

"He never would have lasted with Lukey," Karam said to Dempsey.

"Who's that?" Herren asked.

"Luke Urban," Karam said. "My old high school coach."

Dempsey laughed.

"He never would have lasted with my old high school coach either," he said.

Karam, who coached Dempsey back in the sixties, laughed knowingly and a little sadly. "Ain't that the truth."

Chapter 3

ON A MORNING when the sun was blocked behind large clouds and the sky seemed streaked with shades of gray, Skippy Karam left Durfee in the black Mercury, given to him by some boosters, that he got for winning the state title in 1988, went down to the traffic light, crossed President Avenue, and headed toward New Boston Road. On his left was a large vacant lot, the grass long and unkempt, with a larger field behind it. This is the old football practice field, across which he and his 1950s teammates used to walk every afternoon from the old Durfee High School in the center of town. The real field was behind it. It too is now only overgrown grass and long-gone memories, part of it obscured by the small Fordney Street housing project.

It's times like these, times when he drives through Fall River, the memories running through his head, reminiscences of how different the world was when he grew up, that he again realizes how far he's come since his childhood.

He drove up New Boston Road, took a left on Oak Grove Road, past the cemetery on the right—what Skippy calls the "Protestant cemetery" where many of the old Fall River mill families, including Lizzie Borden, lay buried—and headed south. At Bedford Street, a main thoroughfare that runs from Eastern Avenue west into downtown, the road changes names and becomes Flint. He kept driving south, on a street now lined with wooden three-decker tenements, houses nestled next to each other, the very image of a New England mill village. It's his old neighborhood, called the Flint, and on the corner stood a handful of stoop-shouldered men, their weathered faces sculpted by time.

"They've been here for a hundred years," he said, pulling the car over to the corner to offer his hellos.

At the end of the street is Alden Street. To the left is an gray stone mill with boarded-up white windows, a building dating to the Industrial Revolution. FLINT MILL is etched into the top facade of it, with the dates 1872–1883. It speaks of another time, the Fall River of legend, back when it was called "Spindle City" and the mills produced cotton cloth that was sent around the world.

He took a right onto Alden Street, past three-decker tenements. To his left was another building, the back of what used to be the Fall River Knitting Mill.

"My grandfather's store was on this corner," he said.

"What kind of store?" I asked.

"Variety."

"What was the name of it?"

He laughed. "I don't think it even had a name."

At the end of a short street is a tan club, the Lebanese-American Club. One block behind it another gray-stone mill looms so large it dominates the entire neighborhood. On the corner stands a white three-decker.

"That was my grandparents' house. They lived on the second floor."

He took a right turn onto Quequechan Street and stopped. The second house on the right was 342, a tan three-decker.

"We lived on the third floor," he said, suddenly running the past through his mind as if it were a newsreel. "The church was across the street. Next to it was the club. There was a patch of dirt where my father had put a hoop up for me. I used to shoot a lot by myself, and my father would watch me from the third floor across the street."

He already had been nicknamed "Skip," the legacy of a sailor suit he'd been given as a child. His father, Tanous Karam, has come to Fall River from Lebanon when he was twelve years old. Two years later he started working in the Berkshire-Hathaway mills, several hundred yards to the south on Quequechan Street. He would work there for forty years. He began as a loom fixer, and later, by going to night school, elevated himself to assistant night manager. Because he didn't have an education, he never could be the night manager, but he attended night school faithfully, learned English, eventually earned his high school diploma, came to realize that education was the ticket to advancement, the passport to a better life. He also believed in loyalty, both to his family and to his company. He worked extra hours. He volunteered for things. He even would train men that would later be promoted over him. The result was there always was a job for him in the company, even during those tough times when others were laid off.

Skip's mother, Barbara, also believed in education. She too had grown up in the Flint, the daughter of a mill worker; she too had seen people not able to get ahead, locked in an endless cycle of no education and no advancement.

When Skippy was a child, the Flint was one of the poorest sections of Fall River, narrow streets full of three-decker tenements that had grown up in the shadow of the mills. It also housed a strong Lebanese community, even though the dominant ethnic group in the Flint was French-Canadian. In the thirties, St. Anthony of the Desert Church was built on the corner of Quequechan and Alden Street and became the spiritual home of the Lebanese in southeast Massachusetts. The Karams lived across the street, on the top floor of a triple-decker. There was no hot water, no bathtub, and rats reigned everywhere. They were forever jumping out of the garbage pail, running across the bathroom floor. Whatever the family did, they could not get rid of the rats.

"I would run upstairs and a rat would be running down," Karam said.

The neighborhood got its name from John D. Flint, a tin peddler, who first came to Fall River in 1850. Before the Civil War the area was mostly rural, but by the time Flint arrived, the city was changing with the building of the large textile mills. By this time Flint also owned his own store, and he saw the mills as an investment opportunity. By 1871 he'd invested in three cotton mills in the area. Along with a partner he spent roughly $60,000 to buy land and began building two large mills: to get workers he began advertising in the Fall River *Evening News*, and soon textile workers from both Lancashire, England, and Canada came to work. The Wampanoag Mill was built in ten months, capable of making eight million yards of cloth annually. Ten tenement houses, owned by the company, were built nearby. At the same time, virtually across the street, was the Flint Mill. It contained forty-two thousand spindles, more than the Wampanoag Mill, and gradually, as the population of the area swelled, the neighborhood south of Bedford Street and west of Eastern Avenue became known as the Flint.

Karam's mother was a seamstress at the Fall River Knitting Mills, a couple of blocks away to the west, toward downtown. She worked days, his father nights. There was an Old World quality to his childhood. When he disobeyed, his father would make him kneel in the corner of the room in silence. His paternal grandparents lived next door, their small variety store a block away. On holidays he and his relatives would go to his grandmother's house, where all the men would be served the meal first. His grandparents spoke only Arabic, his parents both English and Arabic. The church mass was in Arabic. Lebanese kids were taught to call every Lebanese woman "auntie," the men "uncle," everyone else "cuz." The dominant figure in the community was the priest, Father Joseph Eid, who had been born in Lebanon and done missionary work in the Orient before being asked to come to Fall River. He spoke six languages, and was also a poet.

Sports were one of the few things in Fall River that brought the different ethnic neighborhoods together. It was not uncommon for CYO baseball games to draw over two thousand people. Tanous Karam played soccer, took Skippy to Red Sox games, encouraged him to play sports. He even coached Skippy's CYO baseball game, a team that won the city championship.

"I was the only child for eight years, the only grandchild," Skippy said. "In other words, I was a spoiled brat. I didn't have anything, but in the important ways I had everything."

He would play on the field behind the Fall River Knitting Mills where his mother worked. He played at nearby La-fayette Park, only a few blocks away geographically, but in many ways a different world, a French-Canadian one, one that revolved around the Notre Dame Church. He saw his first Durfee game in 1944 at the Boys Club, along with his father. He was eight years old, and right away he was se-duced by the glamor, the crowd, the cheerleaders, the cheers, the raw emotion that seemed to run through the gym like an electric current.

"The Durfee guys wore warm-up jackets. I thought that was the greatest thing in the world."

He came of age playing CYO sports and listening to Dur-fee basketball games on the radio. His middle school team won the city championship when he was a freshman, and the next year he made the varsity. In one of the first games Luke Urban put him in and he immediately lost the man he was guarding. The next whistle he was substituted and Urban was quickly in his face.

"You didn't know where your man was," he yelled at Karam. "From now on look at his face, look at his teeth, look at his number, look at everything. But don't lose your man."

That was the beginning.

"Everyone was scared shitless of him," said Karam. "Even years later. Lukey was like a god. You wouldn't have dreamed of talking back to him. One time when I was a sophomore on the football team he told everyone to run three laps and then hit the showers. But by the time we got to the showers we realized that the juniors and seniors were still out on the field. Lukey storms into the locker room and tells us that he didn't tell us to come in and we'd better get back there and start running. So we dry off, put our uniforms back on, and start jogging around the track. By this time there's no one left on the practice field. The juniors and seniors are in the shower room. Lukey's nowhere to be found. And we still keep running, running, running. Now guys are starting to get sick. But no one's going to stop because he had told us to run. Then we see the juniors and seniors come out of the locker room, all dressed, and they're laughing at us. Then Lukey drives by and asks us what we're doing, says he didn't tell us to keep running. Thank God he happened to drive by. Because we'd still be running."

By the time Karam arrived in high school, Louis John Urban already was a legend in Fall River, a saga that had begun years before. Urban had grown up in the city's South End in the early 1900s, used to deliver milk to some of the local factories before he went to school. It was work that made his hands and arms extremely strong, and though he was only five-eight he was a great athlete, a career that seems to belong on some adolescent fiction shelf. He only played one year of sports at Durfee, but even that had been good enough to get him to Boston College. When he graduated in 1921, he'd captained the football, basketball, and baseball teams and also was the hockey goalie, even though when he first started playing hockey he didn't know how to skate and had to use double-runners. He was Boston College's first football All-American, so well regarded that a few years ago when BC picked its all-time football team, Luke

Urban was the end. He also actually coached the basketball team for two years while he was a player.

He went on to play professional football for the Buffalo Bisons in the old NFL, played in a championship game against George Halas and the Chicago Bears. He also played professional baseball for the Boston Braves for the better part of two seasons. Later, he coached both football and basketball at Canisius.

And he came back home to Fall River quite by accident.

As the story goes, he came down from Buffalo in 1940 to be the new Boston College football coach. But BC refused to give him a signed contract, so he said no thanks, and made a side trip to Fall River to visit his brothers. As fate would have it, one of them mentioned that Durfee was looking for a basketball coach, and that was it. He coached that season, and the next year moved his family from Buffalo and became a physical education teacher at Durfee, not to mention the coach of the three major sports. The legend was about to begin.

The first game he ever coached at Durfee was at some gym he felt was unacceptable. So he had his team hold the ball, won the game something like 6–4. The principal was so upset he threatened to fire him. But Luke survived that, and became one of the most influential men in Fall River. He was a man with a definite charisma, a presence that immediately commanded both respect and fear. He did not believe in the old Grantland Rice adage that it's not whether you win or lose, but how you play the game. He believed in winning, and winning alone. He could be unbearable after a loss, and his tirades soon became legendary. One of the stories forever floating around the city was that one Thanksgiving, after losing to New Bedford, he came home and cleared the entire Thanksgiving table with a swipe of his hand.

Winning the state basketball title cemented Urban's stranglehold on the city. There had been a celebration for the team at Durfee, and as the students lined both sidewalks on Rock Street in May 1947, a light blue De Soto was driven up Rock Street and presented to Urban amid wild cheers.

Urban told the crowd that in his entire athletic career he never had been honored by the way Fall River was honoring him now, saying, "I will do everything in my power to continue to do what is expected of me." He closed his talk by saying he thought it would be a splendid idea to take everyone for a ride in his new De Soto.

It's impossible to overstate the influence Urban had on both Fall River and on an impressionable Skippy Karam. He coached the three major sports. Summers, he managed Fall River's minor league baseball team in the New England League. He was the role model, the most visible symbol of the city's persona, as tough and gritty as millwork. He swore at the players, berated them, tolerated nothing less than perfection. He thought nothing of physically challenging a kid who was being insubordinate. One time in the late fifties he threw a ball off the head of a kid named Tommy Arruda, then dragged him into the showers and turned the water on him. He often would line up next to his football players and tell them to hit him. One kid did and broke Urban's leg. But as legend has it, Urban said "Good hit" as they carried him off the field.

He believed in discipline, in doing the things the right way, and in his personal court he was both the judge and jury, a court with no appeals. If an infielder in baseball folded his glove on a ground ball so that Lukey could not see the palm of his glove, that infielder ran a lap. Urban worshiped at the shrine of discipline, and expected his players to do the same. He also believed in what his son Luke calls "reverse psychology."

"The better a player you were, the more he was on your ass," he said. "It was just the way he was."

Urban's son, nicknamed "Topper," literally grew up with Durfee sports. Some of his earliest memories were going to games. He was the mascot for the basketball team and sometimes his father, in a fit of anger, would throw the resin bag at him instead of a player. He grew up to play all three sports for his father, excelling at football and baseball, later playing them both at Columbia. He was in the Marines for twenty years, sent twenty-seven months in Vietnam, served all over the world, and retired as a lieutenant colonel. Yet he never would smoke in front of his father, because he knew his father disapproved of it.

"Here I was," he said with a laugh, "I've been shot at, shit upon, done everything, and I wouldn't smoke in my own house if he was there. It was the just the way he was."

Urban also believed in structured basketball, disciplined basketball. Urban's teams did not run. They did not freelance, what he derisively often referred to as "scallywag basketball." He was adept at nursing a lead, and thought nothing of starting to hold the ball in the final quarter. He believed firmly that the ball never was to bounce against a zone defense and that one of the worst basketball sins was a bad shot. The old Boys Club, their home court, had a blue line on one side of the court and a red line on the other, painted lengthwise. Urban always instructed one guard to run along the blue line, the other along the red line. He called the plays. And it was all very simple: If you were a player and you didn't like it, too bad. Luke Urban didn't run a democracy.

Halfway through his sophomore year, Karam broke into the starting lineup on a team that was one of eight that went to the Tech Tournament in the Boston Garden. It was the first time he ever saw a jump shot, a sneak preview that the game was changing. It was 1951. The next year Karam was the best shooter on the team but, in Urban's controlled offense, sometimes only took three or four shots a game. Durfee won the Eastern Massachusetts championship that year, the team staying for three days at the Hotel Manger that adjoined the Garden, a rat-trap whose unofficial slogan was "Bang her at the Manger." Professional basketball was still in its infancy, the Celtics were still a few years away from the arrival of Bill Russell and the start of their great dynasty, but the Garden was still magical, a long way from the Boys Club in Fall River. Even now, so many years later, Skippy still remembers that the Garden held 13,909 at the time, *13,909*, a number that seemed wrapped in romance.

The next year Durfee lost in the state finals, and soon Karam's high school years were quickly coming to a close. His parents always had wanted him to go to college, for college took you out of the mills and the second-shift world of the neighborhood. As a young child his mother used to read to him, and later she headed the Aldrich School PTA, unheard-of for a working mother in the 1940s. In a sense this quest for education went against the mores of the Flint, where many of the kids quit school at sixteen to go into the mills. In fact, Skippy's mother met with some razzing and quizzical looks from women she worked with when Skippy did not leave school at sixteen. During the summer school breaks his father would put him in the mill, make him go to work every day to experience firsthand the monotonous, brain-numbing work, to make his son realize he didn't want to end up in the mills, the large stone fortress where too many dreams in the city had gone to die.

But Skippy had been an indifferent student at best. Durfee had overwhelmed him. It was too big. There was too much freedom. It seemed so far away from the structured world of the Flint and the neighborhood schools he'd gone to all his life, schools where if he acted up in class his parents always seemed to know about it the next day. He played both football and basketball at Durfee, reveling in the status that came from being a good athlete in the city, his world revolving around sports, his dreams confined to the present tense.

"I was awed by Durfee," he said. "I was completely lost. I could never concentrate. I would look at a book and see basketballs flying around. I blew four years."

He looked at the future and only saw haze, undefined images of uncertain location. Some New England colleges were interested in him because of his basketball ability, but college basketball was different then, especially in New England. The schools were not "big-time," not yet ready to overlook academic standards in the quest for basketball success. The schools looked at his transcript and backed off. He thought of going into the Air Force.

Instead he went to Tabor Academy, a prestigious prep school on the water near Cape Cod, recommended by an older friend who convinced his family that prep school would do wonders for him. It was less than an hour from Fall River, but it could have been the far side of the moon. Tabor was an old New England boarding school, where students wore white bucks, rep ties and blue blazers to class and teachers spoke in hushed tones about the Great Books. Skippy showed up in blue suede shoes. Academics were stressed: There was a study hall every night between six and eighty-thirty, and a Saturday morning study hall. He lived in a house on the campus with four other students. He got along well with the coach, who invited him over to his house for tea and cookies, talked to him about his future, something Urban never had done. Skippy liked it, but at the end of the year, as his classmates talked about where they would be going to college in the fall, he still had no place to go. Once again, he had not done well in school, nor had he excelled on the college boards. Once again, his poor grades were robbing him of opportunities to play college basketball.

Finally Father Eid, his priest back in the Flint, called Providence College and he was accepted there. Providence College was only about forty-five minutes away, a small school whose charter was to serve boys from the Catholic dioceses of Providence and Fall River. The basketball coach told him there was no more scholarship money left, but if he made the freshman team and played well maybe there would be some the following year. He only lasted three weeks on the freshman team, before the commuting and the fact he didn't have a scholarship disheartened him. He made the varsity the next year, still without a scholarship, but riding the bench, frustrated, he quit the team and began playing semipro for the Fall River Barons.

He continued at Providence College, but it was never easy. As a commuter, often hitching rides between Fall River and Providence, he didn't know many students. He didn't participate in any social life. When he had thought of college, he'd envisioned manicured green lawns and brick buildings covered with ivy, a larger Tabor Academy. Instead, Providence College was a small school with only a few buildings, a small campus. He might have been going to college, but his life was still back in Fall River.

"My senior year I had two classes in the morning and by noon I was back hanging in front of the Granite Block Spa on Main Street," he says.

Shortly after graduating from college in 1958, he found a teaching job in Westport, a small town that abuts the southeast corner of Fall River. He taught social studies, reading, general math, and physical education, and doubled as the baseball coach and the assistant basketball coach. The next year he became the head basketball coach.

"I knew nothing about coaching," he said. "I knew about playing. But I didn't know shit about coaching."

He was the varsity coach for one year, then Urban announced he was going to retire from the Durfee job in 1961. Karam applied, not really thinking he had a chance. He was not interviewed. He was unaware of the politics that surrounded the job. Then one day the Fall River superintendent of schools called him and said Thomas "Skip" Karam was the new Durfee basketball coach. He was twenty-five years old, not too many years removed from the Flint, and he was the Durfee basketball coach in a city that had come to view basketball success as a given.

"I had no idea what I was getting myself into," he said.

* * *

He found out the first game. As fate would have it, it was against New Bedford, Fall River's sister city fifteen miles away, the big rival. As the day of the game approached, Skippy found he couldn't eat, couldn't sleep. The pressure seemed to sit on his shoulders like some giant weight, smothering him, a kind of pressure he'd never felt before. Whatever he did, he couldn't escape it, this horrible feeling his reputation in the city, his identity, his very essence, was all wrapped up in how successful his team was going to be.

Making it worse was that Urban was still around. For a while he even did the color on the radio broadcasts, the pro- verbial second-guesser, the old coach who always seemed to be looking over Karam's shoulder. Urban had become the athletic director, was still in the school every day. One day, feeling cocky now that he and Urban were colleagues, Karam walked into Urban's office and said in jest, "It's about time you're doing some work."

Urban gave him a long, hard stare.

"Who do you think you are talking to me that way?" barked Urban, once again falling into the familiar role of coach to player. "Don't you ever talk to me that way."

So much for being colleagues.

That first year Karam's team won its first sixteen games. All the while he felt like some kid who had sneaked into the game on a free pass. He read books on coaching. He watched innumerable games, trying to discern the secrets of other coaches. He took much of what he remembered from Urban. He stole a little from what he remembered from Joe Mul- laney, his coach at Providence College. He watched more games.

In the beginning he wanted to have the control Urban had had, but he also wanted to deal with the kids too. It was the one complaint he'd had with Lukey, the sense that he had no interest in you off the court. Urban didn't ask what your fu- ture plans were. He didn't inquire about what might be hap- pening in your life. It was as if the players ceased to exist the minute they left the locker room, their personal lives dissolving into mist until they rematerialized on the court the next day. If Urban happened to pass one of the players in the hallways during the day, he wouldn't speak to him. Skippy wanted to be different.

From the beginning he also was sarcastic, often profane with his players. Some of it he undoubtedly borrowed from Lukey, but he also had grown up with sarcasm, one-liners that had an edge to them. His mother was a sharp-tongued woman not averse to needling people. Razzing also had been the currency of the street corner, how people related to each other. Needling people, what was known as "busting balls," was as much a part of the neighborhood as the triple-deckers and second shift. So was swearing. Skippy couldn't remember when he didn't swear. Years later he thought that the swearing had been a defense, a way of sounding tougher than he really was, for in a city where fighting and toughness were respected, Skippy never had thought of himself as tough. But as a kid he was known for his bad language, and when he began coaching, the swearing was part of his innate vocabulary. The kids and their parents seemed to accept it.

He was demanding that first year, but in retrospect, it was an easy team to coach. On the first bus ride he was surprised at how quiet it was, how so many of his players were studying. They were self-disciplined, self-motivated, didn't make mistakes, didn't turn the ball over. They knew how to play. They had played for Urban; they easily adjusted to Karam.

"Skippy was almost tentative," remembered Barry Machado, a starting guard on that 1961 team. "That first year it was like he was feeling his way. But it was a time when kids were very obedient. A coach would say 'Jump' and we'd ask 'How high?' We also knew he was one of the stars of the constellation. He wasn't Farrissey and he wasn't Attar, but he was right below them, that next level. He hadn't played at Providence College, but he had proved himself in the pickup culture in Fall River. Therefore he had credibility. We liked Skippy."

The first game Karam lost was to Fairhaven, a town on the other side of New Bedford. The coach, a man named Mel Entin, had been there for years and hadn't gotten along with Urban. So Karam started off the game not particularly liking him, and as the game began getting away from him, he liked Entin even less. At one point, seeing Entin get on the officials, Skippy snapped.

"Hey, Mel, why don't you referee too?" he yelled over at Entin.

"Hey, Sonny, go back to Westport," the other coach yelled back.

"He put me right in my place," Karam loved to tell people. "I never got on another coach after that."

Yet whatever he did that first year, no matter how successful the team was, all he heard was they were all Lukey's kids, that it really was Lukey's team. *Lukey's kids. Lukey's team.* This refrain haunted him as he traveled around the city, the irritating sound track to his supposed dream job. He lost in the finals of the Eastern Massachusetts tournament at the Boston Garden that year, a great year, but it did nothing to remove Urban's weight. It was still there two years later when he lost again in the Eastern Massachusetts finals.

In a sense that scarred him, for the inherent message was that whatever he did was never enough. He internalized the pressure until it became part of the baggage that went with coaching basketball at Durfee, part of his life. Then in 1966, five years after he began coaching in Fall River, he won the state championship. It should have been the culmination of everything he'd accomplished so far, the dream actualized, Urban's ghost finally exorcised. Yet when the game ended he felt not elation, but relief.

"I thought I'd be happier," he said.

In retrospect, he learned a lesson that's stayed with him throughout his coaching life: *The only thing winning is, is not losing.* It doesn't bring elation. It doesn't even necessarily mean satisfaction. It merely means that you didn't lose, and losing is a form of death, a hollow, empty feeling that never seemed to diminish, no matter how many games he won.

In the early seventies Skippy saw coaching start to change. The remnants of the counterculture spread through the country's youth like some out-of-control virus. Even in Fall River.

One day in practice he didn't think his starting center, whom he considered a great kid, was playing hard enough.

"Start running," said.

"For what?" the kid said.

"Because I told you to," Skippy barked.

"I'm not going to run," the kid said.

Skippy couldn't believe it. Nobody talked back to him. Ever.

"If you don't run, you aren't starting tomorrow night. Are you going to run?"

"No."

It was the first time a kid ever had been truly insubordinate, and Skippy quickly sensed it had become a symbolic battle of wills. He made the entire team run, then realized that his best player was merely trotting, his own protest for his punished teammate. So the next night he didn't let the two kids play, because he still believed what he always had believed, that a coach without control had nothing, that a coach without control was like an emperor with no clothes. The incident blew over, but he knew a new era had come to Durfee.

He also came to learn the price tag for being the Durfee coach. First there was the criticism, the inevitable second-guessing, the blaming of the coach for everything from when he takes his time-outs to how many games he wins. There were parents who didn't like him because their kids didn't make the team or didn't play enough when they were on the team. There were parents who thought Karam was too hard on their kids. None of these sentiments ever really died, old battles still remembered as the years went on. One night the father of one of his star players, a man he had gone to high school with, met him in a darkened parking lot, ostensibly to fight him because he didn't feel his son was getting enough shots. Skippy eventually had talked him out of it, but it had been one of those bizarre moments he'd never forgotten.

And there was the jealousy which is directed at anyone who lives in the public eye. In this case it was not just Skippy, but his brothers too. In the past decade his younger brothers—Bobby, commonly referred to as "Boo Boo," and Jimmy—had become two of the biggest movers and shakers in Fall River, one in investments, the other in development. In 1988 the Sunday *Standard-Times*, based in New Bedford, had done a magazine cover story on the Brothers Karam, the lead being that the man most responsible for shaping Fall River in the late twentieth century was, perhaps, Tanous Karam. It's not an altogether improbable boast, but there was a certain backlash too, the feeling that the Karams had become too powerful, too much of an influence in the city.

Then there were people in Fall River who thought Durfee basketball was like some spoiled province, full of pampered players and excess. A faction inside Durfee, made up of teachers, administrators, and students, believed the basketball team got too much attention, too much of the limelight, at the expense of the other sports. They saw Skippy receive a car for winning the state championship in 1988; they saw the players get a trip to Disney World. And they resented it. The only slogan posted in Karam's office at Durfee reads, "People love success; but they hate successful people."

He had probably learned about envy as a high school basketball player. It was the first time his world had expanded beyond the Flint, and the big thing was to head downtown, called going "up Main Street," and hang out in front of the

Granite Block Spa in his blue suede shoes. Or else walk into one of the local pool halls and play his buddies. But some old men in the Flint, Lebanese men, couldn't understand him wanting to leave the neighborhood. "Why do you want to go downtown and hang out with all those rah-rahs?" a cousin said to him.

What's the alternative? Karam thought. *To stay here in the Flint where everyone just sits in the clubs and gambles?*

So things always were more complicated than they might seem on the surface. There were debits and credits when it came to being the coach, an ongoing ledger sheet. But the realization still pained him. Maybe nothing hurt him more than to hear that a friend or a parent had second-guessed him, hadn't been loyal. In his view of the world, loyalty was prized, one of those childhood lessons he'd learned from his father, and in many ways it was a black and white world, the colors rigid and monochromatic: You were either for him or you were against him.

But there were the highs that came with the job too, the fix that came with being the Durfee basketball coach, of being right there in the white-hot glare of the spotlight. There was the sense of competition he'd always had, the drive that had pushed him out of the Flint in the first place so many years ago, the burning desire to win, as if winning were somehow validation. There was the satisfaction he always felt in taking a group of kids and molding them into a team, seeing them develop and improve, seeing them start to play the kind of basketball on the court that he'd envisioned in his head. It was the essence of coaching, and he'd always loved it. Even the people who occasionally second-guessed him never really questioned his coaching ability. Skippy Karam could coach. He had proven that a long time ago.

Last year he had won his six hundredth game, complete with local television cameras, newspapers, attention. When the game was over, he'd been mobbed by his players, surrounded at center court. He was well respected in the Massachusetts high school basketball world, had accomplished virtually everything there was to accomplish as a high school basketball coach, already had been inducted into the Massachusetts Coaches Hall of Fame. There were times when it seemed Karam was better known in Fall River than the mayor, and there was no question he'd already created a legacy that would live on in the city as long as there was high school basketball. By all standards of measure Skippy Karam was at the mountaintop of the world he'd created for himself. The only things that seemed to get in the way were the expectations, the unrelenting, omnipresent pressure of another season.

Sunday morning.

"How was the party last night, Danny?" Karam yelled, as Callahan missed a layup in one of the opening drills of practice. "You guys should be playing for the Edgehill All-Stars"—Edgehill being an exclusive drug and alcohol treatment center in nearby Newport, Rhode Island.

Herren sat on the first row of the rolled-up bleachers, not practicing because he had congestion in his chest that made it painful to breathe.

"How would you like to wake up and hear that voice the first thing in the morning?" he said with a yawn. "I hate Sunday morning practices."

The field house was cold, drafty. There are no windows. Karam prowled in his black warm-up suit with the red trim at one end of the court, determinedly watching, his eyes missing nothing. Dempsey, seemingly still wiping the sleep away from his eyes, stood at the other end, a cup of coffee in his hand. The bleachers were pushed back, making the gym seem bigger. The gray tartan floor with the red trim looked scruffy, like an old carpet rubbed by too many feet. The players were going through a full-court layup drill, three at a time in a weave, passing and cutting behind the man who the ball was passed to, a timeless drill, one that Karam had practiced for Urban. The players ran up and down in virtual silence.

"Let's go," Karam yelled. "Make good passes."

Another group ran down the court, then another, the passes crisp. A third started down the court, but Mikolazyk, a small guard who is vying for playing time, threw a pass at Pavao's feet, the ball skidding out of bounds.

"Nice pass, Kevin," Karam said disgustedly. "We can't even play against air, never mind another team."

The Sunday morning practices are important to Karam for two reasons: Durfee usually plays Tuesday nights, so it gives him an opportunity to get two practice days in before a game, and he believes it helps to curtail the players' Saturday night activities. It's usually a hard practice, lots of running, and there have been many players over the years who came to regret some of those beers from the night before.

For many of them the drinking had begun in the ninth grade, when they first got to Durfee. It was ingrained in the culture, passed down from the older kids to the younger ones like some secret code. A few had started as early as the eighth grade when they were in middle school at Morton, sneaking a few beers before going to birthday parties. It had been a kind of a joke then, something new and exciting that made them seem cool, older.

Caron remembered going to huge outdoor parties off Airport Road in the northeastern part of the city when he was in the ninth grade.

"I thought it was the coolest thing," he said.

He didn't drink himself then. In truth, the year before he had been a little intimidated by the thought of drinking, intimidated by the fact so many of his friends were already doing it. Often that year he would ride around in senior Todd Majkut's car while Majkut and his friends drank.

"Want a beer, Jeff?" Majkut would ask.

"Nope," Jeff would say.

"You will," Majkut would answer.

Majkut was right.

It started for him last year, but even then he approached drinking warily. In his view of the world it was simple: Drinking was bad. Basketball was good. Drinking kills basketball. So he rarely drank on a Saturday night if the team had practice the next morning. And if he drank a couple of weekends in a row, he started thinking he was a loser, no different than the kids he saw around him who seemed to live from weekend to weekend, with no goals, no vision of any future that extended beyond the next party.

There never was any trouble getting beer. Someone always had a fake ID that said they were twenty-one; a couple of the players had been getting served in package stores since they were fifteen, not all that unusual in a city where there always were "greenhorn" package stores that seemingly would take the money of anyone who could crawl to the counter.

"The best was we got the Domino's Pizza guy to buy for us one night," laughed Caron. "He came to the door to deliver the pizza and someone paid him to make a beer run for us."

Nor did there seem to be a whole lot of difficulty in routinely drinking on weekends, though one might expect parents would be more of a presence. That always was Skippy's lament, when he'd hear the stories of weekend parties and too much drinking: Where were the parents? Why couldn't they seem to control their kids?

"A lot of the parents got their own problems," Caron said. "I think my parents have a good marriage, but I was thinking of all my friends the other day and most of their parents are either divorced or thinking of getting divorced."

Often the kids hung out in Peter Suneson's basement, which had a separate entrance. Suneson's parents had divorced when he was young and since his mother often worked nights as a nurse, the basement had turned into a sort of clubhouse. Sometimes some of the kids would sleep over, a weekend crash pad. They even had an unofficial name for it, "The Speakeasy."

He too has deep Fall River roots; both his father and uncle are former Durfee athletes. He too started going to Durfee games when he was young, has been friendly with Herren since the first day of kindergarten. Teammate Matt Boardman lives across the street. Suneson also was a Milliken League star, but now alternates between the jayvee team and a reserve varsity player. He is a junior, and already has been the starting quarterback for two seasons, football replacing basketball as his favorite sport. Unlike some of the others, he's a good student, for his parents stressed education early. Also unlike some of the others, he yearns to one day leave Fall River.

"My father always told me there's a big world out there and I should see," Suneson said. "He told me that Fall River can be real small."

There is a restlessness about him, a rebellious streak.

"I like to shock people," he said, with a mischievous glint in his eye. "Like showing up at a dance in cutoffs."

He had become a cult hero to the Durfee student section when he came into games, whether jayvee or varsity, the crowd yelling "Old Man Sunny" every time he touched the ball. It's a nickname he picked up one night when, a few too many beers in him, he fell off a couch.

"Look at Sunny," said Callahan. "He acts like an old man."

It stuck. Old Man Sunny.

Yet there were times when Suneson felt he was a prisoner of his image too. Times when he tried to be serious, but no one would take him seriously. Old Man Sunny.

Herren also was beginning to realize drinking could get in the way of basketball, for the simple reason that in the fall he had started to gain weight, and the added weight robbed him of some of his quickness. No longer was drinking just some harmless thing that he did on weekends because that was what everyone did. Now it had consequences, and for the first time in his young life he sensed he had to start making choices.

"I realize now that I probably drank too much for a kid my age," he said. "But it was because of the lifestyle I was living. I was fifteen years old hanging around with eighteen-year-olds and I did what they did. But basketball is more important to me than drinking, and now I know I have to watch it."

One night I went to a party with a group of them, Herren, Callahan, Pavao, Mikolazyk, and jayvee players Brendan Gettings and Eric Couto. It was at a girl's house in the Highlands, not too far from Karam's house. Her parents were away, and there about fifteen kids in all, a small party by local standards.

"How many have you had?" Herren asked Callahan, who was sitting on the couch with a Budweiser in his hand.

"Heavy teens," he said.

"Yeah, right, Cal," Herren said. "If you were into the heavy teens, you'd be passed out now."

Callahan laughed.

After a while they all played a card game. The penalty for losing: having to chug beer. In a sense drinking was the great equalizer. It made everyone the same. On the court Herren was different, but here, at the party with his friends, he was no different than anyone else.

"Chris will never do anything to be the center of attention," Callahan said. "Suneson will stand on his head in the middle of the room, or do a handstand or something. Chris would never do that."

Apart from the music—rap, heavy metal—I was struck by how similar it was to parties from my own high school days thirty years earlier. The same dialogue. The same put-downs. The same peer pressure to drink, get drunk, as though being able to consume a lot of alcohol earned a macho merit badge. The parents always away somewhere, either out of town or gone for the evening. There was something timeless about it, the boys getting drunker, more sophomoric, the girls rolling their eyes, but also going along with it.

The only other difference was the language. Where twenty years ago there were two kinds of talk—the speech boys used with their friends, and the one they used when girls were around—now it was all the same, words like "fuck" and "motherfucker" used so repeatedly in mixed company that they long ago had lost their ability to shock, had become part of everyday speech.

By the end of the evening, the party had swelled a bit, and some kids were smoking grass in the kitchen. But it was far from boisterous. This wasn't a wild party, or anything out of the ordinary. This was just a bunch of kids on a typical weekend night.

"I can count the number of kids who don't drink on one hand," Caron said. That statement would be true in Fall River and thousands of American towns.

"Let's go," yelled Karam, clapping his hands. "I bet you all had a lot more enthusiasm at the party last night."

"I hate it when when he says shit like that," Herren said. "It's like he's got spies all over the city. Whatever we do, he seems to know the next day. Last Thursday he was a nut. Wired. I thought he was going to throw me out for sure. He was a maniac. Wicked on my case."

"What got him started on you?"

"He was yelling something at me and I turned my head and waved my hand at him. It drove him nuts. That's why I did it."

"So you like provoking him?"

He paused a beat, fidgeted in his seat. There are times when Herren always seemed to be fidgeting, unable to sit still for very long, the sense that there was all this energy with no place to go. There was a moodiness to him too, one minute his face blank, his eyes vacant, the voice soft and undistinct, off momentarily in some private world where no one else was allowed, and the next his voice animated, the energy back. One minute he could be full of teenage bravado, strutting about like he was the star in his own movie, the next he could be surprisingly pensive, as if there always were some private battle going on, his behavior hanging in the balance. When he began talking again, the bravado was gone.

"Not really. He just drives me crazy sometimes. But I love Mr. Karam. I wish I was a really great player so that when schools came to recruit me, I'd tell him that if they wanted me they had to take Mr. Karam as an assistant."

It was not an offhand remark. There is a sensitive side to Herren that often got overlooked amid his growing celebrity. After the agonizing Duxbury game, he had sat in the corner and stared at the wall, as if trapped in some personal hell. He showered and began walking slowly out across the gym floor to the bus and the ride back to Fall River, when he saw Shawn Thames walking, head down, in front of him. He knew he had yelled at Thames during the game. He also knew it had been Thames's first game and that he'd been scared, that he hadn't been ready for the kind of situation he'd been thrown into. So Herren caught up to Thames and threw his arm around him, the two of them walking toward the bus, the white star whose missed foul shot had lost the game and the black sophomore who'd just painfully discovered that playing in a varsity game for Durfee was a different world than anything he was used to.

But Herren often lived inside a cocoon, a personal world, one that had little to do with the world outside Fall River. He was an indifferent student, not because he didn't have the aptitude, but because it wasn't a priority. He did sporadic homework, usually leaving school without any books, was mostly content to do barely more than the minimum, though his teachers almost universally said he could be a good student if he wanted to be one. He spent a large part of most school nights talking on the phone, either to a succession of admiring girls or his friends. Outside of basketball and hanging out with his friends, he didn't have a lot of interests. He didn't watch much television. The last movie he'd seen was *Hoosiers* when he was about twelve. His brother Michael, who had opinions on everything from local politics to world events and loved to expound on them to anyone who would listen, was forever criticizing him for his supposed indifference to anything other than his immediate personal world.

"Chrissie can't even name the Beatles," Michael would say.

"Who cares?" Chris would answer back. "Why should I care about them?"

He read little, and when he did it was basketball books, *Raw Recruits*, or Larry Bird's *Drive*. He seemed to live exclusively in the present tense, and maybe nothing came to symbolize that more than his not having a driver's license, though he was more than a year over the eligible age.

"I don't want it," he said about his driver's license. "I don't need it."

"What do you mean you don't need it?" I asked.

"Everywhere I want to go, someone will take me," he said.

He also was one of the few juniors in the school with legitimate college aspirations who had failed to take the PSAT test the year before, the test that not only prepares sophomores for the SAT test, but also gives them an indication of how they might score on it. He just never got around to signing up for the test. He seemed oblivious to the idea that how he did on the SAT test might determine where he went to college. It was just this sense of obliviousness that so frustrated Karam, for often he would look at Herren coasting his way through Durfee and see himself so many years before, squandering his college basketball career because of his scholastic indifference, believing that his actions would be devoid of consequences.

"You know, they have books you can buy to help you prepare for the SATs," I said to Herren.

"I don't need them," he said.

"What do you mean, you don't need them?"

"I don't need them," he stressed. "Notre Dame sends me vocabulary words."

"Do you ever look at them?"

"Once in a while."

"Name a word."

He paused for a moment. 'N-E-F-A-R-I-O-U-S," he said finally.

"What's it mean?"

An impish smile streaked across his face.

"Evil," he said.

Friday night Durfee had rolled over St. John's of Danvers, ahead by seventeen at the half. Herren had scored eight out of his team's first ten points, finishing with twenty-three points and eighteen rebounds, two points more than Caron. He had not gotten the forty he had promised, but he could have. Herren was at a different level than his competition that night, more gifted athletically, able to beat his man anytime he pleased, able to get to the basket virtually at will, essentially able to do what he wanted. He moved with a sure physical grace, had a presence on the court that was almost leonine, quick, strong, explosive. Shortly before the end of the game he had dunked at the end of a fast break to the vast delight of the student section that sat across from the Durfee bench, an exclamation point for the evening.

It was one of those games that makes a team feel good about itself, an easy victory, a Friday night home game before a decent crowd, a chance for the subs to play and for Karam to toss one-liners at the people who sat behind him, Durfee basketball the way it's supposed to be.

At least Callahan had thought so. Like so many of the others on the team, he had grown up playing in the Milliken League and going to games as a kid, dreaming of one day being out there on the court at the field house, the big stage that's Durfee basketball. Now that it's actually happening to him—and he's starting, no less—he's almost in awe of it all, so thrilled to be playing that he doesn't particularly care how well he's playing. So it doesn't bother him when Karam yells at him, for he's in the middle of a childhood fantasy, complete with the parties and the smiles of girls in the corridors and the attention that comes with playing for Durfee, and so what if the price tag for that is Mr. Karam yelling at you every once in a while?

The first team was now working against a zone defense and Karam was telling them to move the ball, not to let it bounce, make the zone react. A lesson he had learned back in the early fifties from Lukey. Over and over it went, until he began substituting.

"Mr. Karam, can we get a drink?" Caron asked.

"Yeah, you guys really worked hard," he replied sarcastically. "No. No drinks. No one leaves the court."

There are thirteen kids on the team, most of them seniors: Jones, Pavoa, Cioe, Mikolazyk, Eric Santos, Matt Boardman, Chris Campbell, John Eagan. Except for the first four, the others get very little playing time. Karam is known for not playing a lot of players, for not substituting often. It's a residue of another basketball era, the one he'd been shaped by, the way it's always been. He probably would be better served by using some of his younger players as reserves, but he feels a loyalty to the seniors who sit on the bench and rarely singles them out for individual criticism. He is like Urban in that respect too; the kids who play are the ones who get yelled at. Karam walked over to the bench where Herren was sitting.

"Can you imagine him at a Division I school?" he said to Dempsey, talking loud enough so Herren could hear him. "He'd lose his scholarship in ten minutes."

It bothered him that Herren was not practicing, for he suspected his malady was the result of too much partying the night before and that Herren, because of his obvious stature, had an obligation to practice hard and set the tone for the others. He's sensitive to the impression Herren is given star treatment, even though all the kids know he is and that's just the way it is. So he wanted Herren to know he disapproved of his taking the morning off.

"Chrissie, you're really hurting?"

"I can't breathe," Herren answered, giving a cough as an exclamation point.

"I guess you won't be able to play Tuesday night, then. Because if you don't practice tomorrow, you're not playing Tuesday."

Herren shrugged, walked through the doors and back toward the locker room.

"Do you think he'll practice tomorrow?" I asked Karam.

"What do you think? He'd have to be dead to miss a game."

The practice continued for a while before Caron started limping, the same foot that had been bothering him for over a week now. He hopped over to the front row of the bleachers, grimacing in pain. The gym fell silent. Karam gave an exasperated sigh. Last Sunday he had lost Jones with an ankle sprain. Now here was Caron hurt again. All this on a team that wasn't deep to begin with.

Caron limped into the trainer's room, sat on a bench with his foot in a bucket of ice. He had played against Duxbury with his foot bothering him, and less than a week later he'd hurt it again. Worse was the fact that what was causing him the pain supposedly came from a structural deformity, for which the only cure would be surgery.

"It's been killing me," he said, "but I could take a couple of weeks off then come back and hurt it again the next day. So what's the point?"

He knew he needed a big season if he was ever going to realize his dream of getting a Division I scholarship. Last year had been a great year for him, what he'd always envisioned for himself at Durfee. He had been the starting point guard, the surprise of the season, the kind of tough, smart, good-shooting kid that always seemed to roll off Fall River's assembly line. On a team with Herren and three seniors he'd been overlooked, but he'd benefited from that too. Teams were so intent on the others that he'd gotten a lot of open shots. He had made opponents pay dearly. Throughout the playoffs he seemed to make every shot he took, plus playing a steady floor game. He'd only been a sophomore, but already had proven to be an excellent high school player, one who had the ability to play college basketball somewhere.

But in the Darwinian world of college recruiting and talent evaluating, judgments already were being made on him, as if he already had a Division II stamp on his forehead and there was nothing he could do could eradicate it. He was only about six feet tall, and in a college game that's become dominated by super-quick, athletic black kids, he already was being viewed as too small and maybe a step slow. It was not a knock on him, but an example of what Division I basketball has become, an extremely athletic game where physical gifts and potential are often more prized than basketball skills. If Caron had been three or four inches bigger, his shooting ability and overall basketball savvy no doubt would have made him a prized commodity at the Division I level. But he wasn't, and those same skills now seemed to translate into Division II.

He didn't dismiss that. He knew a Division II scholarship meant a free education, something worth about $80,000, knew what a windfall that could be for his parents. But the dream had been to play the kind of college basketball he saw on television, the big crowds, the glamor, Dick Vitale's voice, the carrot dangled in front of virtually every kid who ever bounces a ball in earnest. Unlike many of the kids on the team whose sole basketball dream had been to play for Durfee, Caron always had hoped for more. Now he was beginning to sense that his dream was going to be difficult to achieve, that everything was happening very quickly, his future being decided by forces beyond his control.

Making this season seem more urgent was the swirl of attention that already followed Herren, the letters from schools that came to Durfee every day, the calls to Karam's office from assistant coaches, the omnipresent reality that Herren was in demand by the basketball biggies, all the things Caron once had envisioned for himself. So although a few Division II schools in New England were showing serious interest, he wanted more. And now he was hurt again, his foot once again in a bucket of ice, trying to control the swelling so he'd be able to practice the next day and be ready for the game against Boston College High on Tuesday night.

Unlike some of the others, Caron had a strong sense of self. He knew what he liked and what he didn't, his attitudes often assuming the rigidity of a seventeen-year-old. He seemed removed from the peer pressure that often engulfed his peers. He had a girlfriend he was serious about, thus didn't hang out in the basement of Suneson's house with Herren, Pavao, Callahan, and Mikolazyk. He was one of the few kids on the team able to detach himself and look at both the team and the city from the outside, somewhat critically. He was goal-oriented, and he often would look at many of the kids in the school and think of them as "losers," kids with no goals, no ambitions, no futures. He was a good student, though he knew he could be a better one if he worked harder at it. He was smart and perceptive, yet he was a product of Fall River too, shaped by its values, occasionally imprisoned by the idea that the world stopped at the rotary at the start of Route 24 and the highway that led to Boston.

"What books do you read?" I asked as he sat with his foot in the ice bucket.

"Nothing, really," he said. "I just read sports books. Joe Namath. O. J. Simpson. Jim Brown. All the Bird books. I know everything about every player that ever lived. But I probably only read one fiction book in my life, something called *A Baseball Fantasy*. I know I should read others, but they don't interest me."

"What books have you read in English class?"

"I don't read the books," he said. "They suck. I just read the *Cliff's Notes*."

"What are you reading now in English?"

"We just got a new one and it sucks wicked bad."

"What is it?"

"*Jane Eyre*," he said, pronouncing "Eyre," as if it were Lake *Erie*.

"Jeff," I said. "It's *Jane Eyre*," pronouncing "Eyre" like *air*.

Without missing a beat, he said, "It still sucks. It sucks so bad they probably don't even have a *Cliff's Notes* for it."

Both Herren and Caron were ready to play against Boston College High School. The game was in Boston—in South Boston, really—across the street from the Boston *Globe* newspaper offices on Morrissey Boulevard. The team was lined up in a corridor waiting for the jayvee game to finish. Minutes later the BC team, in their white uniforms with maroon and yellow trim, came into the same corridor. The trash-talking started quickly.

"We're going to kick your ass," a BC kid said.

"Like fuck you are," Cioe said.

"You guys aren't shit," another BC kid said.

"We don't have to be to kick your ass," Herren piped in.

It went on like this, back and forth, teenage machismo in a corridor lined with pictures of past teams. It's the legacy of the playground, trash-talking is, a practice that's now as much a part of basketball as expensive sneakers and missed free throws, from the NBA to some lowly pickup game. It's a game within a game and these Durfee players have been doing it for years, as far back as the Milliken League. One of the worst sins in Fall River is to be called a pussy, to back down when challenged; thus trash-talking doesn't affect them the way it might a more suburban team, especially Herren and Caron, who instantly rise to the challenge.

It's also an integral part of the Fall River persona, the subtle one that says we're from Fall River, we're supposed to be tough, certainly tougher than some pseudo-preppies at Boston College High.

Now it all seemed to be intensifying when Karam came around the corner and saw what was going on.

"Knock it off," he said. "When are you guys going to grow up?"

"They started it," Caron said.

Karam shook his in disgust.

"I don't care who started it. Knock it off."

It's always something, he thinks. *We can't just come up here and play a game and go home anymore. It always has to be something to take the fun out of it.*

"Chrissie, stop bouncing the ball," he said.

Herren, again full of energy, bounced the ball hard on the floor, then caught it and slapped it. Karam just stared at him.

Once again, Durfee has drawn people to an away game. Michael Herren and his circle of friends are there. Minutes before the game started he came down near the court, staring out at the two teams.

"I hate BC High," Michael said. "They think they're fucking Irish-Catholic royalty."

He was visibly nervous, like a parent there to see his son play for the first time. There is no competition between him

...... 75

and Chris, although it's becoming obvious that Chris will have a chance to erase a lot of Michael's all-time Durfee records. Chris has said that if in the last minute of the last game of his high school career he found himself only two points shy of his brother's record as the all-time scoring leader, he wouldn't shoot the ball. Once, he'd been asked in a local television interview who was his favorite player of all time, and he had named his brother Michael. The interviewer, expecting the usual response of Larry Bird or Michael Jordan, had given him a quizzical look, but Herren had meant it. He used to love to watch his brother play, and now that the roles were reversed, Michael fervently rooted for Chris, as if his younger brother now carried his own basketball dreams too. Michael was fully aware of the situation his brother found himself in, thanks to the controversy that hovered over his own career.

"Christopher really walked into a hornet's nest because of me," he said, "I hope to God that he can take things I did negatively and learn from them. That's my job as a big brother."

The game quickly showed Durfee's deficiencies. BC High was big. They played a zone, pinching Herren out at the top of the key shading Caron on the wing. Their game plan was simple: Turn the game into a halfcourt one and don't let Herren get to the basket, make Durfee win by having to hit perimeter shots. Once again the Durfee inside players were no factor, putting virtually all the pressure on Herren and Caron. The result was a slow, physical game, one that Durfee appeared in danger of losing. You only had to look at Karam's clenched face to realize he knew it too.

"What the fuck is that?" he yelled to one of the referees as Herren was bumped on a drive to the basket and no foul was called. "I can hear the slap from here, for chrissakes."

"Enough, Skip," the ref said as he ran by.

Karam glared at him.

Three years ago he'd been thrown out of a playoff game, then had to go before the disciplinary board of the Massachusetts Interscholastic Athletic Association. The charge had been bumping a referee and there was speculation the board was going to suspend him for the entire year. He'd been suspended for two games instead, after John Corriero, the Fall River superintendent of schools and a onetime Durfee classmate of Karam's, had testified strongly on his behalf, saying that he'd seen the ref initiate the bumping. Ever since, Correiro thought Skippy was a marked man.

Karam waved his hand at the referee in disgust, a pained look on his face. He doesn't want a technical; the game is too close. He knows his team is in trouble, that it's going to be fortunate to escape with a victory. He cannot remember a Durfee team that began a season 1–2 and the thought of doing it this year fills him with dread. At halftime he tells Herren to look to pass the ball inside more, try to take advantage of the holes in the BC High defense. As soon as the second half started Herren quickly hit Callahan for two layups, turning and subtly nodding his head to Karam after each of them. A few minutes later Durfee began to take control. With fifteen seconds left to play, they're only leading by one, trying to hang on. Then Caron makes two free throws and they escape, 63–60.

"It's going to be like this all year," said Karam, his blue shirt stained with sweat, his red tie loose around his neck. "We're just not very good."

He stood outside the locker room, in an area that led to the showers, but his coaching night was not yet over. Dempsey had told him that Steve Breese, a six-foot-six sophomore and the biggest kid in the school, wants to quit the jayvee team because he doesn't think he's playing enough. Not that Breese deserves to play. He is out of shape, weak, his body soft and overweight. He appears nowhere near ready to play competitive basketball, even at the junior varsity level.

There is a youthful quality about him, a young kid trapped inside an overgrown body. But he's six–six, can catch the ball, has a decent shooting touch, and who knows? An old coaching adage says you can't teach height.

Karam wants Dempsey to play Breese regardless, for at a school that never seems to have any height, he has to be patient with any kid who's six-foot-six in the tenth grade. Another old coaching adage says big players often develop late, need time to grow into their bodies.

"That's the trouble with jayvee coaches," Karam was forever telling Dempsey. "They want to win jayvee games, where their real job should be getting kids ready for the varsity. No one gives a shit what the jayvee record is. No one remembers."

Dempsey knew this. His competitive juices made him want to win jayvee games, but he also was very cognizant of playing kids who he thought would help the varsity.

"Breezie will never help you, Skippie," Dempsey was forever telling Karam. "He never plays on his own. He doesn't work at it. He doesn't want it bad enough."

Now Breese wanted to quit, feeling that Dempsey was never going to play him, and he didn't want to be on the team if he wasn't going to play. This was not unusual. Gone were the days when kids were content merely to be on the team, were willing to wait their turn, proud to even have a Durfee jayvee uniform. Much of it now was instant gratification, the feeling that if I'm not playing, why not quit and go do something else? His brother already had quit the jayvee team a few weeks earlier. Breese didn't particularly like Dempsey, referred to him behind his back as "a dick," thought that Dempsey didn't like him. Now he came over and stood in front of Karam, towering over him, yet still full of scared innocence.

"Why do you want to quit?" Karam asked.

"Because I never play," he said in his soft, high-pitched, adolescent voice that belied his size.

Karam shook his head. He stood back a step, cocked his head to the side, as if seeing Breese for the first time.

"Breezie, if you want to quit, go ahead," he said disgustedly. "But if you do, you're going to walk around school for the next two years like a big six-foot-six sack of shit."

Chapter

ON A STIFLING HOT August morning in 1892 Andrew Borden, a wealthy Fall River businessman with one of the oldest and most influential names in the city, and his second wife Abby Durfee Borden, were found hatcheted to death in their home on Second Street in the downtown section of the city. Seven days later Andrew's youngest daughter Lizzie was charged with the murders. So began one of the most mystifying murder cases in the history of American crime.

Abby Borden had been killed at approximately 9:45 in the morning, Andrew a little after 11. In the house at the time were Lizzie and Bridget Sullivan, the Irish maid. So the obvious question was, if the two were killed by some intruder, how did the intruder go undetected in the house for nearly an hour and a half?

Lizzie was thirty-two at the time, living at home with her father, stepmother, and older sister Emma. By all accounts she seemed an unlikely killer. She was a member of the Central Congregational Church, one of the most affluent and prestigious in the city, did work for charities, was quiet and reserved, a proper young lady in a small, provincial, Victorian city where the rules of decorum were rigid and uncompromising. In an age where the only options for women were marriage or to live at home with parents, both Lizzie and Emma already were considered spinsters. Her only apparent vice was a desire to live in the Highlands, a place appropriate to her father's money and social status in the community. Her father, though, had little desire for status. What motivated him was the accumulation of money. He continued to live in the small house on Second Street, one in which the two daughters had an uneasy relationship with their stepmother, a house in which there was little evidence of affection.

There also was speculation it was a house in discord. The two sisters had resented the fact their father had given Abby the deed to some property he owned, property Lizzie and Emma thought they were going to get. Abby also had complained in the weeks before the murders that someone was trying to poison her. The day before the murders, Lizzie had tried to buy a form of poison from a local druggist.

The day of the murders had begun like many of the days in the Borden house. Bridget the maid had come downstairs at 6:15 and begun making the breakfast of mutton and johnnycakes, a large breakfast considering the heat of the day. At the breakfast were Andrew and Abby Borden, plus John Morse, Andrew's brother-in-law from his first marriage, who had spent the night. Lizzie, sick the night before, came downstairs at roughly nine, didn't eat breakfast. Morse already had left for the morning, though he was expected back for lunch. Emma, the older sister, was away for a few days, visiting friends in Fairhaven, a small town on the other side of New Bedford.

Shortly afterward, Andrew Borden left to go downtown on his daily errands and Abby told Bridget she wanted her to wash the windows. Lizzie supposedly went back to her room, then came back downstairs and went into the kitchen to iron some handkerchiefs. Just before 11 Andrew Borden returned and was let into the house by Bridget, since he had forgotten his keys and the front door was triple-locked. Bridget told him that Mrs. Borden had left to visit a sick friend. He went into the sitting room and began reading the paper. Lizzie, to get out of the heat in the kitchen, had relaxed in the backyard for a while, then had gone into the barn to look for some lures for an upcoming fishing trip. She later testified she thought she heard a groan, and went into the house, where she found her father slumped on a couch, covered with blood. His wallet, plus a silver watch and chain and a gold ring, were on his body. The police and a doctor were quickly summoned, after which Abby was found upstairs, also dead.

Less than a hour after Andrew Borden's body was found, several hundred people had gathered in the street outside the house. There was incredible public interest in the case. Who had done it? Why had they done it? How could the descendants of two of the oldest families in the area be killed in their own home? How could something so hideous happen in the middle of the day on a busy street just off downtown? The murders had happened just four years after Jack the Ripper terrorized London, and the idea of some axe-crazed murderer patrolling the streets of Fall River had the city in a frenzy. SHOCKING CRIME, A VENERABLE CITIZEN AND HIS AGED WIFE HACKED TO PIECES IN THEIR HOME . . . POLICE SEARCHING FEVERISHLY FOR THE FIENDISH MURDERER, screamed the headline in the *Herald*, one of the city's three newspapers.

As soon as news of the murders had gone out, everything in Fall River seemed to stop. There were so many people in front of the house on Second Street that it was impossible for carriages to move in the street. Many of the mills and businesses had shut down because workers failed to return from lunch. By the sixth day afterward, the day of the inquest, it was the same scenario. On the second day of the inquest, Lizzie was charged, the news flashed to the crowd outside.

The case attracted international interest and was covered

in newspapers around the East, some reporters traveling from as far away as New Orleans and San Francisco. The trial started in New Bedford in June of the following year. Lizzie was prosecuted by two district attorneys, one of whom went on to become attorney general of the United States. She had three defense attorneys, including a former governor of Massachusetts, who later billed Lizzie $25,000 for his services.

The trial had everything from a headless hatchet that might or might not have been the murder weapon, testimony from one of Emma's closest friends that Lizzie had burned a dress shortly after the funerals, and relentless cross-examinations. It lasted ten days, but the jury was only out for about an hour when it returned with a "not guilty" verdict. The courtroom erupted in cheers. Throngs of people passed by Lizzie's carriage in a processional before she left the courthouse. There was relief at the verdict, especially among the closed, rigid society of the Highlands, for Lizzie was one of them, linked with them by breeding and social class, though her father had chosen to live downtown on Second Street. This was "old Fall River," the village within a city that was unofficially called "the people you know," the people who controlled everything. There were others in the city, though, who resented the decision, feeling she got acquitted only because she was one of Fall River's leading families.

Interestingly, Lizzie spent the rest of her life in Fall River.

"A good many persons have talked to me as if they thought I would go and live somewhere else when my trial was over," she told a reporter. "I don't know what possesses them. I am going home and I am going to stay there. I have never thought of going anywhere else."

Shortly after the trial, she and Emma, using their inheritance of roughly $400,000—huge money in 1893—moved into a big Queen Anne-style house in the Highlands less than two miles from the murder house. It was on French Street, had fourteen rooms, four bathrooms, a carriage house, spacious gardens. When she moved there after the trial, she changed her name to "Lizbeth" and called the house "Maplecroft," a social no-no in what passed for Fall River society. She even chiseled the name into the top stone of the front entrance in what became known as a monument to bad taste.

Eleven years after the verdict, Emma moved out of Maplecroft, never living there again. The rift supposedly was caused by Lizzie's friendship with Boston vaudeville actress Nance O'Neil, a relationship, complete with rumors of lesbianism, that in the rigid social world of the Highlands was considered nothing short of scandalous, especially for a woman who'd been accused of murdering her father and stepmother. Emma always had been in public mourning, often wearing black, believing that after the tragedy that had befallen them it was their civic duty to live out the rest of their days in quietude. Lizzie didn't agree. She had spent much of her young life yearning for social acceptance, and now, with a house in the Highlands and the money to enjoy it, she wanted to take advantage of all the things she once felt deprived of.

Lizzie would live the rest of her life in Fall River, dying in 1926 at the age of sixty-eight. She never married, nor did Emma. Lizzie lived thirty-six years after the murders, yet never was able to escape them. After the jubilation of her acquittal, her status in the city continued to decline, to where in the last years of her life she was essentially ostracized, especially by the Highlands society she had so tried to impress. Forget that she had been found innocent in a court of law. In Fall River it was much more complicated. She was too notorious, the crime too heinous for her to ever be able to escape the ramifications. The *Globe*, one of the city's newspapers, continued its campaign to impugn her, one that started shortly after the murders and continued every August 4 with an anniversary story. Years later she supposedly told a friend that she liked to travel to such places as Boston, New York, and Washington, places where no one recognized her.

And yet, as Victoria Lincoln writes in her book *Private Disgrace*, Lizzie "never considered leaving the city that had formed her and cast her out. Throughout her life she still clung, as she had in high school, to the wistful perimeter of the small world that never gave her full acceptance—yet still flung its protective, familial cloak about the story that was its own private disgrace."

But if she had been acquitted in June 1893, her acquittal didn't solve the mystery.

Did she do it? If she did, what happened to the murder weapon? Or the clothes she was wearing at the time, clothes that surely would have been splattered with some amount of blood?

And if she didn't, who did?

It's now a hundred years later. Maplecroft is still there on French Street, a little run-down now, with grass that needs cutting. It's no longer the elegant home it was in Lizzie's day, but still in the Highlands, still a good address on a good street with a view of Mount Hope Bay at the bottom of the hill. There's even a basketball hoop over the garage, the ultimate irony: Lizzie and basketball, the city's two main passions, finally linked together.

No matter that it was her stepmother, not her mother, who died that hot August morning in 1892. Or that her father was hit by ten whacks, not forty-one. Or that a jury decided that Lizzie did not kill either her father or her stepmother. "Lizzie Borden took an axe and gave her mother forty whacks. When she saw what she had done she gave her father forty-one." There's not a kid in Fall River who doesn't grow up hearing it.

There have been numerous books on the murder, a Broadway play, a ballet, an opera, and a movie, in which a nude Elizabeth Montgomery, her hatchet dripping with blood, walked from room to room as if in a trance. There have been many theories, everything from Lizzie did it, to Morse did it, to the illegitimate son of Andrew Borden did it, to some fiendish passerby did it, to the idea that Lizzie was an incest victim.

Evan Hunter, who as Ed McBain is one of the most popular writers of detective fiction in the country, theorized that Lizzie was a lesbian and killed Mrs. Borden when she discovered her and Bridget Sullivan, the Irish maid, in a lover's tryst.

One of the more interesting of the Lizzie Borden books is Lincoln's *A Private Disgrace*. Lincoln had grown up in the Highlands as a child, in the same social strata as Lizzie, and remembered her as the strange older woman in the neighborhood that all the kids made jokes about. She theorizes Lizzie had epilepsy and thus killed her father and Mrs. Borden in the midst of a seizure.

It's Lincoln's argument that Lizzie had been tried and found guilty in the Highlands long before the actual trial began, yet the community had publicly rallied around her because she was one of their own.

"I knew something about her limitations and her small town ambition . . . I know something of her temperament, lost in fantasy and at the same time strangely deficient in imagination, blind to the real world of people and still so terribly anxious for its acceptance, its admiration—so self-defeatingly anxious," Lincoln writes. "Those who knew her best and spoke of these limitations, ambitions, mechanisms of self-defeat have often seemed to me to be describing themselves—and my own early childhood—when they spoke of her. She was Fall River."

She was Fall River.

"Born in Fall River, die in Fall River," Michael Herren likes to say, the pride evident in his voice.

His aunt Kathy Bellanger had said how she had looked at

him moments after he had just finished his Durfee career, after winning his second consecutive state title in the Worcester Centrum, watching him accept the spoils of victory, and knew it never again would be as good athletically for him as it was at that very moment: It just couldn't be.

She was right.

Michael Herren had been the Massachusetts player of the year two straight years, a high school All-American, and one of only two players in Massachusetts high school history to be All-State three years in a row; the other was Patrick Ewing. But he was the wrong size for a college basketball player in a league as highly competitive as the Big East. He was the classic "tweener," too small to be a forward, maybe a step too slow to be a guard. He'd been a great high school forward at six-foot-four, but to play at Boston College he was going to have to make the transformation to guard, a position that required both the foot speed and the ball-handling skills that never had been the strongest parts of his game.

It's hard to imagine anyone who ever had a more dramatic high school basketball career than Michael Herren. He was the focus of everyone's attention since his freshman year at Durfee. As early as the sixth grade the word already was out on him, and when he arrived three years later as a freshman he didn't disappoint. He started immediately, a gifted player with visible charisma. He had a maturity far beyond his years, largely the result of his father's habit of taking him everywhere, so that Michael grew up around older people.

"There was more pressure on him as a freshman than I've seen with any other senior," said Jack Campbell, a Durfee physical education teacher who was Karam's assistant for thirteen years. "People had been hearing about him since he was in the fourth grade."

By his own admission it was his sophomore year that things started to get "completely insane" for Michael Herren.

The parties. The drinking. The fights. The feeling that it was all starting to take on a life of its own. The fighting started innocently enough. He had learned to fight in the Fordney Street projects when he'd been young, for the simple reason that fighting was a way of life there. He'd learned early that you never backed down. Wasn't that the quality that made him such a great player, that he didn't back down, that he wanted to win more than his opponent did? By the time he arrived at Durfee, his basketball reputation preceding him, almost immediately there were kids who challenged him, older kids who wanted to find out if Michael Herren was really as tough as he was touted to be. In Fall River, where fighting was part of the fabric, whether for respect or to right perceived wrongs, confrontation was virtually inevitable.

"There's a certain pecking order," said Michael. "You start to get a reputation in the tenth grade. Then older kids challenge you. It just kind of snowballs."

Michael also was everyone's big brother. Just as Chris would do years later, Michael surrounded himself with a small coterie of friends he played with, and within that world he was the big brother, the protector, Fall River's version of Holden Caulfield trying to stop everyone from falling over the cliff, the catcher in the rye. One of his friends got hassled at a party? Michael would come to the rescue. Some older kid had threatened Chris at Morton Middle School? Michael would be there the next day. He and his friends would be at a party in some neighboring town and someone would say something disparaging about Mr. Karam or Durfee basketball? Those were fighting words too.

To him, it was different sides of the same coin: You took no shit on the court, you took no shit off it. It was all about winning, about asserting your will in a given situation.

"We'd have an intramural tournament and Michael would say, 'Count the number of games my team wins in a row,'" said Jack Campbell. "And then his team would win something like forty-one games in a row. He was like that in practice. Every day. He would play one hundred and ten percent every day."

His last game as a sophomore had been in the Boston Garden, a loss in the semifinals of the state tournament. Durfee had been playing Cambridge Rindge and Latin and this is how Leigh Montville, the *Sports Illustrated* writer, then a columnist for the Boston *Globe*, described him:

> The eyes couldn't stay off Herren. He was involved in everything. He was involved in the good, the bad. He was involved in the ugly. One minute he was scoring, clenching a fist to the Durfee crowd, yapping. The next minute he was committing a charge, clenching a fist, yapping at the referee, yapping at himself. One minute he was up. The next minute he was on the sidelines at the end of the third period, blood rolling down his face from an eight stitch cut across the top of his left eye from an elbow, unable to sit still as the trainer applied a temporary bandage.
>
> "I've got to get back," the kid was yelling.
>
> "Be still and I'll get you back," the trainer was yelling in return.
>
> "Tell the coach to call a timeout to start the fourth quarter," the kid was yelling. "Tell him."
>
> The kid ended the night with 14 points, only three in the second half. He ended with the eight stitches. He ended with a bunch of roses someone had given him in his hands and his mouth still moving.
>
> "That's just the way I am," 15 year old Mike Herren said. "I play basketball like a kid."
>
> He paused.
>
> "I am a kid," he said.

Two years later Montville caught up with Michael Herren, again in the Boston Garden in the state tournament, this time squeaking by Cambridge Rindge and Latin. This time he described him as having the exuberance of a ten-year-old who has been raised in only warm and happy surroundings, told about how he shook hands before games, kissed babies, high-fived strangers, signed autographs afterward, approached each game as if he were the ringleader of a grand circus, and of course never stopped talking:

> The kid talked in a hurry. The words tumbled out of him without punctuation, words and more words. He moved his legs as he talked, moved his legs without moving his feet. Kinetic energy. There was nowhere left to go, nothing left to do, but the motors were still running. Words.
>
> "You think I'm something now," he said, legs moving in place, energy everywhere. "You should have seen me as a freshman. I've mellowed out."

Eventually it all took on a life of its own, the success, the fights, the reputation, Michael and his merry band who dominated high school basketball in Massachusetts, sometimes beating teams that on paper they shouldn't have beaten. Not that he was the only legitimate player on the team. Juddy McDonald, his best friend all through Durfee, got a scholarship to the University of Richmond, later transferred to St. Michael's, a Division II school in Vermont, where he had a successful career. Matt Attar ended up starting for Drexel. Jason Correiro had a fine career at UMass-Dartmouth, a Division III school two towns away from Fall River. But it had been Michael's will, his refusal to lose, that had defined those state championship teams in 1988 and 1989.

By the time he arrived at Boston College, there already was a certain legend surrounding him, as if no one knew what was real anymore and what wasn't.

"I've never been around a kid who had such a cloud hanging over him," said Boston College coach Jim O'Brien. "Guys used to come into the dorms looking for him, guys from all over who wanted to challenge him. And one thing about Michael. He never backed down. I felt sorry for him. He was like some old gunfighter who was trying to retire and people wouldn't let him. I think it was great for him to go down south to Belmont Abbey, to get away, to go someplace where people didn't know him."

Maybe more importantly, Michael Herren also was never able to emotionally leave Durfee in the year and a half he spent at Boston College, as if all his basketball dreams had been actualized when he won his second state title as a senior.

For the first time in his basketball life he looked around and there was no Juddy, who had been his teammate since they had been seven years old. No Jason. No Pat Malloy. No Matt Attar. No John Murray. No Lamar Stevens. None of the kids who had been with him forever, had been his support system, none of the friends who always had been with him when he used to be a contemporary version of Shane with a jump shot, riding into some alien gym to take on all comers. He looked around and saw thirteen new teammates, knew he had to start all over again, and in a deep, private part of himself, knew that something was gone forever.

In a funny way he'd always known that basketball never would be the same after Durfee. He understood as early as ninth grade that he never was going to be a professional basketball player, that he didn't have the physical gifts for it. Even then he'd known he was an overachiever, that his determination and his uncompromising thirst to win were his biggest strengths. By the time he was in high school, right in the middle of his incredible success, he knew how difficult it was going to be to play in a league as competitively demanding as the Big East. He had been to Five Star, the showcase Pennsylvania summer camp, had played against some of the best high school players in the country. He always had done well against them, winning awards, making all-star teams, but he'd also learned that many of the true elite players were more gifted athletically than he was.

"When I was in the ninth grade I told Skippy, Jr., that I was going to play in the Big East someday and he slapped me and said, 'Don't talk like that,' " Michael said. "But I knew I'd get there someday. But I also knew I was never going to be a marquee player at Boston College. I thought I'd be able to start for a couple of years, have a good career."

It hadn't happened.

In January of his freshman year, after a couple of games when he'd played well, he broke his leg in the Meadowlands, missed the rest of the year. The next year he left school at the end of the first semester.

"One night after I left Boston College and didn't know if I wanted to go back or not, I was walking by Durfee," he said. "It was late, maybe two or three in the morning, and I was walking home. I was all by myself and I walked past the field house and then I walked through McDonald's parking lot where we used to hang out and then I cut through the projects on my way home and it was like walking through my entire past. I guess I knew then that it was probably better if I got out of here for a while."

"I remember one time in October of his freshman year," his mother said. "He'd been home for the weekend and I had driven him back to school. He got out of the car and started walking toward his dorm and I realized he was wearing his Durfee jacket. I almost started to cry. I wanted to run after him and tell him to take it off, that it was over."

Would it be different for Chris?

Would he be able to escape Fall River, to move on to the next chapter, or would this be the high point of his basketball life, as it had been his brother's?

These were the questions I asked myself as I watched the season start to unfold. For after playing basketball in college myself in the late 1960s and both watching and writing about it ever since, I had come to know that it often takes more than talent to make it in sports. It takes mental toughness and commitment and dedication and all those other clichés that often are taped to locker room walls. Sometimes it even takes luck, the good fortune to be in the right place at the right time.

Did he have these other qualities, or would it be his destiny to be just another high school star whose career couldn't find a second act? For that was everyone's secret fear, from Karam to Dempsey to anyone close to the situation, the fear that Chris ultimately would self-destruct the way his brother had, a comet that sped brightly across the sky only to burn out just as quickly.

To watch Chris play was to see all the possibilities, to realize that he had the talent to transcend the Luke Urban Field House, to have the kind of college career he now seemed destined for. Then he would loaf through a practice or go off into some private funk, and you would realize that it was more complicated than just talent; that it also was all about Fall River and the legacy of the past, this city that both idolized its heroes and devoured them too.

Lizzie Borden couldn't transcend Fall River.

Neither could the majority of the city's high school basketball stars.

The theory among some residents is that Fall River is an attitude, almost a world unto itself, the result of both provincialism and a certain feeling of inferiority that comes with growing up in a city which few seem to ever leave.

Fall River and the rest of southeastern Massachusetts is virtually ignored by Boston and by the political and social forces that control the state. It's not Cape Cod, with its tourists, its beaches, its charm. It's not suburban Boston. It's closer to both the Rhode Island cities of Providence and Newport than it is to Boston, yet it's ignored by Rhode Island too. There is a sense of self-containment about Fall River, one fostered by family roots that run deep and the attitude that the world is bordered both by Route 24, the highway that leads to Boston. This feeling of containment is both Fall River's strength and its weakness.

For all of Durfee's basketball success there really has been one kid who successfully played big-time college basketball: Ernie Fleming. He started on the same Jacksonville team with Artis Gilmore that went to the Final Four in 1970, losing to UCLA in the national championship game. In the past forty years or so there has been a handful of others who have played Division I basketball, mostly at mid-level schools in New England. A few others have had excellent careers at the Division II level. But for all of Durfee's success over the past fifty years, few players have gone on to make an imprint on college basketball. Outside of Fleming, none had done it on a national level.

One reason for the lack of college success was that Durfee teams rarely had any size, so many kids had to be played out of position, thus hurting their future chances in college basketball. A second was that Durfee teams traditionally were known for their grit and toughness and solid coaching, not necessarily their outstanding natural talent. Finally, there was something inherent to Fall River that made it hard to leave and be successful somewhere else.

The first basketball hero was Andy Farrissey in the late forties. He was the first star, the leader of the teams that had started it all, someone mentioned when the names of the greatest players in Durfee history are bandied about.

He still lives in Fall River and one winter afternoon he was sitting at the bar at the Belmont Club, a downtown establishment without a sign, a bar that looks like a house. It's one of those places that's seemingly been around forever, the ultimate insider's place, where little kids used to come to the rear window and take home buckets of beer for their parents and where there's a "death book," full of signatures of the departed.

Farrissey is in his sixties, now, a thin wrinkled man with white hair. It's been a lot of years since he was the one who led the Hilltoppers to the Boston Garden, but he can still see it in his mind, a newsreel he can stop anytime he wants.

"All activity in the city stopped when we went to the Boston Garden," he said, a far-off look in his eyes. "Everything stopped dead. It was like going to an inauguration."

He had grown up in the Corky Row section of the city, an Irish enclave that essentially ran from City Hall to South Park, had virtually come of age in the Boys Club. By the time Farrissey got to high school, Durfee was about to start making its mark on Massachusetts high school basketball. Urban already was there, with his patterned basketball and his discipline, his way of harnessing the children of immigrants into fierce athletic teams. Farrissey became his first real star.

In the fall of 1948, after his spectacular Durfee career had ended, he went off to the University of Rhode Island, at the time one of the biggest basketball names in New England, a team that had gone to the national finals in 1946 and was coached by the legendary Frank Keaney, the man credited with popularizing fast-break basketball. Farrissey left before the season started, and came back to work in his father's meat business. He never went back to college.

"I've regretted it all my life," he said.

Winters, he played in the city league. Summers, he played with Bob Cousy on Cape Cod, Cousy then a young player for the Celtics. They would barnstorm around the Cape, often playing outdoors in Yarmouth. For a while he traveled around New England playing against the Harlem Globetrotters, back when the 'Trotters had such greats as Goose Tatum, Marques Haynes, Sweetwater Clifton. Then at twenty-five he stopped. Just like that.

"I put the ball down and never picked it up again," he said.

He ran for the City Council when he was twenty-five, won easy, capitalizing on his local fame. Four years later he ran for mayor, lost, later was on the council again.

"Let's see," he said. "I've been on the City Council. I've

run for mayor. I've had successful businesses. But people around here still look at me as a Durfee basketball player."

He paused, a dreamy look on his face.

"It was probably the best days of my life," he said wistfully.

"I never had toys," said Chris Herren.

"When I was three I had a basketball in my hands. A basketball was my toy. I never sat around the house playing with toys. I was outside playing a game. Something to help you get better as an athlete, not to sit in the house and play with dolls."

The first time Chris ever saw his brother play basketball, he was about seven, Michael about twelve. It was in the Milliken League and not only was Michael the best young kid in the city, he already was the center of attention, flamboyant, emotional, intense, already possessed of a charisma rare for someone so young.

"He was in the layup line and some kids in the stands were giving him shit," Chris recalled. "They were yelling at him, calling him names. Then the game started and my brother made a layup. Without stopping he ran right over and cracked a kid. Beat the shit out of him. It was awesome."

Chris can't remember a time in his childhood when his brother was not the star, or that the focus of his house wasn't sports. It's the environment he grew up in, and it shaped him as strongly as growing up in a monastery would have shaped a young priest.

Not only had his father, Al, been an excellent high school player, Durfee basketball had almost been his religion. It had been more than just a game to Al Herren back in the late sixties when he was at Durfee, it had been his identity, the culmination of his ambition, what had transformed him from just another poor kid from "below the hill" into someone with a certain status in the city. In a sense he always was the outsider, the one who had to prove it. His family was not from Fall River. He didn't have the deep Fall River roots like so many of the other kids had.

Al Herren's parents had come to Fall River from Alabama when they were eighteen years old. His father had found a job in the Firestone rubber plant, a red-brick fortress on the Taunton River just to the south of the Braga Bridge, the old American Print Works. They lived in a tenement on Almond Street at the very bottom of the hill where Al shared a room with both a brother and a sister. His father was a big, strong, hard-drinking, hardworking man who got up every day at four in the morning smelling of Old Spice and went off to work. At night he frequented the neighborhood bars, where he was known as "Alabama." He would be in Fall River for nearly thirty years, but it was never really his home. Home was Ragdale, Alabama, a small town about an hour north of Birmingham. Fall River was merely where his job was. His emotional ties, his allegiances, were to the south, the Alabama of his youth, and shortly after Firestone closed in 1970 he and his wife quickly moved back there. The Herrens had seven children. Al was the fifth child, the third oldest boy. There wasn't a lot of money.

"I always was aware that other kids had more than I had," he said. "Very much so."

It was a tough neighborhood, "Below the Hill," one in which ethnic differences didn't seem to matter because everyone was too concerned with getting by, a neighborhood where work was prized, not education. It also was a neighborhood where you learned to fight early because you really had no choice.

"If you didn't fight, you got beat up," Al Herren said. "It was that simple. To find your own peace, your own little corner, you had to use your fists."

Basketball became his own little corner. Not only was he good at it, he liked the immediate gratification of it: You shot the ball, it went in. Then you did it again. By the time he got to Durfee, basketball had become everything, school just something to sit through before practice started.

"I loved Skippy," he said, "to the point that I don't tolerate any bitching about Skippy in my house. When I played, Skippy didn't have to tell me twice. He didn't have to pump me up. My practices were like a war. If you were on the other team in practice, I hated you. If I played outside in the park, I played every game like it was my last game. Guys would tell me to lighten up and I'd tell them to shut up. I didn't know any other way. If Skippy told me to punch a guy in the balls four times, I would have done it five. I bought the whole package. I was a devotee. Where I came from, we didn't have too many guys taking piano lessons, if you know what I mean."

In the spring of 1970, his senior year at Durfee, he discovered his girlfriend Cindy Carey was pregnant. It was the time, he says, when "reality punched me right between the eyes." He was all set to go to play ball at Roger Williams, a small college in nearby Rhode Island, but things suddenly had become very complicated. He never entertained any thought of not having the baby, not getting married, because "Cynthia was always a goddess to me," but it wasn't easy. His parents were getting ready to move back home to Alabama and by the winter of the following year he found himself with a wife and an infant living in his sister's basement, all the while commuting to Providence every day to go to school and also trying to play college basketball. It soon got to be too much. He quit school and got a job at the Fall River Water Department as a laborer.

All around him the country was changing, the increasing protest against the Vietnam War, the counterculture finding Fall River, a time of increased personal freedom, the challenging of all the old stereotypes. His friends were starting to grow their hair long, smoke dope, go to rock concerts. He and Cynthia were at home rocking Michael.

"Everyone was rebelling, but I didn't have time for that," he said. "I had to make a living."

He began going to a local community college at night because he didn't want to spend the rest of his life digging holes in the ground. He began to care about his courses, care about school. He calls it his "wake-up call," the time that changed his life, made him start to see things in a different way, to become politicized, the first time in his life he began realizing that he could do well in school too. In 1976 he campaigned locally for Fred Harris, the Oklahoma senator trying to get the Democratic nomination as a populist. He was working for Family Services then, a private, nonprofit social agency, helping in the various Fall River housing projects. For a while he and Cynthia lived in the projects on Fordney Street, only a couple of hundred yards from where they live today.

In 1983 he decided to run for the state representative, one of three spots in Fall River, though he never had run for anything in his life before. He campaigned for over a year, going door to door in his sport jacket and tie on humid summer days, eventually visiting some doors three times. There were seven people in the race, but in the end Al Herren outworked them all, using a lot of the same characteristics that he once had shown as a Durfee basketball player, a ferocious tenacity and a relentless desire to win, all fueled by the lesson he'd learned on the playgrounds of his youth: It's not about participating. It's about winning.

It's the lesson he gave to his kids, though each accepted its hard truths differently. Michael bought it all, made it the article of his faith. Playing for Durfee was the ultimate, like being touched by the godhead. And you had to win, no matter what, for losing was incomprehensible. Michael internalized these lessons early and they defined his childhood, as simple and clear-cut as a drive to the basket.

With Chris it was a little more complicated. Even though his father knew at an early age that Chris was the better natural athlete, Chris didn't love sports the way Michael had. He also didn't like the pressure of trying to follow in Michael's large and imposing footsteps. He never was allowed to play sports at his own pace, to dabble in them the way other kids did, trying them out, trying to determine where they fit in his life. He was expected to play because that's what you did in his house. He was expected to be good because his brother was. He was the little brother, with all the ramifications.

"My father and brother used to get mad at me because I didn't want to play sports," he said.

His mother was different.

"I didn't care if my kids played sports or not," she said. "I can remember when Chrissie tried out for Little League and I picked him up and he was crying. He said he didn't want to play. I said fine, you don't have to. That night Al went out and bought him a new glove and played catch with him in the yard and the next day Chrissie came to me and said he wanted to try out again. But I think if I had pushed him that first day he wouldn't have wanted to do it again."

There are times when Cynthia Herren feels she has spent her entire life watching Durfee basketball. In a sense she has. She grew up with five older brothers and a twin sister. There was not a lot of money, and she can remember looking in her mother's closet as a young girl and seeing only two dresses. They lived near Sacred Heart Church, and one of the priests there then was Father James Porter, who in 1992 was charged with sexually molesting hundreds of boys back in the 1960s when he worked in Fall River and other southeastern Massachusetts towns. When she had been a small child, Father Porter often used to tuck her into bed.

Her father, Charley Carey, once had been a great athlete at Durfee in the late 1930s, a good enough baseball player to play professionally in the St. Louis Cardinals organization for three years. Her oldest brother Charlie had played for Urban in the late 1950s. Her brother Donald had been a starter on Karam's first team in 1961. Her brother Dennis also had played for Karam. She had liked sports as a girl, but it was a different world then, long before girls' sports became popular and provided both opportunities and identity for girls, a world where the boys played and the girls cheered. She became a cheerleader, her sister Kathy a majorette.

"My parents always went to my brothers' games and me and my sister would tag along," she said. "But they never came to see me cheer. The message was that what the boys did was important. What we girls did was not."

Charley Carey is in his early seventies now, and he grew up in a different Fall River, one caught in the awful throes of the Depression. No one had any money. There was a lot of unemployment, including Carey's father, who had immigrated from Ireland as a youth and had been laid off from his job as foreman of Bowen's Boat Yard on the waterfront. Carey was one of eight kids, and most of the time they rented a house on Maple Street, off Robeson Street, in the stretch between the Highlands and downtown.

"We always ate," he said, "but we didn't have anything. If you had a nickel in your pocket, it was a big deal. You could go a month without having enough money to go to the movies."

What they did have was sports. They also had Ruggles Park, just off Robeson Street, a playround with ball fields that looked out over the downtown mills. He was an outstanding athlete at Durfee, playing football, basketball, and baseball, and one day a gym teacher at one of the middle schools took him and five or six other kids to try out for the Cardinals in Blackstone, Massachusetts, about an hour away. There were about four hundred kids there, one of those grassroots tryouts where major league baseball in that era searched for talent, and at the end of the day Carey, who was an outfielder, had been impressive enough to get invited to a Cardinals' minor league spring training camp in Columbus, Georgia. So in the spring of 1940 he went to Georgia, his first time ever away from home. Again, there were four hundred kids, and they stayed in private homes and received meal tickets to eat in a cafeteria. That tryout led to another camp in Springfield, Missouri, before he decided to come home.

"After I bought a train ticket I had about ten cents left, so the only thing I ate from Missouri to Providence was a peanut bar," he said.

He went back later in the summer to a team in Caruthersville, Missouri. It was Class D baseball, a league with only four teams. A long way from Fall River. But it was a job, with the hope of a future, and in Fall River in 1940 nobody seemed to have a future.

"The town was just like *Gunsmoke*," he said. "No sidewalks. No sewer system. When it rained, everything flooded and it looked like Venice, Italy."

He went back to baseball the next year to Washington, Pennsylvania, broke his ankle, lay in the hospital for two weeks, and came home. The next year he gave it one more try, in the "Three I" League in Evansville, Indiana, before realizing he probably never would get to the major leagues.

He was married by this time, to Mary Martin, his Durfee sweetheart, who once had been the former head cheerleader at Durfee, and he went to work in Railroad Express. Then came the birth of his first child and the war, and a stint in Italy. When he returned in 1945, he came back to a different world. His older brother Bill had been killed at Anzio. Carey had a young family that was soon to get bigger, eventually would be seven kids in all, five boys, then the twins, Cynthia and Kathy. All this in a city that still hadn't come out of the Depression. He joined the electrician's union and began to raise his family.

Mostly, they lived on the second floor of a three-decker tenement on Seabury Street, which runs from behind Anderson-Little and goes north, adjoining Ruggles Park, which became like a surrogate backyard where his kids always played. Ruggles Park is still there, a little seedier, a little more run-down, graffiti on the backboards on the basketball court. The court is in the section of the park that's elevated and from it you can look out over the factories off in the distance, a Fall River still life.

The twins were the last born, Cindy and Kathy. Two girls with five older brothers in a family that revolved around sports, in a city that revolved around sports. One of Cindy Herren's childhood memories is going to a Durfee game to watch one of her brothers and being told to sit there and be quiet.

"All my brothers had a shelf for their trophies," she said. "Charlie had a big shelf and Donald had a big shelf. Billy and Michael had smaller shelves, then Dennis had a big shelf. I saw it as very competitive and I didn't like it."

Yet at the same time, self-praise was not accepted within her family. That was her father's legacy, for he never talked about his own athletic exploits. Once she had found one of his trophies in the basement, all covered with dust, and had brought it upstairs, excited. He had quickly told her to put it back where she had found it. As a girl growing up, she hadn't even known her father once had played minor league baseball, for the simple reason that he never had talked about it.

When she was a young child, she slept in the same bed with her sister and her brother Michael, shared a bed with her sister until she was twelve. Cindy remembers when her oldest brother Charlie went off to college and her father sold their family car to help pay for it, began walking to work. There never had been enough money; it always had been a struggle, no different than the struggle many Fall River families went through, in a city where the past seemed to promise more than the future.

By the time she got to Durfee, she already knew that to be a girl in Fall River was somehow not as important as being a boy. In a city that defined itself by sports, by winning, by competition, girls were almost peripheral, cheerleaders for the boys, judged virtually exclusively on their looks. She was a cheerleader, attractive, and within the constellation of Durfee was one of the shining stars. But she already had begun to sense that a girl in Fall River had limited opportunities. Her brothers had been encouraged to go to college. There was not the same encouragement for her. She had wanted to be a physical therapist, but the only program in the area was at a college in Boston and she knew the financial drain was going to be too difficult. She had decided to go to nursing school instead, to St. Anne's in the city.

Her boyfriend at Durfee was a dark-haired kid named Al Herren, and on those bus rides in the winter of 1970, Karam was always yelling for Cindy Carey to sit in the front of the bus and not in the back with Al.

"I don't think I had any sense of self in high school," she said. "My sense of self was my relationship with Al. I didn't see a life beyond Fall River."

That spring she discovered she was pregnant. She was eighteen, and her world suddenly had become very complicated. Nice Catholic girls like Cindy Carey were not supposed to be pregnant in the spring of 1970, even though all arond her in that turbulent spring were the shootings at Kent State, a society in the midst of massive change, a lot of the old values being examined like specimens under a microscope. She felt shame. She felt as though she were a social leper. She felt she had disappointed everyone.

She and Al were married in September 1970; Michael was born the following January. She was still in the hospital, feeling socially ostracized, when one day Karam walked into her room with a present for the baby, a tiny outfit.

"I've never forgotten that," she said. "I've always loved Skippy for that."

* * *

She had come to see her pregnancy as a responsibility, a commitment. Later, she would come to understand that it gave her a sense of direction too.

She went to work four months after Michael was born in 1971, first at the local Stop & Shop. Two months later she was laid off and went to work for the telephone company. She's been there ever since, starting out as an operator and rising through the ranks to management, an unlikely path for a woman. But in those early years, newly married and with a son, at a time in America when many other kids her age were letting their hair grown long, experimenting with drugs, questioning the society that had spawned them, things were difficult. Once she pawned both her and Al's high school rings for grocery money. They lived in public housing, struggling from one paycheck to the next.

Chris was born in September 1975. She went back to work two and a half weeks later, working nights. She believed in letting her two kids express themselves, tried to give them reasons when they were disciplined, child-rearing out of the permissive early seventies.

"If I could go back and do it differently, would I?" she asked rhetorically. "Yes. Sure I would. We made some mistakes. But we were children having children."

She really wasn't ready for all the attention and notoriety that swirled around Michael in high school, as though it had taken on a life of its own and she was powerless to do anything about it.

"I saw it as outrageous," she said, "a lot more negatives than positives."

In a sense it resurrected a lot of negative memories of her childhood, the emphasis on sports, the competitiveness, a world that seemed to exclude women. She often thought she was living in some Boys Club, an insular, macho world that had remained relatively unchanged since her childhood.

All the while she continued to work. Now she is one of

the people who supervises installations. It's something she's proud of, for she's done it on her own, independent of her husband or her family. She now works in Rhode Island, forty minutes from Fall River, and puts in a lot of hours, arriving at work at seven in the morning.

"It's not what I would have chosen for my life," she said. "But I do it well."

One senses that her children's notoriety is also something she wouldn't have particularly chosen, if she had had the chance. She goes to all the games, but sometimes she looks around at all the people who seem so obsessed with it, and wonders why she doesn't enjoy it more. She looks out on the court during games and sees Kevin Mikolazyk and Peter Pavao, Jeffrey Caron and Danny Callahan, kids she's known since they were small children, and wants them all to have fun, to be happy. She sees all the attention her son gets, and knows that it's precarious, double-edged, lessons she learned with Michael. She knows Chris could be a better student, but that once his obsession with basketball started, his studies became sacrificed on the altar that's basketball in Fall River. So sometimes she detaches herself, as though looking at it from a distance, and thinks that what is happening to her son is crazy, some runaway train that no one can catch anymore.

"I don't look at how he passes the ball or how many shots he makes," she said. "I look at how he's doing mentally. Whether he seems into it or not. If he's having fun."

From an early age it was apparent Chris had exceptional athletic ability. He first went to Karam's summer camp at Durfee when he was eight. When he was in the fourth grade, he played in a basketball camp at Holy Cross in Worcester, Massachusetts, and was MVP in his age group. He was the best Little League player in Fall River when he was twelve years old. From the beginning he was better than most other kids his age in sports; from the beginning he knew he was supposed to one day be a Durfee basketball player, that his father had played and had worn number 24.

"I never played a game of basketball for fun in my life," he said. "From the time I started playing in the Milliken League, it was more than just a game. You had to win. Milliken League was just like Durfee. I would sit in school on the day of a game and get nervous. I had butterflies when I was eight years old, and I only had one thing on my mind. To fuckin' win that game that night. Because you didn't want to come back to this house after you lost."

He played in the Milliken League for "Karam's," a team owned by Skippy's brother Bob "Boo Boo" Karam, and coached by his father Al. Not only had his father coached his brother, he'd also coached in the league for five years before Michael played, at one point winning seventy-two games in a row. Chris always was on the all-star teams, right there with Caron and Callahan and Pavao and Mikolazyk. They were ten, twelve years old, and it already seemed fated that they would play for Durfee. From the time they were nine years old until they were twelve, they lost only one all-star game in tournaments around New England.

Matt Boardman, a senior reserve, remembers the first time he knew that Chris Herren was something special as a basketball player.

"We were playing Milliken League all-stars," he said. "We were thirteen. All of us. Chris. Jeff. Pavoa. Mikolazyk. Callahan. Eagan. Mr. Herren was the coach. We were playing a team from Mattapan who were our rivals. We were down by ten or fifteen in the second half and Chris just took over. He really didn't used to handle that ball that much back then because he was one of the bigger kids. But this time he just took the ball and scored every time. It just seemed that the game came real easy to him."

Already there was pressure on Chris Herren, the pressure to play well, to win. The Milliken League was Fall River's basketball version of Little League baseball, complete with overbearing parents, jealousies, internecine feuds, the place where a kid first earned his basketball reputation in the city.

By the late 1980s, Michael Herren's era at Durfee, Chris idolized his brother. He looked at Michael and Michael's friends and he saw himself replicating it. He and his friends would go to the games, awed by the crowd, hooked on the same excitement that Karam had felt nearly forty years earlier. Jeff Caron remembers how Michael Herren would lead the team out onto the court, a ball cradled in his right arm, his left arm extended straight out over his head, as the band played and the cheers seemed to bounce off the red banners that stared down from the walls of the field house. There was no question that Jeff and Chris and Pavao and Callahan would soon be running out onto the same court; it all had been predetermined in the Milliken League.

"We used to talk about it all the time in the eighth grade," said Julie Kitchen, a dark-haired senior cheerleader. "About how it was going to be when we all got to Durfee. How the boys were going to play and us girls, we were going to cheer. We all used to sit in the same section at the games and talk about how great it was when we all got to Durfee. Then we'd go home after the games and call each other on the phone and talk about it all over again. It was always about how great it was going to be when we got to Durfee. It was like all we ever talked about. I think we all knew then that it was one day going to Chris's team. That he was just waiting his turn. He's always been the star."

But it hadn't necessarily been easy in the beginning.

The summer after his eighth grade year, Chris had been placed on the Durfee summer league team, became the sixth man. But he felt uncomfortable because he knew most of the older kids didn't want him there, resented the fact that there was some hotshot kid coming up that might take away some of their playing time, even if it was Michael Herren's brother. One night in the summer league Karam had gone to a game, something he did infrequently. Chris mainly had sat on the bench. At one point Karam walked up to the guy who was coaching the Durfee team, told him to put Chris in the game. That was the turning point. He started the rest of the summer.

When tryouts for the freshman team started in November, Chris went out for them. Karam saw him in line and told him to forget about trying out for the freshman team. Karam did the same thing when the junior varsity tryouts started. The opening day of varsity practice Karam put Herren in the starting lineup and that was it, Karam's way of telling the upperclassmen that this was the way it was going to be and they better get used to it.

His first game Chris had been incredibly nervous. It was on the road against Weymouth, a suburb of Boston on the South Shore. People were yelling derogatory things about his brother. He felt everyone was watching him, judging him. Could he really play or was he only on the varsity because of his brother? Was he going to be as good as his brother? He'd been awful in the first half, afraid to shoot, afraid to do anything. Then Dempsey had pulled him aside at halftime, told him to relax, that he was the best player on the court and not to worry about anything. He finished the game with twenty points, ended up averaging seventeen for the year.

Todd Majkut became his unofficial bodyguard, his protector. He was a senior, a tough six–five kid who once upon a time had been befriended by Michael Herren and now was going to return the favor, primarily because Michael once had told him that the way to pay him back for his kindness was to take care of his little brother when he came to Durfee. Chris knew many of the upperclassmen still resented him, often tried to freeze him out. Majkut didn't let them. He would come into the huddle during time-outs and tell the others to give Chris the ball. Often, Majkut would hang out with Chris and his friends, Pavao and Mikolazyk.

Six games into the season, Majkut died in an automobile

accident, going down a steep hill on President Avenue, the road that essentially runs from Durfee up through the back of the Highlands, then down to the Taunton River. There were three kids in the car. They had been drinking. Majkut was the only one killed. Chris heard about it at four in the morning when his brother woke him. He was devastated, didn't go to school for a couple of days. During the funeral service in the church he was the one who placed Majkut's Durfee jersey on the casket. The service was held at a small Polish church in the South End. It was jammed with people, students, a tribute to an athlete dying young.

Majkut's death cast a pall on that season, one that never lifted. The team immediately lost several games in a row, eventually losing to New Bedford in the opening round of the state tournament. Chris felt an emptiness all year, even though he was having a great season for a freshman, already showing the promise of what was to come later. He kept one of Majkut's uniforms in his closet in his bedroom. It is still there.

One cold, windy afternoon Chris Herren was in his kitchen, a narrow room dominated by a table in the middle. He was listening on the phone to a taped recruiting message from Bob Gibbons, one of the national recruiting gurus. He'd been told his name was on the tape and had dialed the 900 number to hear what Gibbons had said about him.

"This motherfucker is just bullshitting to keep me on the line," he said with a laugh. "Bullshitting his ass off. But I'm cool with him. Real cool."

He listened for a couple more minutes, seemed to lose interest, hung up the phone, and settled into a couch in the living room, an open room with white walls that's been added to the back of the small frame house. He was wearing his standard uniform of baggy jeans and loose-fitting T-shirt.

The house is gray with a front porch. It is small, unpretentious, on a quiet dead-end street only a couple of blocks from

Durfee. To the people in the South End it might be considered the Highlands, since it's hard by New Boston Road, which intersects Highland Avenue about a half mile to the west. But it's not really. It's only a block or so from Eastern Avenue, a main road that essentially connects the back of the North End to the Flint and the beginning of the South End. There is no front lawn, the house sandwiched between houses on each side of it. There is a basketball hoop over the single garage in back, its orange rim faded and slanted down. Directly across the street is the house where Chris's grandfather and grandmother live, Charley and Mary Carey. That's where he eats dinner most every night, since his mother doesn't get home from work until later. About a hundred yards away, across New Boston Road, is the field where Durfee once played its football games. Next door is the Fordney Street housing project, a cluster of red-brick buildings where the Herrens lived when Michael was a child and Al Herren worked for Family Services. Mikolazyk lives one street over. Suneson lives farther down New Boston Road, a short walk away, and Caron, Callahan, and Jones are within a mile.

Last summer the Fall River *Herald News* had done an article on Chris's national AAU experience, one that essentially had taken him around the country. In it he'd said how he'd liked the travel, liked seeing different things, but after three days he started "wishing for the rotary," a euphemism for coming off Route 24 from Boston and coming into the northeast corner of Fall River, the rotary that leads into Eastern Avenue, then the quick right onto New Boston Road and home.

But his AAU experiences had been good for him. For a while he had been the only white kid on his team, a Boston-area team known as Boston Amateur Basketball Club (BABC) and coached by Leo Papile, a white basketball junkie in his forties who has befriended many a black kid in the Boston area, shepherding them to prep schools and providing them both a national and regional showcase for their basketball skills. Papile had seen Herren in his sophomore year, fell in love with him as a player, and when several of the black kids on the team encouraged Papile to invite Herren to play for him, he had done so.

"The black kids loved the way he played," Papile said. "They used to say he's 'just like us.' "

In the beginning it had been an adjustment being the only white player on an all-black team, for Chris hadn't been exposed to many blacks before. There was Lamar Stevens, who had played with his brother, and Corey Luz, who had played with him last year, and Shawn Thames this year, but it was still possible to come of age in Fall River and not deal with many blacks, although this was starting to change. So he had learned to fit in with BABC by not trying to fit in, by letting things come to him instead of pushing things, eventually realizing that he and the black kids he played with could be both friends and teammates, though they lived in two different cultures.

"I've never had a problem with a black person," he said. "They've broadened my views on things. I have no reason to be prejudiced."

BABC also got him out of Fall River, at least for a while.

"All my life I've heard that Fall River athletes don't really make it when they leave," he said, lying back on the couch. "Fall River's like the black hole. It's like you're born at either St. Anne's Hospital, or Charlton Memorial, and they put a stamp on your ass that says you can't leave. It's the black hole. But no matter what happens, I'll never put Fall River behind me."

It was a school day, and once again he'd left school without any books.

"You don't need books at Durfee," he said, somewhat defensively. "What do I need books for? I'm not in class to get all As. I'm not in class to get high honors. No one in Fall River is a decent student if you're a basketball player. You don't have to be. It's just not important to me."

"So what is important to you?" I asked.

It was not a careless question. By this point I had spent many hours with Herren. I had given him rides. I had sat around in his living room talking for hours. I had sat in some of his classes at school. I had played many HORSE games with him after practice, just me and him playing shooting games after everyone else had left. I had seen him at his best, and I also had seen him at his worst. I knew about his girlfriends, what colleges he was serious about, about parties and friends and drinking. I had come to know things I was sure not even his parents knew. We were comfortable with each other, and yet most of the time he hid behind his teenage bravado with me, one of the defenses he used to ward off the world.

Part of it was typical teenage way of viewing the world through veils of machismo. Yet part of it also was Fall River, Herren and his friends believing that though they certainly weren't inner-city kids, they weren't suburban kids either. They were working-class kids in a city that always had respected hard work, the kind of blue-collar, lunch-pail work that took no quarter, asked for none. Once, driving by a nearby tennis court, I asked him if he ever played tennis. "Fuck no," he said disparagingly. "It's a faggot sport." Tennis to him was country clubs and people who didn't sweat, a preppy sport that seemed as foreign to him as cricket.

"My friends are what's important to me," he said. "The inner circle. Me. Pavao. Gore. The guys we hang with. It's just a few of us, and no one else is invited in. We don't want new friends. We don't need them. That's just how it is."

He picked up a basketball and began throwing it into the air, still lying on the couch. He flicked his wrist and the ball went up in the air, then back down again, over and over. Every few minutes the phone would ring and he would pick it up and growl "What's up?" into the receiver, the words running together so they sounded like "Wassup," mumble a few unintelligible grunts, and hang up.

"Michael is different than me," he said finally. "Michael has opinions on everything. Ask him about politics and he'll talk for hours. I could care less about politics. I'm uninvolved. I don't give a shit about Clinton or any of them. Michael would have done anything to be able to meet JFK. I don't know fuckin' diddly about JFK. Michael's always telling me I'm so culturally deprived I can't name the Beatles. Shit, of course I can name the Beatles."

He smiled over at me.

"Actually, I couldn't name them, but he's asked me so many times they've sunk in, though I sometimes forget that Harrison guy."

"So you've grown up differently from him?"

"Definitely," he said. "I've grown up in some shit hip-hop generation. Imagine that. But I don't really belong to it. I think of myself in the rock 'n' roll generation. I grew up listening to Jackson Browne, the Eagles, the Stones, stuff like that. My mother likes the Police, the Clash. That's the kind of stuff I like. Not rap."

One day a member of the Durfee girls' team said "Yo, girl" to a teammate and Herren had said how he hated it when white kids acted black, yet he had several black affectations. The baggy jeans that always seemed to be one inch away from falling off his hips. The caps he usually wore turned backward. The walk with the accentuated dip, the ghetto strut. It was all the "homeboy" look. He often called his friends "bro."

Not that his is unusual. Black culture has come to dominate white teenage culture, not just in Fall River, but across the country. All the top athletes seem to be black, the top musicians. Every night Arsenio Hall brought hip-hop culture and all its ramifications to white America. Rap is the sound track to everything, blaring out from car radios, played in the locker room before games, an anthem for a generation. Teenage fashions seem to come right out of Bedford-Stuyvesant, from the untied sneakers to the shaved-sides hairstyles to the baggy jeans, brought to mainstream America by such ambassadors as Madonna and Marky Mark, white performers who leave no doubt that they think black culture is the advance guard of cool, the cultural explorers who constantly reinvent themselves and take everyone else along on the journey. Even in a place like Fall River, where blacks make up only a small percentage of the school population, a city essentially devoid of any black culture, any black heritage, the teenage culture shows the results of the national phenomena of white kids embracing black culture.

Herren exemplified it more than his teammates did, for the simple reasons that he was exposed to it more with BABC and that as Chris Herren, he could get away with wearing anything to school and having it meet with peer approval. It was often said Michael Herren started the crew-cut fad in Fall River a few years back. Chris was now doing it with his baggy clothes and his ripped jeans, a hip-hop ambassador.

He kept throwing the ball into the air, as if it had become his security blanket.

"Where's basketball fit in?" I asked.

"It's everything," he said. "I don't even follow other sports. Football. Baseball. I don't care. I like everything about basketball. I like blowing by people, dominating them. I like winning. I like the fun. I like everything about it."

When he thinks about the future at all, it's a fuzzy version of some undetermined time beyond college where he sees himself playing professional basketball, though he knows the odds against that are incredibly high. But what are odds when you are seventeen years old? What are odds when you've spent your life taking the ball past kids and every morning mail comes in from school around the country, schools that all want you because of your basketball ability?

He went upstairs to get a sport coat he'd borrowed from a friend for a banquet he had to go to that night.

"I had to borrow it because I don't own a sport coat," he said. "I had to borrow a pair of shoes too."

"How about a suit? Do you own one of those?"

"Fuck no."

He made a disgusted look, as if I had just asked him if he wore tights.

"I don't need any of those things. I don't even have a wallet. No ID. I don't know my social security number. I couldn't name a number on it."

He said this matter-of-factly, as if these things were of no importance to him, had nothing to do with his life, as if his life has been reduced to his basketball and his friends, everything else superfluous.

His bedroom is small, only room for a couch. There is no clock. There is a blue rug, but there is no wallpaper, the walls covered with off-white plaster board, some of it with holes. On the walls are phone numbers, over his head, on the far wall, written in pencil on the plaster board.

"This is where I keep everyone's number," he said. "My parents want to do the room over, put up wallpaper, but I don't want wallpaper. I started this in the eighth grade, writing everyone's number on the walls. I even got Sonny Vaccaro's," Vaccaro being another one of college basketball's power brokers. "I called him the other day."

The sun came in through the windows, highlighting the austere quality of the room. He lay back on the bed. In a while he would be going to practice, the boys' team sharing the early gym with the girls' team, one week early practice, the next week late. Once upon a time the idea of the Durfee basketball team being inconvenienced by the girls' team would have been anathema. Now it's just the way things are and no one thinks anything about it.

"What else did you learn from watching what happened to Michael?" I asked.

"Michael always trusted people," he said, "and when

things were going well, he had all these friends. When the nitty-gritty came down, he had six. I learned from that. I never put myself in a situation where something can happen. I don't go to malls. I don't associate with people out in public. I don't like it. Michael used to go to parties everywhere, Somerset, Dartmouth, all over the place. I don't. I stay close by. That's why we party at Suneson's house. We keep it among ourselves."

"So you're concerned with your image?"

"I have to be, because I learned what happens when you're not. I'm much more concerned with things than Michael was. He would fight in front of three thousand people. He didn't care what people said about him. My brother would wear two different sneakers, a ripped shirt. He didn't care. I feel an obligation to little kids who look up to me. I make sure I help the 'special needs' kids out. I make sure I know their names and always talk to them. But I get sick of people talking about me. I don't like people asking me where I'm going to college or what I'm going to do. I hate it."

He took a piece of paper out of a drawer. It was ripped from the phone book's yellow pages. On the back of an ad for funeral homes, scrawled in black Magic Marker, were the words "You can't watch your kids all the time. Your family will soon be reduced in number."

"Can you believe this?" he said.

He was seventeen years old, a junior in high school, and already Chris Herren was beginning to realize that basketball fame in Fall River comes with a price tag.

Chapter

5

CHRIS HERREN took the the ball to the basket in a practice session in the Luke Urban Field House, got hit across the wrist, and angrily threw the ball to the floor.

Karam glared at him.

Herren gave him a look back.

"I'll kick your ass out of here, kid," Karam said threateningly.

Herren went over to the sideline, bent over at the waist, and started rubbing his wrist. Karam shook his head, wondering why Herren thought it was some sort of personal insult to get fouled in practice. Herren wore dark shorts and a white "Big Johnson" T-shirt that read on the back, SOMETIMES IT'S HARD TO STUFF IT IN UNLESS YOU HAVE A BIG JOHNSON.

Eric Santos pointed to the slogan and laughed.

"If Mr. Karam sees that, he'll go crazy," he said.

"So what?" Herren said. "He goes crazy anyway."

It was a few days before Christmas, the air clean and cold outside, Fall River and the rest of the world getting ready for the holidays, but inside the field house it was practice as usual. Everyone seemed on edge. Caron's foot still hurt, and it made him short-tempered, frustrated. He stopped practicing and limped over to the front row of the bleachers. Herren was rubbing his wrist, seemed to show no rush in getting back on the floor. Karam's voice was tense and irritable, insisting the players move the ball, not stand around, getting louder as the practice wore on.

"It's going to be one of those days," Dempsey said, raising his eyebrows. "Either Skippy's going to throw the kid out, or he's going to walk out himself and I'll be stuck with the rest of practice."

The day after Christmas there will be a three-day tournament in Lowell, another old textile city north of Boston, about an hour and a half away, a tournament with several good teams in it. Skippy knows his team isn't ready for it, that all the questions he had going into the season still remain. Here it is three games into the season and it's Herren and Caron against the world. Jones is still hurt, though he's expected to play in Lowell. Pavao's given him nothing, Callahan little. Cioe battles, but is limited. He knows someone will have to emerge to take some of the scoring pressure off of Herren and Caron, for they both must have great games every night to beat a good team. But who is it going to be? He looks at his team and doesn't like what he sees, knows it's going to have to get a lot better quickly or this season is going to turn into a nightmare. They are 2–1, but easily could be 1–2.

His only solution is to have them work harder, but Caron is hurt and Herren's in one of his funks. Skippy turned his attention back to the floor, but already his temper was rising. He hates practice sessions that essentially are a waste of time. This was shaping up to be one.

Caron sat on a row of bleachers and watched Karam patrol the court beneath the huge scoreboard that hangs from the ceiling over the center of the court. Karam barked something at Pavao and Caron shook his head.

"If the scoreboard dropped, I don't know whether I'd save him or not," he mused.

Caron watched Herren go back to practice and immediately take the ball strong to the hoop, his way of making a statement. Caron smiled, as if talking to himself. He liked to think he understood Herren as much as anyone did. He knows this is Herren's way of telling Karam he's now ready to practice. Herren again took the ball hard to the basket. Caron smiled again.

In a sense he's known Herren all his life. Their mothers had been childhood friends, and Herren's aunt, Kathy Bellanger, had been in Caron's parents' wedding. The first time he'd met Chris, he was seven years old, living in neighboring Westport, and going to Karam's summer camp. One night he was supposed to stay over at Herren's house.

"I came into his house and I was wearing these five-dollar pair of sneakers—sidewalk sale, Swansea Mall—and he looked at me and said 'What do you have on your feet?' in this real disparaging tone. I didn't know. I thought my sneakers were cool because Westport kids knew nothing, but he threw a pair of Nikes at me and said, 'Wear these.' That was it.

"There's no one like Chris. He only cares about what's right in front of him. The school could be burning down, but if there were two ants going across the floor he would be looking at them, asking you which one you thought was going to get to the other side of the floor first, wanting to bet on one of them. Everyone else would be running to get out of the building, and he would be watching those two ants."

He paused a second, his eyes still on Chris.

"The whole family's different. I used to love going over there when I was younger. The house was always open, people coming and going. My house is like a fortress. Alarms. Bars on the windows. The Herrens' is just the opposite. Michael's always giving his car to his friends and then forgets about it. You ask him where his car is and he has no idea. They're all like that. You can't not like the Herrens. It's like they don't care about what most people care about.

"I've been in competition with Chris since the first day in the sixth grade when I walked into Morton and he was sitting there like he ran the school. But we're great friends. I think he's an awesome kid one-on-one. If he's in a fight against three guys and I see it, I'm there. But put him in a room with his friends and they all kiss his ass. A lot of them are losers."

He leaned back on the bench, continued to stare out at the court.

"I wish I were a loser sometimes. A one-week span last summer I was living like a loser. I was going to a beach party every night. I would play at Pottersville in Somerset and then go to the beach and drink.

"It was funny last summer. It seemed that whenever Chris went away with BABC we got in trouble. We even got arrested one night. We were trying to find a party in Rehoboth, out in the woods somewhere, 'cause I wanted to punch a kid's face for messin' with my girlfriend. I was even wearing a state championship ring. So I could punch the kid with it. So we're riding around with all this beer in my car. Me. Gore. Suneson. Callahan, I can't remember who else. And we got lost by this pumpkin field and Gore and Suneson start throwing pumpkins at each other and then a cop comes. The cop wants to take us all in. He's looked in the trunk and seen the beer and the pumpkins in the road. But I start talking to him, saying 'Yes officer, no officer,' and I'm good at getting myself out of shit and he's about to let us go. But Gore and Suneson are acting goofy. Suneson keeps blowing cigarette smoke in the cop's face until the cop gets pissed and is going to take Suneson with him.

"Then Gore—that little mutt—says we can't leave without Sunny, so he starts giving the cop some shit because he wants to get himself arrested. Finally, the cop grabs him and then finds out that he's eighteen and Suneson's only seventeen, so he lets Sunny go and Gore goes to New Bedford, where he spends the night in jail. The dumb bastard.

"But then I knew I was acting like a loser and I knocked it

off. Now I consider everything before I go out on a weekend. You'll never see me drinking in front of young kids. I don't want a reputation."

The players moved off and on the floor, and while the first team was standing on the sidelines, Herren and Callahan snuck off into the locker room to get a drink of water, something that's not allowed without permission. A couple of minutes later Karam looked over and saw Herren coming out of the locker room door.

"Where have you been?"

"I was getting a drink."

"Did you get permission?"

"I asked Mr. Dempsey."

Skippy looked over at Dempsey with a raised eyebrow. "Did he ask you?"

"I don't know, Skippy," Dempsey said, exasperated. "A whole bunch of them asked me. I don't know who it was."

Herren stood in a group of players alongside the court while the second team was on the floor against the jayvees. I went over and stood next to him.

"You know that Dempsey just bailed you out there, don't you?" I whispered.

"Big-time," Herren said. "Mr. Karam's looking to throw me out today. I can tell."

"Are you going to make it?"

He smiled. "I don't know yet."

Things settled down after that, fell back into a familiar pattern. Karam would occasionally yell, but his criticism was like flash paper, easily combustible, gone just as quickly. It was rarely directed at either the reserves or the junior varsity team, which often practiced with the varsity. Callahan received the most verbal abuse, then Herren, then Pavao. Caron, Mikolazyk, Jones, and Cioe were mostly spared.

Herren went back on the floor and began to dominate the practice. Sometimes he would get a defensive rebound, then explode out of the pack of defenders and rush down the court, going around people, past them, becoming his own fast break, then throwing a great pass to one of his teammates. Sometimes he would simply take the ball to the basket himself. Over and over it went, Herren putting on a show, his quickness, his agility on the open floor, his great ability to see the court and be able to deliver the ball to his teammates, all his awesome potential showcased. Karam shrugged. He knew how good Herren was when he wanted to play, knew he was the best he'd ever coached in thirty-two years. He wouldn't admit it publicly when asked, knowing that saying that in Fall River would only open a Pandora's box. But he knew.

In a sense Herren had become Skippy's last gift, the truly great player he'd waited for his entire coaching career. Dempsey often thought that Skippy would go out with Herren, that Herren's senior year would be Skippy's final signature on a career that had started in 1960. But Herren's special talent also frustrated Karam, and concerned him. About a month earlier he'd sat Herren down, talked to him about how everyone was going to be watching him, and how he was going to have to be extremely cognizant of his behavior, to opposing players, referees, everyone. Karam knew Michael's ghost still hovered over Chris, that the two bothers were always somehow linked together, even though they were different. So he seemed to take it personally when Chris did something he considered foolish, something he thought was only chipping away at Chris's reputation or his future.

He turned around to Dempsey, his voice low.

"How would you like to have had that ability? If I had had his talent, I'd still be playing."

Dempsey just nodded. He knew too. Many times he stood at practice and watched Herren, thinking about the possibilities. He had been around basketball all his life, knew how talented Herren was, and often he would watch Herren and wonder how far his great natural ability could take him, how far away from this field house, this city.

Once Dempsey had nursed his own Fall River dreams. He had grown up in the South End in the late fifties and early sixties, as much Fall River as the Braga Bridge. His paternal grandfather had been born here; his maternal grandparents had immigrated to work in the mills. His mother worked at Firestone, the large rubber plant near the river that had made gas masks during World War II and whose whistle blew every day at noontime, the same factory where Al Herren's father worked. Sports had been everything in Dempsey's childhood, a life that revolved around Kennedy Park a couple of blocks away, and other parks in the city. One of the younger kids who used to hang around the park was Al Herren, four years younger than Dempsey.

"I always liked Albert," Dempsey said. "He always wanted to play. I remember one summer I brought him to Sam Jones's basketball camp. I heard later that he became a real tough kid, but I never saw that. I never saw him as a wild man or anything."

By the time Dempsey got to high school, he already was aware of Karam's reputation, since his older brother Ted was playing for Karam.

"My brother really liked Skippy," he said, "and by the time I got to Durfee, Skippy already was a legend. At first the yelling bothered me and when I was a sophomore I wanted to quit and play CYO instead, but my mother wouldn't let me. But Skippy has a way of letting you know you're good, and one day he said to me, 'If I had had your talent, I would have been All-American.' After that I knew he thought I could play and the yelling never bothered me."

Dempsey went on to star for Karam's first state championship in 1966, then to the University of Massachusetts after a year of prep school in Maine. He had played with Julius Erving on some good UMass teams, and later with Rick

Pitino. Then he'd come back to Fall River, found a job as a culinary arts teacher at Durfee, and got into coaching. Now it was his ninth year as Karam's assistant and he'd come to understand that there were two sides to his old coach. There was Skippy on the floor, with his anxieties and the pressure he felt, and there was the Skippy off the court. He remembered a summer night in one of his first years as Skippy's assistant. The two had gone to a summer league game, and on the ride to the game Skippy had been joking, relaxed, but that had instantly changed the minute they walked in to the game.

He knew that Skippy's bark was much worse than his bite, that "when he yells at you that it's way of telling you he thinks you can be a better player." He often said how he never had appreciated how funny Karam is when he was playing for him. More importantly, he knew that Skippy never had a bad word to say about a player in public, that he never blamed a player after a loss, always taking the blame himself.

They'd become very friendly, for Dempsey had learned that beneath the tensions that came from being the Durfee coach, Skippy was a great friend, loyal, funny, with a big heart. They always went out after the games, win or lose, and these nights had cemented their friendship.

"One year we had made plans to go out with our wives after the New Bedford game," said Dempsey. "I think it was the first time my wife was with Skippy socially. Turns out we lost and when we all get in the car, Skippy and I start talking about the game and Skippy's wife Betty says, 'I hope we're not going to talk about the game all night.' We're all silent for a minute, then Skippy says, 'What the fuck did you think we were going to talk about?' "

The sixteenth annual Greater Lowell Holiday Tournament was held at the Greater Lowell Regional High School, a modern, sprawling structure along the Merrimack River. It was the second night of the tournament. Durfee had won their first game easily, moving way ahead in the first half, even though Skippy wasn't particularly happy because "we never ran a goddamn play."

Before the second game, they sat in the large yellow and red locker room in their red uniforms, in a semicircle around Karam, who went over the pregame instructions very calmly. The opponent was Cambridge Rindge and Latin, long a basketball power in Massachusetts, the inner-city school in the shadow of Harvard where both Patrick Ewing and Rumeal Robinson had played. It wouldn't be an easy game. Rindge and Latin was an all-black team, athletic, pressing most of the game, and are ranked number one in Massachusetts by the Boston *Globe*. Karam knows this would be a real test, that it would take more than heroics from Herren and Caron if Durfee was to have any chance of winning. Once again he felt that old anxiety.

He saw Pavao get up to go into the men's room.

"Don't get lost in there, Peter," he yelled.

Pavao showed no expression. Then again, he's long accustomed to Mr. Karam. It's his fourth year on the varsity, and in a sense his career at Durfee has never really happened. The irony is that since he lives with his mother in Swansea, a small town a few miles to the west of Fall River, he could have gone to a smaller high school there where he undoubtedly would have been a star. Instead, he wanted to go to Durfee, to play with the kids he'd been on all-star teams with in the Milliken League. So he used his father's Fall River address and commuted every day from Swansea, where he slept on a cot in a room with his two stepbrothers in a small apartment over a garage. Every weekend he came to Fall River with no idea of where he was going to stay, depending on the kindness of his friends, sleeping on floors. He'd been doing it for two years. He thought of it as a big adventure, an existential weekend full of possibilities.

Pavao was not the first kid from a neighboring town to

play for Durfee, a fact of life that's created a certain backlash against Durfee in recent years. It started in the late 1980s when Al Attar, a great Durfee player in the 1950s and now the Durfee principal, wanted his son Matt to go to Durfee, and not high school in Somerset where the family lived. Since Attar was a teacher in Fall River at the time, it was arranged that his son could go to school at Durfee, a practice that became unofficially known as the "Attar Rule." In 1988, Matt Attar teamed with Michael Herren to lead Durfee to the state title. The star guard on that team was Juddy Mac-Donald, who just happened to live that season in Westport, the town to the east of Fall River. No matter that McDonald's family long had been a fixture in Fall River; his father, Willie, had played with Karam in high school, and other relatives once had played for Durfee. Legally, his father now lived in Westport, where he'd moved after retiring from the Fall River Police Department, so that for Juddy to continue to go to school at Durfee, he had to use his grandparents' address. Suddenly the perception was that Durfee and Skippy Karam were recruiting players, a charge that upset Karam no end, for he'd had nothing to do with it.

It also had been Pavao's father's dream for him to play for Durfee. His father, Jerry, walked with a limp, the result of a childhood injury. Pavao's father had grown up in Fall River with his own basketball dreams, had tried out for the team, though he really had no chance to make it. After he graduated from Durfee Tech, the school that trained people to work in the mills, he'd helped out scoring the games, just wanting to be a part of Durfee basketball. For his son to play for Durfee was vitally important to him, the career he never got a chance to have.

When Pavao had been in the seventh grade, he'd been regarded as on a par with Herren in the Milliken League. Standing five-foot-nine when he was eleven years old, he thought he was going to be six-foot-four, could close his eyes and envision himself as a star. Instead, he'd only grown another inch or so, and his potential seemed to stop along with his height. He was a good outside shooter and he played hard. But he didn't handle the ball particularly well, and his fate consigned him to the periphery. Last year he'd been the sixth man, first off the bench, yet Pavao always seemed to tense up when he came into a game. He was perhaps a victim of Karam's tendency not to use his reserves much, and of Karam's coaching style. Some kids let Karam's style roll off their backs; Pavao internalized it. He knew Karam had no confidence in his ball-handling skills and was losing faith in him as he continued to struggle with his shot. Yet he both liked and admired Karam and never questioned his own decision to come to Durfee, even though the basketball hadn't worked out the way he'd fantasized.

"When I was in the seventh grade, me and Chris were the best," he said. "He developed. I stayed the same."

He said this with no emotion, simply a matter of fact, a reality he long ago had gotten used to. Surprisingly, there was little resentment of Herren's growing celebrity among his friends, maybe for the simple reason that he'd become so much better than the rest of them that it wasn't even an issue anymore. Going into the season, the potential cause for friction was between Pavao and Mikolazyk, though they were great friends. They were both seniors, played the same position, and they both had done the math: They knew that if one started, the other wouldn't. There had been some tension the first week or so of practice before they both decided not to let what happened on the court affect their friendship.

Now, on this night in Lowell where he'd lost his starting position to Mikolazyk, Pavao came out of the men's room into a large room with yellow walls and red lockers.

"Pavao, get your ass over here, you banana," Karam said to him. "Now listen up. We're coming back here tomorrow one way or the other, either for the championship game or the consolation game. It's up to you guys."

He paced in front of them in a gray sport jacket and dark slacks.

"Warming up," he said, "let's do layups. Not circus shots and alley-oops to Herren for half an hour. And one more thing. If you don't shake hands before the game, I'm putting five new guys in. What is this bullshit? It's not a war. Now let's go."

The game was an uphill struggle the entire way. Durfee trailed by five with only 1:40 left to play in the game, before another comeback, similar to the one against Duxbury the first game of the season. Herren had had a great game, more evidence why he was being called the best player in the state. He seemed to control the game, driving to the basket, hitting three-pointers, finding the open man, constantly putting pressure on the Rindge and Latin defense. Again, he supplied the last-minute heroics. He made a nifty bucket in the lane, then stole the ball and set up Mikolazyk for a layup that brought Durfee back to within one. With eighteen seconds remaining, Caron's two free throws put them up two, then he canned two more to ice the game, Durfee eventually winning by five. Caron finished with seventeen points, Herren twenty-eight. But the big surprise has been Mikolazyk, "Igor" himself. In his first start he'd scored seventeen points, taking some of the pressure off of Herren and Caron. It was been his best moment in a Durfee uniform.

It had also been a long time coming.

He grew up one street behind Herren; they were childhood friends, ever since he came home crying in the first grade because Herren had been throwing rocks at him. He began playing basketball early in his backyard, then in the Milliken League, where his father, who taught at the Spencer Borden Elementary School only a few hundred yards away, was always his coach. Mikolazyk also had started going to Durfee games when he was seven or eight, awed by the crowds and the team, seduced early by Durfee basketball.

"I thought it was the greatest thing on earth," he had said

one night earlier. "Now I think it sucks. Everything's just too focused on us. This big spotlight that you can't get out of."

He first became aware of how big the spotlight was in the fall of his sophomore year. His parents had been away and he'd hosted a party at his house. As soon as he went back to school, it seemed everyone knew about it. Especially Mr. Karam. Somehow it didn't seem fair: Go out drinking one night and the next day Mr. Karam knew about it already, as though he had eyes and ears throughout the city, a network of spies constantly reporting back to him on the actions of his players.

"I don't like it when he calls us alcoholics and says we should be playing for Edgehill High," he said. "Or when he starts yelling and screaming and acting like he's nuts."

Mikolazyk had come to realize this was it, as far as his basketball career was concerned. Like Pavao, Jones, Cioe, and the other seniors, there would be no college scholarship, no basketball future. His had been determined two years ago, in the tenth grade, when he stopped growing, stuck at five-foot-seven. Sometimes he thought back to when he and Chris had been young kids, when they used to play ball together in the backyard, virtually equals, and how it all had changed.

He'd begun drinking in the ninth grade, and now it's an intregal part of his life. Some Saturdays he begins as early as ten in the morning, goes until two or three in the morning, a long binge when he sees everything through a haze, the edges smoothed over, one big buzz in his head. It's not been the easiest year. His parents are going through a divorce, and he's been to counseling for it. He feels burned out with school. He was an excellent student when he was younger, and knows that if he sits in class and pays attention he can get Bs and Cs without doing any homework, but he no longer has the energy for that, content to merely coast along, considering his classes a joke, school a joke, most everything a joke.

In the early seventies, when I was teaching in a suburban Rhode Island high school, I had known a lot of kids like Mikolazyk, kids for whom the system no longer worked, kids who went through school day after day, week after week, numbed by it, alienated to the degree that none of it mattered, except on the most primitive survival terms, their lives squarely in the present tense. The difference then, it seemed to me, was that many of them had the cloak of the counterculture to wrap themselves in. It had been considered cool to be alienated then, an emerging consciousness that saw all school systems as little more than repressive house organs of the establishment. That had been the jargon of the times and it had given an imprimatur of respectability to a lot of lost kids.

Now it's all changed. In this age of a diminished economy and a bleak future where there's tremendous pressure on kids to achieve or be left behind, this time of multicultural education and a growing emphasis on new immigrants that are changing the country, white working-class kids seem to have been lost in the shuffle. They have little culture of their own. Their rage and sense of impotence is little understood. They've mostly been forgotten. Mikolazyk may be one of them.

Sometimes he goes "slam dancing," listening to punk rock groups like Punk Ska, Murphy's Law, the Mighty Mighty Bosstones. One night he climbed the tower in the shopping center across the street from Durfee, perching several hundred feet in the air, a night that addded to the growing perception among his friends that "Gore is crazy." He liked to go into the small patch of woods near his house, quickly shinny up a tall pine tree with a harness around his waist, then rappel himself to the ground. He looked for danger, and he often found it.

Still, to start for Durfee had been his first sports dream, and on this night he had made the most of it.

Another unexpected surprise was Cioe, who had come

off the bench and battled Rindge players who were both bigger and more athletic then he. Then again, Cioe was nothing if not an overachiever.

He had grown up as one of seven kids in a tenement near downtown, not far from Second Street and the Lizzie Borden murder house. He never knew his father; his mother was on welfare. His surname is from another man he never knew. He never played in the Milliken League, never had hung out with the other players when he first came to Durfee. He tended to view them as richer than himself, cocky, most of them living in the Highlands. He belonged to a different crowd, one that wasn't linked to Durfee basketball, yet he always had wanted to play for Durfee, for he too had gone to Durfee games in the Michael Herren era. He had started on the freshman team, but sophomore year he had missed a lot of school and, in his words, "I fucked up." Last year he had played jayvee, and now, on the varsity as a senior, it had become important to finally be playing for Durfee.

"I was so proud when I started the first game," he said. "It meant a lot to me."

He also has come to like his teammates, even started hanging out with them. Yet his life is very different from theirs.

Last year his girlfriend, who is black, became pregnant. They both decided to have the baby. Soon after Vanessa Cioe was born, he and his girlfriend broke up, so now Vanessa lives with her mother half of the week and with Cioe the other half. He has a crib in his room where the baby sleeps, and he's learned to change her, to care for her. In the morning he takes Vanessa to Durfee where she spends the day in the school's Young Parents Center, a day-care room handling about twenty kids. Cioe keeps his books in the nursery, visits his daughter between classes.

The experience has changed him. It's made him think of the future, start to plan for it. It's also changed his attitude about race, and there are times when one of the players will make an inadvertent racist comment, remarks that cause him pain.

"I don't understand it," he said one day. "They like Shawn Thames, who is black, but then they'll call some guy on another team a 'nigger.' But if I call them on it, they'll apologize. They used to use the word all the time, but not so much now. They've become better now. But sometimes, when they slip, I feel like punching them."

He already has enlisted in the Navy for four years, will leave in June for Orlando, Florida to begin training as an aviation mechanic, because "I want to have a career so I'll be able to take care of my daughter."

The next night the bus was in the parking lot outside the field house as the day turned to dusk, the sky the color of washed-out pewter. Clumps of old snow lay on the fields across the parking lot.

Caron was standing by the front door when Herren came walking up the sidewalk. He was wearing his baggy jeans and a tan shirt, no jacket, though it was the last week in December, winter's chill in the air. The other players all were carrying traveling bags that contained their sneakers, uniform, towel. Santos had his in a large paper bag. Herren carried nothing.

"Go up and ask him where his uniform is," Caron said to me. "I guarantee you he has no idea where it is."

"What are you talking about?" I said. "What do you mean he doesn't know where his uniform is?"

"Someone has it, but he doesn't know who," said Caron with a smile. "It will just somehow appear in the locker room."

"Don't tell Mr. Karam," Herren said, when I told him what Jeff had said. "He'll go crazy."

A few minutes later the players and cheerleaders began filing onto the bus. Karam sat in his customary front seat, Dempsey a seat behind him. The cheerleaders wore their red and black jackets. The players walked by, many of them with Walkmans audible, in their jeans and their baggy jackets.

"They dress like the homeless," muttered Karam.

He stood up to count the players.

"Where's Thames?"

No one answered.

"No one knows where he is?" Skippy asked again, imploringly.

"He didn't call me," said Santos, who also lives in the South End of the city. "He usually calls me for a ride."

"Did you call him?" Karam asked.

Santos shrugged.

"Do you believe this shit?" Karam said to Dempsey. "This is like taking a fifth grade field trip to Plymouth Rock."

The night before, Thames had gotten all the way to Lowell only to discover he'd forgotten to bring his uniform. He had spent the game sitting in the stands, a young gangly kid who looked a little lost. Now he was missing. Here Karam was trying to get him some playing time, knowing that for all his lack of both skills and experience Thames had some athletic ability, and he didn't seem to care.

"Okay," Karam announced. "We'll wait five minutes."

Dempsey started telling Karam a story of how back in 1967, the year Jimmy Walker was one of the best college players in the country, Joe Mullaney, then the Providence College basketball coach, had kept the bus waiting an hour and a half for Walker.

"I'd wait for Jimmy Walker too," Karam replied. "But Shawn Thames isn't Jimmy Walker, so let's go."

The game tonight was against a team from Windsor, Connecticut, another all-black, physical team Karam didn't think Durfee could beat. But they immediately went up by eight in the first few minutes of the game, even though Herren was having trouble shooting free throws. He had gone to the line three times, missing the second shot all three times, when he got fouled again and was awarded two more free throws.

"If he makes two, we give him a trophy," Karam muttered to the people behind him.

Herren missed the second one again, shook his head as he ran back down the floor. It had become mental by now, Herren feeling that he could be standing over the basket and he would still miss.

No matter. Durfee went up seventeen at the half, playing their best ball of the season, and coasted in the second half. It was a night when everything clicked, when Durfee played like Karam had only wished they could, other kids helping out Herren and Caron. Mikolazyk again performed well, hustling on the top of the Durfee press, sticking the open shot, playing like he used to play back on the Milliken League all-star teams. Pavao came off the bench and quickly got fifteen points, shooting the way he was supposed to be able to do. Callahan was playing tougher, no longer as tentative underneath. Cioe came off the bench and battled with his usual abandon. The team was coming together, the other players starting to get more confidence.

Then there was the return of Jones, a six-foot-four blond-haired senior, his first game of the year. Last year he had been the first big man off the bench, had played with a lot of heart, if sparingly. He was not much of a scorer, didn't jump particulary well, but like all Durfee kids he played hard and rarely tried to do what he couldn't do, a trademark of a Karam-coached player. Jones was a lot like Cioe, only bigger, with a few more offensive skills. And like Cioe, he never really thought he'd end up being a Durfee player.

He had grown up in the Highlands with a variety of interests, not just basketball. He often surfed along the coastal beaches of southern Rhode Island about twenty miles away. He liked listening to music, especially such groups as the Grateful Dead and Led Zeppelin, as though he had grown up in the wrong decade. Jones seemed better suited to the early seventies, with his longish hair and bedroom at home that had strobe lights, a leftover hippie. He had turned himself off to school his first three years, barely scraping by, having no interest. That had changed recently, and now he garnered all As, resurrecting his academic career so he's already been accepted to Castleton State in Vermont.

His teammates liked him, though many didn't understand him. They considered him very smart, yet a little weird. On the surface he didn't seem to have their passion for basketball. As a kid, he'd never been an all-star in the Milliken League. This past summer he'd been awful in the summer league, seemed disinterested and out of shape, and both Herren and Caron had wondered whether Jonesy would ever help them.

They didn't know that beneath the surfing and music, beneath the counterculture remnants, there also burned a desire to play for Durfee. Jones too used to watch the Michael Herren teams, had seen the excitement, and now he was a part of it. He had continued to grow while a lot of more talented kids had stopped, and now he was one of the biggest kids on the team, someone whose height made him a player. He thought of being a starter for Durfee as a wild ride, and in his own idiosyncratic way, he appreciated that. Now he was back from his sprained ankle, ready to play his last year of basketball. He didn't think he would try to play next year at Castleton State, for he believed that after Durfee basketball, the game wouldn't have the same intensity.

He had played like Karam thought he could, under control, battling underneath, some inside help for Callahan. His presence had seemed to take Durfee to another level as a team. With fifty-one seconds left in the game, Durfee leading by sixteen, Karam substituted Eric Santos, a seldom-used senior, for Herren.

Herren slapped hands with Santos, turned to the bench.

"Look at him," Karam said to the Greek chorus behind the bench. "Here comes John Wayne."

Herren walked over toward the bench, threw his fist into the air over his head. His teammates embraced him as he got to the bench. He had played a great tournament. Karam cuffed him affectionately on the head. Minutes later Herren was named the MVP of the tournament. He walked up to accept the trophy with no expression on his face, as several rows up in the bleachers his mother and aunt watched.

Skippy was happy. His team had come a long way from the Boston College High game only a week ago. They no longer seemed to be playing two on five. Mikolazyk had been a real surprise. Jones would help, for he played hard. Pavao had enjoyed the best stretch in his career. The hard work in practice had been worth it. They had just beaten two good teams on back-to-back nights, two teams they wouldn't have been able to beat just a week ago. They had been tough and gritty and overachieving, qualities the good Durfee teams always had, trademarks of a Skip Karam–coached team. For the first time since the season started, Skippy looked at his team and liked what he saw.

The locker room was ebullient, full of happiness and macho posturing, the fruits of victory.

"Hey, did you see Gore, that little mutt?" said Herren. "Shooting the lights out. I'm going to change the name on my sneakers to Air Gores."

"Igor . . . Igor . . . Igor," Callahan started chanting.

Mikolazyk laughed and began taking off his uniform.

"Igor," said Jones. "One big head on two little stilts."

Mikolazyk threw one of his sneakers at him.

"Fuck you, Jonesy, you big ugly geek," he said with a laugh.

"You should talk, Gore, you little mutt," Herren said.

"Who are you, Tom Cruise?" Mikolazyk shot back.

"I don't see any broads around you."

"Like you're getting laid so much."

"More than you."

"Yeah, right."

Callahan turned to Cioe.

"Did you see what I did to that big motherfucker? I got him good."

"I got the other one."

"The big one got me in the head with an elbow. It still hurts."

"I suckered the little one good."

On it went, postgame patter, catharsis from all the emotion. After the Duxbury game the locker room had been like a wake, full of frustration and thick silence, the air smelling of defeat. This was the flip side, the unabashed emotion of victory, the reward for the hard practices and the anxiety and the pressure, the feeling that nothing else mattered but this moment, this one sweet, sweet moment.

Karam stood in the doorway. He knew what the kids in the room could not know yet, that the time spent savoring victories is too short, too quickly forgotten. For him the pain of losing far out weighed the joy of winning, so that now, after three decades of coaching, winning gave him too little satisfaction. Winning was not losing, nothing more, a reprieve from those times when he felt his insides were being torn out.

"Let's go," he shouted. "Let's get out of here. We've got a long ride ahead."

No one seemed to be listening.

The players were in the showers, the shouts reverberating through the entire locker room, a chant that got louder and louder.

"BACK TO THE RIVER . . . BACK TO THE RIVER . . . BACK TO THE RIVER."

They were coming back to a city wracked with unemployment and social problems, a city that in many ways seemed to mirror much of the anxiety and discontent that plagued the rest of the country, a city whose past and present were a blueprint for what has happened to so many small cities in the Northeast.

Fall River is situated on Mount Hope Bay, fifty miles south of Boston. The explorer Leif Ericsson was said to have sailed into Mount Hope Bay as early as 1000 A.D., and the area that later became Fall River, originally part of the Plymouth Colony, also was one of the sites of the Indian Wars in the late Seventeenth century. In 1659 some early settlers bought land from the Pocasset Indians—a subtribe of the Wampanoags, who in turn were part of the great Algonquin Nation—for twenty coats, two rugs, two iron pots, eight pairs of shoes, and some stockings.

Among the first settlers were the Bordens, and by the early 1700s Bordens owned land on both side of the Taunton River, land awarded by legal decree. It's locally believed that a Borden started the first sawmill and gristmill, harnessing the Quequechan River that flows sluggishly out of North Watuppa and South Watuppa ponds to the east of the city, then drops 125 feet in less than a half mile over a series of ledges until it goes into Mount Hope Bay at the west end of the city. *Quequechan* was the Indian word for "falling water," and in the early 1800s, after first being called Pocasset and then Troy, the city was called Fall River.

In the early 1800s nearly half of the people were Bordens, the inhabitants mostly farmers. But things were changing; the future was arriving even though no one knew it at the time. In 1811, Globe Manufacturing opened on the corner of South Main and Globe streets, in what is now called the South End. It was started by a man who had worked for Samuel Slater in Pawtucket, Rhode Island, about twenty-five miles away; Slater is credited with bringing the first textile mill to the United States. Two years later the Fall River Iron Works started, then the Pocasset Manufacturing Company. By the late 1920s there were ten factories along the Quequechan River, most of the employees coming from the surrounding towns who saw the new millwork as better than farming. Twenty years later agents were being sent to Canada, England, Scotland, and Ireland to recruit workers.

Fall River became a city in 1854. Its motto was "We'll try."

The latter half of the eighteenth century saw the emergence of an industrial culture as new and bigger mills came to dominate the city. American Print Works had been built in the 1840s, but was enlarged in 1867, so that it was five stories tall and 406 feet long, with a 110-foot bell tower. In addition to the main building there were a boiler house, a chemical shop, a print shop, a dye shop, and a carpenter's shop. From a distance it seemed like a prison, a grim, foreboding, dehumanizing place where the men who worked inside were merely cogs in an industrial process that far transcended them. A year later came the Mechanic Mill, complete with 126 tenement houses for the workers to live in. More and more tenement houses were being built for the influx of immigrants.

The immigrants came and brought their culture with them, their own customs, religion, values, food. The French-Canadians in the eastern end of the city, the Flint, the magnificent Notre Dame church being their spiritual center. The Portuguese in the sprawling South End, the Globe. The Irish in Corky Row, just off downtown. They mostly lived in triple-decker tenements that grew around the mills like beads on a necklace. The result was a city full of separate villages, each one different from the other.

From 1870 to 1890 the city's population quadrupled, from 27,000 to 105,000, as Fall River evolved from a small town in southeastern Massachusetts into the biggest textile city in the country, until it became known as "Spindle City," a nickname that exists to this day. Along with it came the benefits: an elegant public library; two large spacious parks designed by the Olmstead Brothers, who had done New York's Central Park; the construction of fifteen new schools, along with a showcase new high school and a new Boys Club.

By the turn of the century Fall River was the undisputed cotton king, the leading manufacturer of cotton cloth in the world. No other city even began to rival it. There were 105,000 residents, nearly 30,000 of them textile workers, an incredibly high percentage. Immigrants from eighteen different countries were included in the city's population, with French-Canadians being the largest group, making Fall River the city with the highest percentage of immigrants in the country in cities of over 100,000 people.

It was the height of the Victorian era in Fall River, the showcase of which was the Highlands, the area just north of downtown. Many of the houses had been built in the period after the Civil War, large homes that often came equipped with carriage houses and elaborate wrought-iron fences, gazebos, and intricate latticework. This was the domain of the mill owners, the men who controlled the city, sat on the boards, ran the banks, and lived on top of the hill, their geography symbolic of their station in the community.

In retrospect, 1911 might have been the high point. Certainly it was the greatest celebration in the city's history. The event was a week-long tribute to the city's textile industry, featuring parades, a horse show in North Park, fireworks, large crowds that jammed the parade route, and an appearance by President William Taft. Photographs from the era show a bustling downtown, with a giant streamer across Main Street that said COTTON CENTENNIAL. There was a sense of incredible optimism then, the feeling that the vast fortunes were never going to decline, that the mills were unstoppable cash cows. Yet already there was competition from the South, a harbinger of a cruel future.

At the time, Fall River was a microcosm of the northeastern United States, a textbook example of both the excesses and abuses of the Industrial Revolution. It encapsulated the growth of the labor movement, with trade unions, strikes, and appearances by Samuel Gompers, one of the country's leading union officials, and socialist Eugene Debs. It exemplified the inhumane working conditions in the textile mills throughout the Northeast, the child labor, the nearly slave wages, the living conditions that seemed to come directly from the pages of a Dickens novel. As early as the late 1920s there were inquiries into child labor in Fall River, with rumors that some children as young as eight were working in the mills, and by the turn of the century it was thought that 10 percent of the mill workers were under fourteen. Still, the immigrants kept coming.

In 1875 there had been a strike that left many of the city's mill workers destitute. When the workers marched on City Hall, they were met by the mayor and a marshal waving a revolver at them. Less than a decade later a U.S. congressional committee had investigated both working and living conditions in Fall River and found them as bad as anyplace in the country. In 1905 there was a twenty-six-week strike, causing the Massachusetts governor to say in his inaugural address, "The most deplorable conditions exist in Fall River. Here in Massachusetts—the citadel of wealth, culture, refinement and progressive liberality—is presented the melancholy sight of our women and children being fed from soup houses and sent to bed scantily clad in fireless homes."

The final burst of economic prosperity for Fall River began in 1916 with the advent of the United States' involvement in World War I. Many of the mills received lucrative government contracts and the owners even banded together, using the mills that were most ready to handle the extra work while splitting the profits. Three years later 101 mills were employing over thirty thousand workers.

But the end was near.

Rather than putting the profits back into the mills and buying new machinery needed to fight off the challenge from the southern states that had cheaper labor, many of Fall River's mill owners chose instead to drain the profits. The city's Catholic bishop called for Fall River to be saved, for the updating of factories and for efficient management, but it was not to be. In 1924, just fourteen years after the "Cotton Centennial," Matthew Charloner Durfee Borden, the most powerful owner in the city, announced the removal of some textile machinery from his mills to Tennessee.

It was over.

Soon after, Fall River was being called a "city of misery," its unemployment, homelessness, and hopelessness a sneak preview of the Great Depression that was only five years away, its large mills left abandoned like the husks of prehistoric dinosaurs.

More than eleven thousand jobs were lost between 1926 and 1931. The population declined. The city was in receivership then, unable to meet its bills, its finances decided by an outside governing board. At the time it was determined that half of the corporations and half of the citizens could not pay their bills. Shortly after, the American Print Works, the largest mill in a city that once had been the centerpiece of the vast fortune of M. C. D. Borden, closed, the definitive end of an era. This was followed by the closing of the Fall River Line, another sign that the city's glory times were over.

Fall River remained in receivership until 1941, roughly ten years. Services were cut. Municipal salaries were slashed. There are grim stories about desperate people standing in long lines for hours, waiting for social services that no longer were available. The remnants of the textile industry would remain until the mid-sixties, but by the late thirties the garment industry, mostly women and mostly low-paid, had replaced textiles as the city's main industry. It remains so to this day, but it's an insecure industry, closely tied to economic fluctuations.

What We Had, a memoir by James Chace, who grew up in the Highlands and went on to become the international affairs editor for the *New York Times Book Review* and a professor at Columbia, captures the era between the Depression and World War II. Chace came of age in a Fall River where the mills were closing and the city was failing.

His grandfather had been the president of the Massachusetts state senate, yet had used the family's money to finance his campaigns, so Chace grew up with the right lineage and the right name and the right address—the only problem was the money was gone. In a sense his personal odyssey mirrored the city's.

"Where I grew up the streets were clean and shaded by elms and chestnut trees," writes Chace. "But as you passed the city hall toward the Flint and the Globe, the streets were left untended, the trees were scant, and the neighborhoods were made up solely of tenements—gray and pink and brown with tiers of porches that sagged against their pillars. . . . Before the war, then, the city seemed a desolate ruin made up of vast factory buildings, sprawling mansions and rows of tenements for the mill workers, who were largely unemployed."

Even then, there was the sense that for kids Fall River was a dead end, a nowhere ward of lost opportunities.

"Almost no one I knew had much hope of making it except by escaping to another city," writes Chase. "Or by finding an angle at home that would give you a bare living. . . . To be called a con man was a kind of compliment."

Chace describes his experience at Durfee High School in the late 1940s: "The curriculum was much as it had been for 50 years, the best teachers at least that old, and the only significant change the spectacular victories of the basketball team, which had won the state and New England championships."

Little has changed.

Tony Medeiros, now a musician in the Rhode Island–southeastern Massachusetts area, grew up "below the hill" in the sixties, a few streets over from Al Herren. His family lived on the second floor of a tenement, his grandparents on the first floor, his aunt on the third.

"It was very Old World," he said. "We didn't get hot water until 1960. There was no tub, no shower. Everyone had a vegetable garden. You traded on 'tick' at the local grocery store, and it was like all the commerce was done Saturday morning. There was a 'Fish Man,' a 'Bread Man,' an 'Egg Man,' a 'Knife Man,' a 'Milk Man.' Everyone came by.

"Fall River was a very closed world then. You didn't get by because of what you knew, but of who you knew. There was the sense that all the jobs are handed down, even the shitty ones. Everything's handed out. That the only way to get a job was to carry a sign on election day. The feeling that if you didn't know someone there was no sense of even trying for a job. That it would be impossible to go do something on your own. There was a very defeatist attitude about everything."

By 1960 the city had one of the lowest educational levels in the country, the average adult completing less than nine years of schooling. In 1975 Fall River had the lowest hourly earnings in Massachusetts. In the late sixties Interstate 195 was built, bisecting downtown, the highway tunneling underneath the new Government Center, but rather than bringing in tourists, it seemed to cut the city in half, dividing the North End from the South End. Then came the growth of the suburban malls, one in Swansea to the west and one in Dartmouth to the east, two daggers to downtown's heart.

It was a familiar story in the Northeast, by no means unique to Fall River. Malls were built in the suburbs, the downtowns deteriorated, the decay and urban blight became more apparent with each passing year.

It is now roughly seventy years since the textile industry began to fold, years that haven't been kind to Fall River.

The city's schoolteachers haven't had a contract since August 1991, periodically picketing outside the mayor's house, and in early February 1993 two hundred of them picketed outside the Government Center, threatening to seriously consider a strike if a deal was not worked out by May 1. Unemployment, which had been as high as 17 percent, one of the highest rates in the country, was now nearly 13 percent, up since the summer. Domestic violence has become such a problem that Police Chief Francis McDonald has hinted that the department might create a special unit just to handle domestic violence cases.

In early January the granite-faced Anderson-Little, the city's flagship company on Bedford Street, home office for 267 clothing stores across the country, closed, costing 540 jobs. This came on the heels of the announcement in early December that two curtain factories would close, ending 166 jobs, the latest in a long string of failures in the apparel and textile industries. A few weeks later Cliftex, which makes men's clothes and had been in the Durfee Union Mill Complex on Plymouth Avenue for nearly a decade, announced it too would close, 79 more jobs gone.

The closing of Anderson-Little hit Fall River hard, one more sign of tough times. The company had begun as the classic Horatio Alger story in Boston in 1912, founded by a Russian émigré. It had been the first seller of men's clothes in New England and in 1936 it opened its corporate headquarters in Fall River. After World War II a city full of ex-servicemen returned, money in their pockets, invariably looking for a suit. So many eventually came to the factory that a little area on the first floor was established to serve them. Soon the area on the first floor kept getting bigger until the entire first floor became a showroom, one of the first mill outlets in the country. As local legend has it, all Fall River men are buried in Anderson-Little suits.

In late January, when William Jefferson Clinton was sworn in as the forty-second president of the United States, when the optimism and hope of a new administration came alive in the land, Fall River seemed like a tiny microcosm of the vast problems Clinton faced, the grim realities everywhere to see, as omnipresent as the daily newspaper. A front-page story in the *Herald News* said SCHOOL CONDITIONS FAILING, told of decrepit buildings, no safety officers at some elementary schools because the city couldn't afford them. One such school, the Greene Elementary School, built in 1909, has an exposed metal pipe used for heat that runs along the floor in the basement that also doubles as the gymnasium. Gym teachers are forever warning their students not to touch it. The Greene School, like most of the schools in Fall River, has lead paint covering most of the walls and asbestos insulating water pipes. To fix the aging system has been estimated to cost as much as $55 million, but so far no money has been allocated.

In early February would come the news that the city was going to lay off eighty people and that all department heads must slash their budget 15 percent, a promise of dwindling city services. Mayor John Mitchell said the layoffs were inevitable, that the city was facing a shortfall of $5 million for the next fiscal year.

Later in the month came a front-page *Herald News* story that a top-grade form of heroin was flooding the city, already blamed for five deaths. The same day offered a story of a New Bedford man being held in connection with a carjacking incident in Fall River that took place in the Almacs Shopping Center on President Avenue, virtually across the street from Durfee, one of the first reported carjackings in Fall River.

All of this was happening during the time that James R. Porter confessed to molesting dozens of boys while serving as a priest in New Bedford, North Attleboro, and Fall River in the sixties. One of the most notorious pedophilia cases in church history, Porter has been sentenced to six months in jail in Minnesota. In December, the Diocese of Fall River had reached a multimillion-dollar settlement with fifty-eight people. Despite his notoriety and range of allegations against Porter, this was his first conviction. The news was spread over the top of the *Herald News* in big, bold letters.

In early March the head of the United Way of Greater Fall River said "this area has been raped, pillaged and plundered" in the past five years by companies that have either closed or had layoffs, with over three thousand jobs lost through plant closings and another three thousand through layoffs.

Clyde Barrow, an economist at the University of Massachusetts at Dartmouth, said that the region's workforce is part of the problem, that in a global economy manufacturers will have to rely on new technologies and these jobs will require a skilled workforce, something the entire southeastern Massachusetts area lacks.

"The literacy rates are higher in Cuba than they are in this region," he told the Providence *Journal-Bulletin*. "Over 50 percent of adults 25 years old and older do not have high school diplomas. We are still not devoting the level of resources we need to upgrade our work force."

These are all symptoms of a city that's grown old.

Bob Kerr, a Providence *Journal-Bulletin* writer, first came to Fall River in 1972. He had just been hired by the *Journal-Bulletin* and one day was on a visit to all of the suburban offices in the paper's circulation area, the traditional starting point for new reporters. One of them was in Fall River, the eastern edge of the *Journal-Bulletin*'s range.

"There was a bunch of us young reporters and we had spent the day touring all the offices on a very hot day," Kerr remembered. "Fall River was the last stop. No one wanted to be sent there. It was viewed as the 'pits' of all the suburban offices. Six months later I was there."

It was the early seventies, just before the mill outlet boom, the old, closed mills becoming prosperous outlets, selling goods at cheap prices. There was hope: The new high school was built, a new courthouse, and new high-rises for the elderly, some of them constructed by Karam's brothers, Jimmy and "Boo Boo." But it also was the era of Pier 14 and Charlie's Cafe, the two bars on Bedford Street in the shadow of the police station that were as hard-core as it gets, complete with rampant prostitution, drugs, pimps, a human sewer that a few years later would provide the backdrop for a string of ritual murders with Satanic overtones, captured in the book *Mortal Remains*. During the same era, the state of Massachusetts followed a policy of "deinstitutionalization," releasing inmates of many of the state's facilities to the street.

"Fall River was like a magnet," Kerr said. "A lot of people walking around talking to the sky. Guys in overcoats with six-packs under their arms. You used to see half a dozen of them every day hanging in front of the Main Drug on Main Street."

Kerr began learning about Fall River at the Belmont Club, where there was a passing parade of people and personalities. It adjoined the old Mellen Hotel and when City Hall was demolished to make way for Interstate 195 the Mellen became the interim City Hall; thus, Fall River was the only town in the country with a barroom in its City Hall. Kerr used to cover City Council meetings by going back and forth between the Mellen and the Belmont bar. In Fall River, no one thought that was strange.

He had grown up in suburban Detroit, served in the Marines in Vietnam, but Fall River was so different than anything he'd experienced before, a human carnival that Kerr spent many a night watching. For one thing, everybody in Fall River seemed to have a nickname. There was Dracula, so named because he once bit another guy in the neck during a soccer game. There was Fire Hydrant, so named because a dog once urinated on his leg while he was immobilized. There was Disease, although no one seemed quite sure why he was called that. Kerr knew guys for years without ever knowing their real names: Joe the Barber, Bowlegger, Superman, Johnny the Moonshiner, Mad Dog, Pencil Strip Gus. Even a guy who was nicknamed Channel 6 because he forever was trying to fine-tune his hearing aid.

Eventually, Kerr acquired a genuine fondness for Fall River, for its unpretentiousness, its quirkiness, its local color. You could start a political rumor in the morning at the

Main Drug and by evening it was on the talk shows. He married a Fall River woman and bought a house in the Highlands. For years he would try to defend Fall River to people he worked with, people who looked at him askance when they heard he actually lived there.

"I don't even bother anymore," he said. "It's really a very livable city, and the great thing about living in Fall River is there's no one to impress. Even the people who have money. People might want to have their money. But they don't really want to *be* them. But I think Fall River is more depressed now than ever. Even the mill outlet thing has been co-opted. Every city has mill outlets now. There is no cultural life whatsoever. There is no bookstore. The Harbor Mall is a joke. There seems to be a very strong feeling that if you got bucks you get your kid out of Durfee.

"It's become a dirty blue-collar town. The bright kids leave. The ones who stay here have ulterior motives. The Portuguese, who make up a large percentage of the city's population, work, pray, go to school, and take English as a second language, without learning English. Their world is as close to the Old World and still be in America as you can get. Yet the Portuguese really have been the saviors of a lot of the city—the stories of them plunking down full payment for a three-decker in a paper bag, then fixing it up with all their relatives. Entire neighborhoods have been revived because of them, and an entire stretch of South Main Street is really a Portuguese business district—businesses, restaurants, and bars. I think they probably still cling to their cultural enclaves, but come closer to fuller participation in the life of the city than they used to. The old money is gone now. It's in Westport Harbor if it's anywhere. The politicians never have done the city any favors. The state ones come in at election time, make the obligatory mill stops, and then leave. The local ones traditionally have been self-serving. The entire city just strikes me as more depressed than I've ever seen it."

Chapter

6

"LET'S JUST GO OUT THERE and fuck them up," said Herren as his teammates surrounded him in the Brockton locker room, a small area with army-green metal lockers dominating the room. It was Friday night, January 8, nine days after the Lowell Tournament. Three nights earlier Durfee had rolled over Bishop Feehan of Attleboro at home; this was the first league game of the season, Karam had just given his pregame talk, and now Herren was giving his. "Let's just go out and play fucking hard. Forget about everything else. Jeff, forget about your fuckin' foot. Cal, forget about how many fuckin' shots you get. Forget about fuckin' everything. Let's just go out and fuckin' play like animals and fuck them up."

Being the co-captain did not come easily to Herren. He was too much the little brother to be a leader, too moody and self-absorbed. He could be very supportive of his teammates, and once the game started no one played any harder or with more intensity. He could say all the right things, yet it was not his nature to be a true leader.

The players burst out of the locker room, went down the hallway, then up the stairs that led to the gym. If New Bedford is Durfee's big rival, Brockton is second, linked by the size of the respective schools and the fact that Fall River is only about twenty-five miles from Brockton. Yet there is not the animosity between these schools that exists between Fall River and New Bedford. The rivalry draws large crowds, fueled by tradition and competitiveness, but there is not the sense that each game is life-and-death.

It was a cold night in early January, the large, poorly lit gym with dark wood walls crowded and warm with growing excitement. A large white sign with red and black letters said GO BROCKTON BOXERS, the nickname in honor of Rocky Marciano and Marvelous Marvin Hagler, the two world champions from different eras that gave Brockton a national sports identity. A championship banner celebrated a recent state championship football team. Interspersed with these were signs for local establishments, Cape Cod Pizza and George's Cafe (where the champs eat), a high school gym with advertisements on the walls like some minor league ballpark.

Brockton is another city in southeastern Massachusetts that's fallen on hard times, a city of almost a hundred thousand people. Once it was known as "Shoe City," with scores of shoe factories, and as late as the fifties there were still thirty shoe manufacturing companies left in Brockton. Now people are hard-pressed to name two or three. In the late seventies it became the fastest growing city in Massachusetts and there was optimism the city was going to have an economic renaissance, fueled by its proximity to Route 128, the high-tech beltway that circles Boston and the growing population around Route 24, the highway that leads from Route 128 to Fall River.

So much for pipe dreams.

The harsh economic realities of the past few years have hit Brockton as hard as they hit Fall River. The entire area has one of the highest unemployment rates in the country: the Massachusetts Rust Belt, small industrial cities without enough industry. Recently, there has been a cutback in social services, even a reduction of the police force. A Boston television station recently reported that there are ten thousand outstanding warrants in Brockton, but the police lack the personnel to serve the papers. The city is roughly 40 percent minority now, an influx of poor blacks and Hispanics who have fled Boston, bringing with them the attendant social problems of poverty that have turned downtown Brockton after dark into a desolate wasteland. The influx of minorities has made both the city and the high school more transient, as people come and go with fewer allegiances to longtime family history. Brockton is nowhere near as self-contained a city as Fall River.

What's survived is an athletic tradition that's centered around football. Brockton traditionally is the best high school football team in Massachusetts, one of the better ones in the country. In 1988 they entered the season ranked number one in America by *USA Today*. They play in Rocky Marciano Stadium, which can seat eight thousand, and each year graduate three or four kids who go on to play Division I football.

Basketball has not been as successful, but that doesn't mean it's been bad either. Fifteen years ago Brockton High School boasted nearly six thousand students, calling itself the biggest high school east of the Mississippi River. The high school has seven gray buildings, is fed by four junior high schools. When it was built in the early seventies there was talk of having two high schools, but the fear was that two high schools would encourage racial divisiveness, with one school becoming "white" and the other "black." The single school has created a potential athletic powerhouse in virtually every sport, the combination of superior numbers and a city with a rich athletic heritage.

Last year Brockton had beaten Durfee in the basketball finals of the South Sectional on a last-second desperation shot in overtime, though Durfee had defeated them twice in the regular season. It had been a devastating defeat for

Karam, for he knew his team had developed the potential to win a state title, certainly had been more talented than this year's team. Herren and Caron, though only sophomores, were stars. The center had been Steve Motta, a strong six-foot-two Portuguese kid with only one eye, who in a different era would have followed Teddy Roosevelt up San Juan Hill and not asked any questions. One forward had been Corey Luz, a quick black kid who shot well. A quintessential Durfee team, not much height, but quick and gritty and resilient. One that had come within one lucky shot of advancing to the Boston Garden and the semifinals of the state tournament. Now Durfee was here for some payback, but this was a good Brockton team, bigger and stronger than Durfee, with a star player of their own, six-foot-four forward Ben Mitchell, one of the top players in the state.

Right away, Durfee fell into trouble.

Karam got two technical fouls in the first minute and a half of the game, setting the tone. Herren missed a couple of drives into the middle of the lane, and as Durfee started falling more behind, Herren seemed to try to get them back into the game all by himself. Durfee trailed by ten at the half, made a little run midway through the second half before losing by twenty. The fears Karam had harbored before the Lowell Tournament, namely that Herren and Caron would be something less than brilliant and nobody else would be able to compensate, had come true.

It was Herren's first mediocre game of the season, for though he finished with twenty-eight points, he had forced things, been too much the offense. He even had been benched for a couple of minutes before the half for answering back to Karam. Gone was the balanced offense Durfee had played in the Lowell Tournament. Gone was the feeling that other players had settled into supporting roles. Caron was particularly frustrated. His foot was still bothering him, and he rarely seemed to get the ball where he could do anything with it, finishing with only eight points, maybe his worst game in two years. He saw Herren always with the ball and could feel himself getting angry, to the point that the anger began to dominate everything, how he felt about the game, the team, everything. He was angry not so much at Herren as at Karam for allowing it. The other players had been overmatched, worn down by Brockton's size and athleticism.

When the game ended, both teams lined up for the traditional postgame handshake. Except for Herren. He could not accept defeat, was unable to quickly turn off the emotional pitch he played the game with and become the good sport. He had not yet learned to do it, and as Karam watched him not shake hands, he felt the anger boil inside him. Herren had talked back to him in the first half; now this. When was this kid ever going to learn? Both teams started down the stairs toward the locker room. Karam quickly followed.

"You're the reason coaching sucks," he yelled at Herren.

The anger was evident on Karam's face, and as he went down the stairs and down the hallway that led to the large area outside the visitors locker room, he walked quickly, with purpose. Herren sat on a bench, his hands covering his face.

"Learn to lose with some class," Karam yelled.

"I can't."

"You better start to learn," Karam yelled back.

His voice cracked through the silent room. The tension that had been building between Karam and Herren since practice began in November had finally erupted, and the other players instantly recognized it. They stood on the periphery, not talking, not moving, only watching as an angry Karam stood over a disconsolate Herren.

"I'll never be able to," Herren shot back, visibly upset.

"Grow up," barked Karam. "Be a man. Learn to lose with class."

Herren muttered something inaudible.

Karam leaned over, his face inches from Herren's.

"You better start to grow up or you're going to be out of here," he yelled. "I've had it. You're real close to being off this team. Don't open your mouth again."

Karam turned away.

"Now you can go out and get drunk," he said over his shoulder.

"What do you mean by that?" Herren said.

"I mean you better start to grow up," Karam said, turning back toward him.

"Can I say something?" Herren asked, his voice choking up through a combination of rage, frustration, and tears.

"*Shut up. Shut up,*" Karam said. "Just keep your mouth shut."

Herren exploded off his seat and went to the back of the room. Dempsey went to him, put his arm around him.

"Chrissie, keep quiet," he said quietly. "Don't say anything."

"Why can't I say something?"

"Because you're seventeen years old and a junior in high school," Dempsey said, exasperated, his voice louder. "That's why."

An uneasy silence filled the room. The players showered and dressed quickly, stuffing their sweaty uniforms into their traveling bags, trying to get out of the locker room. Karam stood in the hallway, talking softly to his brother "Boo Boo" and Dempsey. Dempsey's face was flushed, as though he'd just witnessed some horrible accident. This had been more than Karam yelling at someone or admonishing someone; this had been an ugly incident, the emotions naked, the frustration raw.

"This really sucks," muttered Caron. He glanced over at Herren, who was hurriedly peeling out of his uniform and into his clothes, then at Karam out in the hallway. "I don't even care anymore. All we do is try and keep them both happy and it can't be done."

A few minutes later Karam walked slowly to the bus that

was waiting outside the door, the weariness all over his face, his shoulders slumped. He was angry at Herren, but not because of the outcome of the game. Karam never blamed the players when he lost, regardless of how poorly they might have played. He always blamed himself. He always looked to himself accusingly. What could he have done differently? Should he have gotten out of the 3–2 zone quicker? Should he have gone to a different offense? Questions rolled around and around in his head like some private carousel, questions that ruined his sleep, haunted him. When he lost, he felt *he* had let everyone down, his players, the school, the city itself, as though he were the caretaker of the tradition and with that came the unspoken assumption that to lose was to somehow tarnish it.

Many people would look at his volatility on the sidelines, his tirades, and assume he must be impossible after a loss. They were wrong. Ironically, he was usually at his best after a loss, at least outwardly. He praised the other team to the reporters. He praised the other coach. He was good with his players, never blaming them, essentially telling them it was only one game, soothing them, quickly putting the game into perspective for them. Instead, he internalized it, withdrawing into himself, feeling he had somehow failed.

The bus crept out of the parking lot, then left on the road that led to Route 24 and the highway back to Fall River. Inside, the bus was quiet and dark, only the drone of the engine. Karam slumped in the front seat, Abe White across from him, Dempsey one seat back across the aisle. The happiness of just a week ago in Lowell was over, as though it had never happened.

Eventually, Herren came slowly walking up the aisle toward the front of the bus, a white cap turned backward on his head, highlighting his face, making him look younger. Sometimes, for all his growing celebrity and notoriety, the aura that now always seemed to surround him, it was easy to forget he was still only seventeen years old, still had moments when he seemed a prisoner of his adolescence. This had been one of them.

But now he was coming to apologize, to pay homage to Karam. He sat in the seat behind him, the repentent son come to sit at his father's feet, and said he was sorry. It did not come easily, because in his view of the world he was losing face, publicly admitting he'd been wrong, and like many seventeen-year-olds, this did not come easily to him. But he said it. Karam nodded his head. One of his strengths is he doesn't hold grudges with his players. What's done is done: Life moves on. They made small talk for a second, the mood lightening.

The bus continued to move down the darkened highway, past the sign on Route 24 that said Fall River was only fifteen miles away. The rest of the players and cheerleaders were in the back of the bus, slumped in their seats. Karam and Herren continued to talk.

"Mr. Karam, do you remember when we came up here two years ago?" Herren asked.

Karam was silent for a moment.

"Yeah, Chrissie. You were a ninth grader then. That's when you were a nice kid."

Herren laughed, fidgeted in his seat.

"You know I didn't like it when you made the remark about going out and getting drunk," he finally said.

"You all drink too much, Chrissie," Karam countered. "Don't tell me you don't. I hear a million stories. If I benched kids for drinking, we wouldn't have a team."

Herren was silent. He didn't like Mr. Karam making references to drinking, didn't like to be reminded that whatever he and the rest of the players did over the weekend, Mr. Karam always seemed to know about it by Monday morning. But he knew this was not the time to make an issue about it. He had apologized; the incident was over. He and Mr. Karam were friends again.

"You know," pronounced Herren to those sitting around him, "my parents always said Mr. Karam is family."

Later in the evening Karam and Dempsey were at Lizzie's, a downtown restaurant-bar a block or so away from the Lizzie Borden murder house, adorned in the style of the Victorian era. The bartender was Kevin Whiting, who had starred on Durfee's state championship team of 1977 and had gone on to start on a good University of Rhode Island team, whom Herren had just passed as Durfee's second all-time leading scorer, right behind his brother Michael.

Lizzie's was Karam and Dempsey's postgame ritual, win or lose. Karam liked it because it usually wasn't over-crowded, a clean, well-lit place, a sanctuary away from the second-guessers. At least most of the time.

"Here, Skip," said Ronnie Fahey, handing him a beer.

Ronnie Fahey was in his fifties, rarely missed a Durfee game wherever it was, had grown up making pilgrimages to the Boston Garden to see Durfee, hitchhiking up Route 138, the old road that meandered through all the small towns, back when Fall River seemed to be a long way from Boston geographically as well as psychically, before there was a Route 24. Now he worked at Hartley's Pork Pies in the South End, a popular local institution. Fahey stood there with the guy everyone calls "Clocker."

"What's this?" Karam asked. "Coaches' Corner?"

Fahey and Clocker knew better than to ask Karam about the game. They had been around him after many defeats and would let him initiate the conversation; the last thing you ask any coach after a loss is what happened. But a guy at the bar turned around and saw Karam.

"How'd you do tonight, Skip?" he asked.

"We should have backed up the bus after the first two minutes," he said.

"You got beat?" the man asked, incredulous. "What happened?"

"We got outcoached," Karam said.

He and Dempsey went into the other room, where the restaurant was located, and sat down at a table. The room was mostly empty, just another couple a few tables away. He liked it this way, a place away from the questions. Following the last game of the Lowell Tournament, the bus had returned to Fall River too late to get to Lizzie's, so he and Dempsey had gone instead to the Down Under, also downtown, on the other side of Route 195. Eventually, his table had consisted of Michael Herren, Nicky Salmon, Mikey Martin, and Brian O'Neil, the group dynamics particularly interesting since Salmon and O'Neil all had played on the '84 state championship team, the ongoing argument being whether that team had been better than Michael Herren's two state championship teams.

It was a passion, almost an obsession. The question of best Durfee team was something endlessly debated, one of the age-old barroom topics, right there with death, taxes, and local politics. The great Andy Farrissey team of '48? The '52 team of Skippy Karam that also had won the New England Tournament? The '56 team of Al Attar, former Red Sox catcher Russ Gibson, and Tommy Arruda, who had made it to Triple A with the San Francisco Giants as a pitcher? The '66 team of Dempsey and Ernie Fleming which won a state title? The '77 team of Whiting and Kenny Faiola that also won the whole thing? Over and over it went, a discussion with no end.

Nowhere are the arguments more intense than between the players on the respective teams, the symbolic high point being a couple of years ago when the players from the '89 team and the ones from the '84 team met at the Bank Street Armory to settle the issue once and for all.

No such luck.

The argument continues. It's an argument Karam was forever trying to avoid. He had learned long ago he could not win in such discussions, so he had sat there that night as Michael and Salmon had once again debated the question, and rolled his eyes. He never said who the best team was. He never said who the best player was. He refused to participate in the popular Fall River parlor game of naming the five all-time best Durfee players.

Now, at least, he was free of all that, just him and Dempsey alone at Lizzie's.

"The kid's only hurting himself," he said. "But he won't listen. I don't know what to do with him."

He sighed.

"What's he doing acting like that? He never used to be that way. Why can't he lose like everybody else does? Does he think losing's tougher on him than it is on anyone else? Why can't he lose like everyone else does? Shake hands and get the hell out of there."

Dempsey shrugged.

All of a sudden Michael Herren came into Lizzie's wearing jeans and a black hat. He saw Karam and Dempsey and immediately came over to them.

"I couldn't watch it," he said, the words tumbling over themselves. "I left in the third quarter. I couldn't watch it anymore. It was making me sick."

He began a diatribe of what was wrong with the team, how the big men didn't box out, how no one played with any intensity, how they didn't remotely play the way they had in Lowell, how they had been a disgrace to Durfee basketball, how they all should be ashamed to put the uniform on.

"Michael, when are you going back to school?" Karam finally asked.

"Sunday,"

"Good, because I can't take it anymore."

Michael was nonplussed.

"Mr. Karam, you got to be tougher on them."

Karam looked as if he'd just tasted something sour.

"Michael, please. Enough. I don't want to hear it anymore."

Michael was undeterred. He continued to offer his analysis of the game, his opinion rigid and uncompromising, a verbal locomotive that had lost its brakes.

Karam put his head on the table in mock surrender. "Michael, enough. It's over."

"These guys got no heart," Michael continued. "They don't want it bad enough. They saw our team, me and Juddy and everybody, and they saw the parties and the girls and everything. But they never saw how hard we worked at it."

"Michael, what do you want me to do?"

"Kick their ass. You've gotten too mellow, Mr. Karam. You never would have stood for that kind of effort from us. Half of them aren't even in shape. Mikolazyk smokes two packs of cigarettes a day."

Karam didn't respond. He didn't want to hear that Mikolazyk smokes too much. Or that some guys drink too much. He didn't want to hear anything. He already had retreated into the private hell he goes to after a loss. He wanted to sit here in silence, sip on his beer, and nurse his hurt, not hear Michael Herren tell him what was wrong.

Their relationship was like a marriage that had its rocky times, its times of great conflict, but was cemented through deep affection and a shared history. Skippy Karam had been coaching for twenty-five years and thought he had seen it all, coached it all, that nothing could come along that he wasn't prepared for. Then along had come Michael, with his unbelievable exuberance and will and dominant personality, what Boston *Globe* sportswriter Leigh Montville once likened to a ten-year-old who had been raised in warm and happy surroundings: Look at me, look at us.

It hadn't been easy.

Skippy had never approved of his players showboating or showing up opponents; he was much too old school for that. Then along had come Michael with his fist in the air, his emotion pouring out of him as though it were sweat, his unabashed enthusiasm for everything he did on a basketball court. Michael Herren and Skip Karam, the eternal optimist meeting the born pessimist. In the beginning Karam had tried to put reins on Michael, before realizing Michael's personality was so tied to his performance as a player that he fed off the emotion, was driven by it. They were like a basketball version of Ralph and Alice, and Skippy liked to say Michael Herren was the one kid responsible for both putting him in the Massachusetts' Coaches Hall of Fame and turning his hair gray.

Yet there was deep affection too.

To Michael, it didn't matter that Mr. Karam yelled at him or tried to control him. He loved Mr. Karam unconditionally. Back in 1989 when his Durfee career had been finishing, Michael had told the *Standard-Times* of New Bedford, "The man's a legend, a great, great coach. Everything I know about basketball I learned from him. I respect him as much as I respect anyone and you just don't forget people like that."

The only thing Karam had regretted about coaching Michael was that he knew there were people who misinterpreted him.

"With all his antics I can understand how they dislike him, but I feel bad he's turned so many people off," he had said at the conclusion of Michael's career. "He's really a good kid who likes to win and he's certainly one of the most dynamic players to come out of this area in years."

Karam also was fond of telling a story that was an example of their relationship. It had happened during a state tournament game in Michael's senior year. With Durfee in command in the closing minutes, Michael had made two aborted drives to the basket and a screaming Karam had called him over to the sidelines.

"I wanted to go into a stall and I was screaming at him to hold the ball out," said Karam. "When I called him to the sidelines, he said, 'Coach, please stop yelling at me, you're embarrassing me.' That's the first time anyone ever said that to me, but that's Michael."

But now all Karam wanted Michael to do was stop talking about the game, stop talking about his team.

"Please, Michael, no more. I can't take it," he said.

"All I know is that I couldn't watch anymore," Michael said. "It was making me sick."

Karam looked at Dempsey and shook his head.

Michael didn't seem to notice.

"I can't wait to go back to school," Michael said. "I have to get away from this. I don't care anymore. My brother's on his own. I can't want it more than he does."

"Callahan, if you can't run any faster than that, go home," said Karam.

The schedule had given Durfee a week off before they were to play New Bedford at home, so it was back to the gym, back into Karam's laboratory. It was a Wednesday afternoon, a dreary winter's day, the sky dull gray, the part of the season where practice has gotten tedious, playing against the same people every day, over and over. Herren was quiet, going through the motions, devoid of the spark he so often played with. Caron had a sullen look on his face. Mikolazyk wasn't there, the word being that he was in detention for having been caught smoking in a lavatory. So when he walked in a few minutes later, trying to sneak into the practice, Karam was quickly all over him.

"Gore, if you can't get here on time, why don't you just go home?" he said. "Because I don't care."

Mikolazyk said nothing.

Karam glared at him, told him to start practicing.

The varsity was scrimmaging against the jayvee team and the more Karam looked at it, the more he didn't like what he saw. So when Callahan was outmuscled for a rebound, he blew his whistle.

"Callahan, you haven't hurt anyone all year, but I heard you beat up your sister last week."

Pavao laughed.

"What are you laughing at, Peter?" snapped Karam. "Do you think you're tough? Always jumping on piles like you're some big tough guy."

The laugh ran away from Pavao's face.

"You guys are all a piece of shit," muttered Karam. "Start running. Everyone."

The players start running in a group around the court. Karam watched them with a frown on his face. "We had our best practice of the year yesterday," he said. "No bitching. No ball-throwing. Everyone working hard. Why? Because Chrissie wasn't here. He stayed home from school. Today he's back and it's a waste of time."

He shook his head.

"He was a great kid as a freshman, never said a word. Even last year he was no problem. But the minute he came back this year it's like he's pushing me, testing me. I never had this before. I don't understand it. He's got everything in the world going for him, but some days he'll come in here and just go through the motions, or give some kid a look when he gets fouled like he's Chris Herren and he's not supposed to get fouled. What's that shit about? I don't understand it. He's got everything in the world going for him and he acts like everything's against him."

The players' pace had slowed considerably.

"You should have done fourteen laps already," Karam called out to them. "Pick up the pace, fellas, or you'll be running for the rest of practice."

It picked up; more laps.

"You guys having a good time?" Karam asked.

More running.

"Having trouble breathing, Gore?" Karam said. "I wonder why."

They ran for a couple more minutes, Karam finally blowing the whistle. The players were visibly winded, breathing heavily, some leaning over and pulling on their shorts.

"Mr. Karam, can we get a drink?" Herren asked between deep breaths.

"What's the matter, no water at that hotel of yours?" Karam asked, a reference to the new practice in Fall River of a bunch of kids renting hotel rooms to have weekend parties. "No drinks. You guys don't play hard enough to deserve water."

Karam turned to walk away and Mikolazyk gave him the finger, angrily thrusting his middle finger upward and aimed at Karam's back.

As the second string began scrimmaging against the jayvees, the first string stood on the sidelines. Herren whispered something to Bobby Rodriguez, the student manager. Rodriguez looked wary, began shaking his head no, but Herren insisted. Rodriguez went through the blue door that led back into the locker room area, returned a minute later with a bottle of water. He gave it to Herren, who knelt down behind the line of players and snuck a drink, then handed it to Callahan, who did the same thing. Down the line the bottle went, each player sneaking a drink as the others shielded him.

Who said there was no team togetherness?

Caron's foul mood was apparent. After the bad game against Brockton, his ankle still hurt. He knew he could be playing better. He could see the way the season was developing, how everything was being geared to Chris. Last year he had been the point guard and Chris had been on the wing. Now the situation was reversed. Chris had the ball, controlled everything, and he often stood on the wing waiting for the ball that either never came or, when it did it, arrived at the wrong time, too late for him to shoot. He tried to give himself little pep talks, to tell himself not to let it bother him, to control his frustration; then he would come to practice and it would start all over again, this wave of anger that seemed to wash over him.

There was an obstinate streak in him, a Fall River attitude, one that said, this is the way I am and the hell with anyone who doesn't like it.

"I think I was born to be in Fall River," he said one day. "When I lived in Westport when I was a kid, I think I scared people. People thought I was a weirdo. All the kids in Westport had long hair. I had a 'beezer'—a crew cut. Everyone listened to Bon Jovi. I fuckin' hated Bon Jovi. I didn't even listen to music until I got to Fall River. Kids in Fall River are tough. That's the norm. In a way I'm very narrow-minded and I kind of like it that way. I wish it were the fifties. Like *The Sandlot*, or *Hoosiers*. Short hair. Blue jeans. T-shirts. Chuck Taylor sneakers. Plain. That's what I like. I think I'm a lot like my father."

His father, Rick, grew up near Columbia Park on Bedford Street, on the same street where the family now lives. It was the fringes of the Flint, but his neighborhood was mostly Italian, even though both his parents were of French heritage. The late fifties and early sixties were still a time when the different ethnic neighborhoods formed separate provinces in Fall River, and Fall River was Rick's world, all he knew.

Rick Caron's father was a state policeman, but his childhood world revolved around sports. CYO was big in Fall River then, and he played basketball and baseball, both with success, especially basketball. But when he got to Durfee, he sensed he was on the outside of Durfee basketball. He was five-foot-nine, 140 pounds, a year younger than the rest of his class, so he knew he never was going to be a Durfee star, but he had the feeling that who made the team and who didn't sometimes was determined by small-town politics, not just ability.

"Durfee basketball was a lot of kids whose fathers had

played, or who had older brothers that played," he said. "It was never stated, but you just kind of knew that they were going to play too. I didn't have an older brother, so I didn't try out."

He had grown up listening to the games on the radio, but in high school Durfee basketball didn't overly concern him. In 1966, his junior year, the team won the state title, Karam's first, a team that featured Bobby Dempsey and Ernie Fleming. There was a parade down Main Street in celebration, the players riding in convertibles, past the cheering crowds. Rick Caron was just another face in the crowd, one of the many kids in the city who loved basketball but did not play for Durfee. He continued to play CYO basketball, worked after school in a men's shop on South Main Street, for eighty-five cents an hour.

When he graduated in 1967, he had been working part-time for Stop & Shop, a grocery chain with stores in three New England states, so he began full-time, glad to have a job. He thought about becoming a state trooper like his father, even went to the police academy for a while, but in the end he didn't want to leave the security of Stop & Shop. He's been there ever since, working mostly in stores in neighboring Rhode Island.

In 1972 he married Jane Mitchell, who had grown up a couple of blocks away from the Careys, near Ruggles Park and the Sacred Heart parish. Remnants of the counterculture were all over Fall River then, but Rick Caron essentially ignored them.

"We started out with a big group of guys and some started with the long hair and pot and all that and kind of fell by the wayside," he said. "I always had the sports."

He had begun helping out coaching Little League when he was just a teenager and never stopped. He also started coaching a team in the Milliken League. Jeff was born in 1976, and Rick kept coaching. He's been doing it ever since.

He is proud of Jeff, for he feels that whatever success

he's accomplished at Durfee has been on his own, in that didn't have a father or brother who had played before him, hadn't started out with a connection to Durfee basketball. In many ways Rick Caron is still the outsider. He often sits by himself at the games. He's never talked to Karam about Jeff. He's stayed detached, to the point that his wife has criticized him for it, thinking that Jeff would have been better served at Durfee if her husband had been involved more, even though it wasn't his nature. He believes—rightly or wrongly—that everything would have been geared to Chris Herren no matter what his talent level. In his view, that was just the way it is in Fall River.

He looks at his son now, with his dreams of playing Division I basketball, of getting a scholarship, of transcending Fall River, and realizes how different it is from when he was coming of age.

"We didn't have big goals," Rick Caron said. "We didn't have big dreams."

There is no bigger game on the schedule than New Bedford, and there's an unwritten law in Fall River that until you do it against New Bedford, you really haven't done it at all. Big games either in the state tournament or against New Bedford make a player part of the folklore that's Durfee basketball. Big games against the other schools on the schedule eventually get forgotten, blur in significance. It's a rivalry that's gone on for generations, the most pronounced in southeastern Massachusetts, one part tradition, one part hate and acrimony. Luke Urban loved to fuel it in the twenty years he coached all sports. He was forever telling his teams that New Bedford considered his players "cement heads," or "greenhorns," anything he thought might motivate them.

It's also a rivalry that comes with racial tension. The two schools have been playing football since 1893, sister cities only fifteen miles apart, two cities that on the surface are often linked together and share many of the same social problems all small cities in the Northeast face, but have different histories, different ethnic makeups.

The largest ethnic group in both cities is Portuguese, but while the Fall River Portuguese trace their roots to the Azores, islands roughly eight hundred miles from Portugal, the Portuguese in New Bedford mainly come from the Cape Verde islands, a Portuguese colony off the coast of Africa, a group that wasn't recognized on the census until 1980. The U.S. Immigration Service also confused things by its custom of categorizing arriving Cape Verdeans as either "Portuguese" if they looked white, or "African Portuguese" or "black Portuguese" if they appeared black.

The other difference is that Fall River had few black kids, and New Bedford had many, since New Bedford always had a legacy of being hospitable to blacks, a tradition that dates back to before the American Revolution and includes the whaling days of the 1800s, when sometimes half the boats were made up of blacks as crew.

There have been innumerable fights through the years, stories that are part of the mystique that hovers over the rivalry. Charley Carey, Chris Herren's grandfather, remembers being at New Bedford for a game in the early 1970s, a time when racial tensions were like kindling just waiting for a match, not only nationally, but in New Bedford too. His son Dennis, a Durfee player that year, had been jumped by a group of black kids after the game. He had pulled a kid off his son and wrestled him to the ground. Afterward, Carey had needed an escort to get to his car.

The height of the ill feeling may have come during the Michael Herren years, for his very presence was like waving red at a bull. One night, on the way home from New Bedford, the Durfee bus was stoned going beneath an overpass on Interstate 195, kids crouching down on the floor of the bus, cheerleaders screaming, a few minutes of panic. One night a group of people from New Bedford showed up at Herren's house, looking to rumble. Another night, after a game at Durfee, there was a vicious fight that spilled out into the parking lot.

Ed Rodrigues became the New Bedford coach thirteen years ago. He had grown up in New Bedford's South End and used sports as a passport to college, where he played four years of basketball. He is thirty-nine now, was a "dropout prevention" teacher at New Bedford High School, and never had forgotten what basketball had done for him, a lesson he was always instilling in the kids who played for him.

"Basketball did everything for me," he said. "It got me a college degree. It got me a teaching job. A nice home. A nice car. I tell them that, and then I tell them that it was hard for me growing up too, a tough section in the South End. But it happened to me and it can happen to you."

He had been only twenty-six when he got the job, after going 56–0 as the freshman team coach, the young turk out to carve out his own coaching reputation in the area where Skip Karam already was a coaching legend. It was perhaps inevitable they would clash, a high school coaching version of two gunfighters in the middle of a dusty street in the Old West, the old pro and the kid who wanted to challenge him. Forget the rivalry for a second. People in New Bedford always had respected Karam, and Rodrigues often felt he was being compared to Karam and found lacking, not the most enviable of situations for any young coach. Karam, on the other hand, felt Rodrigues never gave him any proper credit when Durfee won. The start of Rodrigues's coaching tenure coincided with a few mediocre Durfee years, so that for a while, Durfee couldn't seem to beat New Bedford, a fact of life that Karam found increasingly intolerable.

"Our relationship wasn't so great in the beginning," Rodrigues admits. "It's better now. I grew up a little."

One turning point happened a couple of years ago when Karam's mother died and Rodrigues and his wife came to the wake. That changed things for Skippy. He still felt competition with Rodrigues. He still would rather lose to anyone else. But the wake had changed the way he felt about Rodrigues. For Rodrigues, it was more of an evolution, the gradual realization that for all the competition between him and Karam, they had become almost mirror images of each other, both sharing the same pressure, both the victims of ridiculous expectations. Nothing less than a state title would do—or at least winning the South Sections and going to Boston Garden.

That was the monkey on Rodrigues's back. For all his success as a coach, at one time beating Durfee eleven straight games, New Bedford never had made it out of the South Sectionals. Meanwhile, Durfee had won three state championships. No matter that Rodrigues had won numerous Big Three league titles and roughly 80 percent of his games. No matter that his team had qualified for the state tournament twelve consecutive times, and reached the semifinals of the South Sections seven times and the finals once. His team's relative failures in postseason play have become a personal albatross, one that's become so heavy that a few years ago he came close to quitting, fed up with the unbelievably high expectations, the criticism, the unrelenting pressure.

"We always are compared to Durfee," he said. "We can win ninety percent of our games. But if we don't beat Durfee, it's like we've failed. It's not fair, but that's the way it is. I've learned to live with it."

As if fate had scripted it, tonight also was Karam's fifty-eighth birthday.

"If I get interviewed after the game, I'm going to say that we won for Mr. Karam on his seventy-fifth birthday," said Herren.

Last year Durfee had beaten New Bedford twice easily, but this is an experienced New Bedford team that goes ten deep, with eleven seniors, one junior, and a sophomore named Marcus Wills, who already is being called New Bedford's next great player. He is a slim black kid who had been on the jayvees last year, but had played very well over the summer, both in summer leagues and camps, and had emerged as New Bedford's leading scorer. Like all Rodrigues's teams, this one pressed full-court the entire game, relying on its overall quickness and depth to wear down opposing teams. They were 7–2, their losses coming to Andover and to St. Anthony's, the Jersey City, New Jersey, high school that's coached by Bob Hurley, Sr., and is generally regarded as one of the top high school programs in the country.

All the ingredients were there: The Durfee band blared the fight song in the far corner, the cheerleaders cavorted, Durfee with their white shorts, black and red tops, New Bedford in red. Two radio stations. A cable television station. Reporters from Fall River, New Bedford, and Providence, there to do a feature on the biggest basketball rivalry in the area.

"We'll be answering phones all night," said Tim Geary, a sportswriter for the *Herald News*, the Fall River newspaper. "Alumni from the two schools who live around the country all call. They'll all want to know who won."

Karam was wearing dark slacks, a blue shirt, red plaid tie, and a dark sport jacket that he quickly discarded as soon as the game started. A few yards away Rodrigues watched in a bulky white sweater with red trim. The field house was jammed, people standing five deep in back of the east basket.

Durfee was ahead 46–39 at halftime, maybe their best half of the season. Herren already had twenty-one points. He had been simply sensational, taking the ball through the New Bedford press, either scoring on drives to the basket or making excellent passes to his teammates. He even had scored on a a spectacular alley-oop, catching a Caron pass that was

...... 175

thrown high and off to the right of the basket with two hands and slamming it home, a great athletic feat that made the field house erupt in pandemonium.

He was off in some private space, a place where time got distorted. Athletes refer to it as going "into the zone," an essentially hypnotic state that allows athletes to perform at their highest level, yet remain relaxed. This phenomenon is little understood, but there are sports psychologists who believe great athletes are somehow naturally able to work themselves into this state more often than the ordinary athlete. Michael Jordan supposedly drifts in and out of the zone during games, though he's not sure how he does it. As he told Cameron Stauth in the *The Golden Boys*, the unauthorized inside look at the Olympic Dream Team, sometimes when he's in this state he "would feel a 'ball of power' surround him—a field of energy that gave him total control." In the first half Herren had experienced the same sensation, a feeling he's had before in other games, times when he loses all track of time, his consciousness altered.

Still, Durfee was only leading by seven, the game far from over. New Bedford was appreciably quicker, more athletic, their full-court press capable of instantly getting them back in a game. It was a gambling style of play, the downside being they often gave up easy baskets. The plus side was that when it worked, their offense thrived off the press, converting turnovers into easy scores, using their defense to establish the pace of the game.

The players came into the locker room in jubilation, full of energy and emotion. They sat on the benches in front of the red lockers, expectant, still wired from the first half.

"This is far from over," Karam said, standing at the blackboard in front of the room. He knew that halftime scores meant little, especially against a pressing team like New Bedford, and that all teams leading at the half had a tendency to let down when the second half started. "We've got to play defense and we've got to rebound. It's not over."

He was a prophet.

New Bedford narrowed Durfee's lead to just three with a little under nine minutes left to play, then in the course of a couple of minutes their press did the trick, forcing Durfee into turnovers a couple of times and taking the lead on Wills's three-point play with just over seven minutes left. Herren seemed tired, as if his heroics in the first half had taken all the energy out of him. During free throws he leaned over, his hands pulling on the bottom of his shorts, breathing deeply. As he faded, the rest of his team seemed to fade with him. The momentum had shifted, and Durfee players suddenly started standing around, a little confused, hounds that had lost the scent. With four minutes to play, New Bedford had increased their lead to nine and it was clear Durfee was done. The large crowd grew silent, save for the group that sat in the bleachers behind the New Bedford bench.

"HERREN SUCKS . . . HERREN SUCKS . . . HERREN SUCKS," they chanted in the closing minute. Herren, who had scored thirty-two points in defeat, was expressionless.

The final score was 91–79.

Afterward, Karam stood in the hallway between the shower room and the small office. A couple of reporters were around him, a television camera. His blue shirt was stained with perspiration. He looked drained and tired.

"We couldn't sustain it," he said simply. "We had a great first half, but we just couldn't keep it going."

Behind him the Durfee players moved in and out of the shower room in silence. At the far end of the locker room Rodrigues was saying, "Look, it's always special beating Durfee. But we go back and forth. Of the last thirty-one games we've won sixteen."

An hour later Karam and Dempsey again sat at Lizzie's. It was supposed to have been a surprise birthday party for Karam, but now the large white cake lay uneaten on the table in front of them.

"We can't play any better than we played in the first half," he said. "But Chrissie got tired. Hey, the bottom line is we can't stop anybody. We've given up eighty-nine and ninety-one points in two games, and how are you supposed to beat anyone doing that?"

Every once in a while someone would stop by the table to wish Karam a happy birthday. He was good with them, gracious, self-deprecating, pretending to make light of the game. But when the people had left, and the cake still lay uneaten on the table in front of him, he said, almost to himself, "New Bedford. Of all people."

"Come on, Skippy, cut the cake," said Dempsey.

Karam took the large knife and was about to cut the cake when in a mock dramatic gesture he pointed it at his chest and pretended to fall on it.

The fight started minutes after the game ended.

It was three nights after Durfee had lost to New Bedford, and the schedule didn't get any easier, a rematch with Duxbury and the Curley brothers. Since Durfee had lost two games in a row, their record now 6–3, this had become a huge game, Duxbury entering the game ranked number one in the state in the Boston *Globe*'s weekly poll.

It also was the first time during the season that the outside basketball world had found its way to Durfee, this time in the person of Tom Konchalski.

He is forty-six, a former Queens math teacher, who publishes a booklet that lists virtually every basketball player in the East who can hit two jump shots in a row. He began following high school in basketball in New York City in 1958. The city was a fertile breeding ground of high school players then, perhaps the best in the country, and many of the better southern schools had guys in the city who would both evaluate talent for them and try to steer it in their direction. The process was called the "underground railroad" then, and many of the best teams in the country were stacked by New York kids who had taken the "A" train out of the city, often

The ghost of Fall River past: Lizzie Borden
(Fall River Herald News)

The bustling downtown district, on a Saturday afternoon, perhaps the 1930s.
(Fall River Herald News)

Two views of Fall River today: a city bisected by a highway, and the remains of the
Oliver Chace Mill. *(Frank Pollard, Fall River Herald News)*

B.M.C. Durfee High School *(above)* and a Durfee parade *(below)*.
(Frank Pollard, *Fall River Herald News)*

Thomas "Skippy" Karam, at courtside.
(Providence Journal-Bulletin, photo by Richard Benjamin)

Chris Herren slices between defenders. *(Fall River Herald News)*

Watching a jayvee game *(left to right)*: Dan Callahan, Peter Suneson, Jeff Caron, and Chris. *(Bob Thayer photo)*

Michael Herren *(left)* and
Chris, the two greatest scorers
in Fall River history.
(Fall River Herald News)

Peter Pavao shoots
against New Bedford.
(Fall River Herald News)

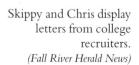

Skippy and Chris display
letters from college
recruiters.
(Fall River Herald News)

lured by some sugar daddy working unofficially for a school, Damon Runyon characters as New York as an egg cream.

In the sixties Konchalski was Tennessee's man in the city, primarily because an older brother once had played for then-Tennessee coach Stu Aberdeen. Konchalski's claim to fame occurred in the early seventies, when he ostensibly delivered Bernard King and Ernie Grunfeld to Tennessee. He also was working for Howard Garfinkel, one of the biggest power brokers in college basketball. Garfinkel ran his Five Star Camp in the Poconos, the first of the showcase camps, and published *High School Basketball Illustrated*. Konchalski eventually went to a lot of the high school games Garfinkel no longer wanted to attend, then bought the high school report thirteen years ago.

Now he sees hundreds of games a year, travels throughout the Northeast to do so. At the beginning of the season he had Herren ranked in his "golden dozen," the twelve best juniors in the Northeast. He had called him the "toughest kid on any block" and referred to Herren as the "white tornado," a nickname he'd previously given to former South Carolina star Kevin Joyce, back when he'd been in high school in New York.

"Right now he lacks the ability to score from the outside, and part of that is a macho thing, the need to always take the ball to the basket," Konchalski said. "But he has a tremendous will to win. If Chris Herren had been a Jesuit priest in the thirteenth century in upstate New York, the Iroquois would have cut out his heart and eaten it for courage."

He was sitting with Leo Papile, Herren's AAU coach. Papile had told Konchalski he was about to enter a "time warp," that going to a Durfee game is like travelling back to the early sixties.

Papile was forty, a bear of a man with dirty blond hair that hung to his shoulders. He was fond of wearing open shirts and gold chains, one of those basketball junkies who, by his own admission, had spent his life in the "bowels of basketball." He grew up in Quincy, a blue-collar city south of Boston, a place where sports were important, and could remember going to Fall River for an Easter tournament at the Boys Club. He played football and basketball at North Quincy High, including a state tournament game in the Boston Garden against Durfee and Al Herren.

He left North Quincy in 1971, spent a year at a small college in New Hampshire playing football, hurt his knee, then came back to Boston and began coaching a semi-pro team called the O'Brien Club. He was nineteen years old and what he knew about coaching could fit in a thimble, but it was like being an apprentice in a basketball workshop. The players he coached were older; some, like Bob Carrington and Ken Boyd, had spent some time in the NBA, and often they went around New England playing in money tournaments.

In 1977 Papile got in on the ground floor of the Quincy Chiefs, a new team in the Eastern League, as head coach and general manager. He was twenty-five. It was professional basketball on the far side of glamor. Little gyms in little places. Gyms where the locker rooms were always too small and there never seemed to be enough hot water. The players made $50 a game. They traveled in cars, often driving to Pennsylvania on a Saturday morning, playing the game, then driving back that night. The old ABA had folded and players were everywhere. Two of the players on the Quincy Chiefs were Walter Luckett and Frank Oleynick, the subjects of the excellent book on basketball in inner-city Bridgeport, Connecticut, called *Chase the Game* by Pat Jordan. Luckett once had his picture on the cover of *Sports Illustrated* before ever playing a college game, and Oleynick played briefly for Seattle in the NBA. On those long car rides to an obscure game in some small gym before only a smattering of people, Papile would listen to the stories, learning the game from the inside out, immersed in the subculture.

That summer he started a fledgling AAU team, made up

of some of the best kids in the area, and took them to a couple of national tournaments. The national AAU scene was far less sophisticated than it is today, just a few tournaments here and there, not the national showcase for young talent it has now become. Still, there were four kids off his first team that ended up in NBA camps, proving to Papile that there were kids in Boston who could play with anyone in the country if given the right conditions, though Boston was not traditionally regarded as a great spawning ground of basketball talent.

Papile would spend the next nine years on the periphery of college basketball, first as a part-time assistant to Rick Pitino at Boston University, then as an assistant to Kevin Mackey at Cleveland State, though he lived in Boston the entire time. All the while he was building his kid team, now called the Boston Amateur Athletic Club, part of an AAU network that now includes virtually all the top high school kids in the country. He has coached virtually everyone in Boston considered a genuine player, including NBA players Patrick Ewing and Dana Barros, nine pros in all. And along the way he's immersed himself in the black community of Boston's Roxbury section, part coach, part big brother, part surrogate father to the black kids who play for him.

"I guess I am into downward mobility," he said with a laugh. "But you couldn't make this up. I should have written it all down somewhere, but no one would have believed it anyway."

He first met Chris Herren back in 1989 when Chris was in the seventh grade. Chris was playing for Buddies, an AAU team in New Bedford run by Jim Taveres, along with a lot of Durfee kids. But every time BABC appeared at a similar tournament, Chris was intrigued by them, all the older black kids who dunked and played with the indelible style of the inner city.

"It seemed Chris was everywhere that year," Papile said.

"He knew all about our team and sometimes he'd even go through the layup line with us, this little white kid with this angelic face."

It wasn't until two years later that Papile knew Chris was going to be a great player. It had been a spring tournament in Boston and Dempsey had brought a team from southeastern Massachusetts. Only a freshman, Chris had been the best player on his team, and the older black kids for BABC had been impressed, not exactly a common occurrence. Chris and a couple of them had even begun to be friends, periodically calling each other on the phone. The following winter, Dempsey had run into Papile at a college game and asked, "What about Herren? He belongs with you guys."

So it had begun in the spring of '92. Chris joined BABC, the only white kid at the time. Right away he was accepted. The stars on that team were Jamal Jackson and Shannon Bowman, both older, and Chris had acquiesced to them, subordinating his own game, making sure they got the ball, using his passing skills far more than he had at Durfee. The team had gone 75–2 that summer, playing all over the country, winning the national AAU championship in Jacksonville, Florida.

It had been a great experience for Chris on several levels. It had placed him around black players for the first time, an important developmental step in the evolution of any white player—the harsh reality being that until a white kid does it against black kids, he's suspect as a basketball player, regardless of how good he's supposed to be. It had enabled him to play against many of the best high school players in the country, which gave him the opportunity to start acquiring a national reputation. It also got him out of Fall River for the first time, away from the baggage that surrounded him there. For the first time in his basketball life it didn't matter who his brother was, or how many points he scored, or whether Durfee won or not. He had to create his own identity, not merely borrow one that already had been scripted for him.

From the beginning he'd impressed Papile with his unselfishness, his willingness to subordinate his ego, his ability to quickly fit in with a team of inner-city black kids.

"He doesn't care about how many points he gets," Papile said. "He doesn't even care about how he plays. He only cares about winning. He only cares what the scoreboard says. And there never was any adjustment problem. My kids are all street urchins and Chris fit right in."

This past fall the dynamics had changed. Chris was a BABC veteran by then, there were other younger players, the Curley brothers being two of them. His game had become more assertive, more like the way he now played with Durfee. He was one of the team's certifiable stars, a bona fide hero at the Tobin Gym in Roxbury, in the heart of the inner city, where BABC played many of their local games, the charismatic white kid who dunked like a brother.

"He's a hero to the kids in the Tobin who watch us play," Papile said. "He walks in the gym and it's like Jordan just walked in. The little kids run to him."

Papile also thought Konchalski sold Herren's ability short. For Papile had become Herren's biggest fan, believing he could one day be a pro, that his potential was unlimited.

Tonight the field house was crowded, the fans lured by the promise of a good game against Duxbury. With all the success over the years, people in Fall River have gotten spoiled, no longer get very excited over blowouts and teams on the schedule they consider inferior. This night, though, was a Durfee game by-the-numbers. Across the court from the bench was the student section. Down to one side the band blew and drummed in their red and black uniforms. On the far wall hung a huge red banner with black letters saying THANK YOU FOR BEING DURFEE STUDENTS. Behind the bench were parents, the Greek chorus, some of the people who sat there every game, every year. A standing-room-only section was roped off and packed behind one basket.

At one point, Matty Curley leaned over to Caron during a time-out and said, "I wish I could play here all the time."

It was a game worthy of the atmosphere.

There had been a fight in the first half, both Mike Cioe and a Duxbury player being ejected from the game. With ten and a half minutes left to play, Duxbury led by eleven, the inside presence of the six–nine Mickey Curley too much for Callaghan and Jones to handle. Then Karam changed defenses, going into a halfcourt trap. The strategy immediately started to change the rhythm of the game. Durfee went on a 16–1 run, both Callahan and Jones becoming more assertive, and Durfee went on to win 68–59, their best game since the Lowell Tournament.

As the two teams were going through the traditional postgame handshake in front of the Durfee bench, people milling around everywhere, a burly Duxbury fan bumped Karam. His son, Skippy, Jr., who had been sitting a few rows behind his father, immediately jumped on the Duxbury fan.

Within a few seconds there was pandemonium, bodies flying, punches being thrown, two cops trying to break everything up. Karam's jacket was off, his white shirt out of his pants. Herren had ended up on the floor, pushed over by two guys who were fighting. People were yelling and pushing each other, and just when it appeared to escalate into something truly ugly, it subsided just as quickly. Another flash fire, extinguished for lack of oxygen.

Al Herren stood on the periphery of the brawl. He had run over from his seat across the court, in jeans, sneakers, and a camel-hair overcoat. By the time he got over there, the fight had been broken up, so now he stood in the aftermath, when he saw me standing next to him.

"Welcome to Fall River," he said with a grin.

Chapter
7

THE 450S IS A hallway on the fourth floor of Durfee, right by the entrance to classrooms lined with green lockers and a green carpet that looks as if thousands of sixteen-year-old feet have walked on it. On this morning Herren, Callahan, Mikolazyk, Pavao, Caron, Cioe, and sophomore Brendan Gettings were congregated at the top of the stairs in their uniforms of jeans and T-shirts, young princes in the courtyard of their own castle. Sometimes they lined the hall so that girls had to walk through them in a gauntlet.

"Chris likes to smack some girl's ass, then make believe someone else did it." Caron laughed. "He does it all the time."

They all have their lockers here. Herren, Pavao and Mikolazyk share the same locker, by choice, not school policy. They wear each other's clothes. They share each other's books. They share each other's chewing tobacco. They share everything. In a sense they've become a surrogate family, have created their own little insular world in the middle of a school with roughly three thousand students, a world with its own secrets, its own social structure, its own mores.

The 450s is their meeting place during school. They come

back between classes. They meet in the morning. They meet after school. In a school of three thousand, in a large building, the odds are strong that you could walk around the school all day and rarely see a basketball player. Not true. Not if you come to the 450s.

"Who's got dip?" Herren asked, rummaging through his locker. "Gore, you little monkey, where's the dip?"

Virtually all of them chew tobacco, have done so since middle school. They've been chewing for so long that a part of the gray wall between the hallway and the stairway is stained brown, the residue of innumerable expectorations. "I don't know anyone in Fall River who hasn't done dip," Herren said. "Even some girls do it."

The bell rang shortly after eight, the corridor suddenly swarming with kids, a mass of T-shirts and jeans, Los Angeles Raider jackets, B.U.M. Equipment sweatshirts, starter jackets, and $100 sneakers, all scurrying off to class, a swirl of energy through the corridors, a heightened buzz of conversation. Herren moved through the corridor as though followed by his own sound track, nodding to this kid, saying hello to another, playfully punching another in the arm. He wore dungarees, a yellow sweatshirt, and black Converse sneakers. He was on his way to English class and a room that seemed to come directly from a John Hughes film about high school: cinder-block walls, blue rug, desks in rows. A large poster on a wall, "A History of the English Language," displayed a portrait collage of Shakespeare, Othello, Hamlet. The blackboard in the front of the room had words for a vocabulary quiz: *vestige, picayune, iota, magnitude.*

There were twenty kids in the class, twelve of them girls. The teacher was James Tavares, a man in his forties, someone Herren liked. It was a level-two junior English course—the levels running from one to four with one being the most demanding—and the subject of the day was Jonathan Swift's "A Modest Proposal." It's an essay that uses satire as a bludgeon, writing about cattle at one level while criticizing the English landlords for their treatment of Irish tenants on the other.

"Swift was seeing a dehumanized society," Tavares said, "a society in which people were being treated as though they could be bought and sold, things you could make money on. Commodities."

A commodity.

"Who's the biggest commodity in Fall River?" I asked Herren afterward.

He looked perplexed.

"Someone who is bought and sold," I said. "Seen only as an object."

His eyes shone with the glint of recognition.

"Me?" he asked.

He was on his way back to the 450s, where he went after every class, a brief gathering of the tribe, before heading off to history, a class taught by Jack Carey, his mother's cousin, a wiry, gray-haired man in his forties who refused to let Herren call him by his first name.

There were thirty-one kids in the class, the boys and girls dressed similarly in sweatshirts and jeans, warm-up jackets, baggy clothes. One burly kid had a beeper on his desk. Two girls wore black leather, as if extras in *West Side Story*. Once this style of dress would have been considered a form of social rebellion. Now it's de rigueur, simply considered cool. The American flag stood in front of the room. Maps covered the cinder-blocked walls. The desks were scrawled and carved with graffiti, full of slang and names and local code.

After telling them that Roosevelt, Churchill, and Hitler all had mastered radio, Carey played them Franklin D. Roosevelt's speech to the country two days after Pearl Harbor, one of his famous "Fireside Chats." The room was silent, save for Roosevelt's voice coming through the static. Down in the back of the room a kid in a red shirt put his head on the desk and started to sleep. When the speech was over, Carey addressed his class.

"Why did people listen to him?"

"Nothing better to do," said the kid with the beeper.

Carey explained that all of this was before television, before videos, before a generation had been weaned on action and colors that moved before their eyes, all the things that reduced their attention spans and made listening to some twenty-minute speech a form of academic torture.

"What kind of sentence structure does Roosevelt use?"

"Boring," said one of the girls in the leather jackets.

"It was boring because you had to sit and listen and concentrate for twenty minutes and that was difficult for you," said Carey.

"Yeah," Herren added. "It's real boring for us."

There was the sense that the teachers and the students stared at each other from a distance, one that was not only chronological and generational, but also rooted in different ways of perceiving the world, as if they were a product of two different Americas. The teachers had come of age in a linear world, one essentially governed by reading and books, one in which to listen to a twenty-minute speech was not unusual. The kids were a product of channel surfing, the endless roaming of channels in search of something more entertaining, a world of videos and VCRs, a world of visual images that constantly changed before their eyes, images they could control with their thumbs. Was it any wonder that so many of them looked at a teacher in front of the room, trying to teach them something in the traditional linear fashion, as something horribly outdated, a magician who has run out of tricks?

"Kids are much more difficult to deal with than they were twenty years ago," said Carey as the kids filed out of the class. "And no one really wants to deal with them anymore. You can see that the school committee is sick of dealing with kids after two hours. You listen to them talk and you can read between the lines."

* * *

Controversy has surrounded the high school ever since it opened in 1978, the first new public high school in Fall River in nearly a hundred years. The first controversy was where to put this new school. There's always been a conflict in Fall River between the South End and the North End, the prevailing thinking being that the North End, which includes the Highlands, gets preferential treatment over the poorer, heavily Portuguese South End; that it's the kids from the North End that traditionally are the better students, the class officers, the athletes. So here was the new school built in the northeast corner of the city, miles from the South End, forcing some kids in the South End to take two city buses to get to school in the morning, while to the kids in the Highlands it's a neighborhood school.

The second conflict was the name. Since the new school was being funded with public money, there was sentiment it should be called Fall River High School, not the continuation of a family name. The public rebelled. Their high school always had been Durfee; they wanted it to remain so. The compromise was B. M. C. Durfee High School of Fall River, the name on the brown wall of the field house.

Third was the controversy surrounding its construction. The company that eventually got the contract had never built a school before; three Fall River politicians went to jail for kickbacks, including one of the wealthier men in the city.

Before the school opened, there were numerous newspaper stories about it, all designed to portray the new building as some educational version of Shangri-la, full of wondrous new things that the old building hadn't offered: the largest high school library in New England, a sophisticated media center, a pool with seating capacity for six hundred people, a football stadium to seat over four thousand people, a field house to seat nearly twenty-five hundred, modern locker rooms and shower facilities.

Shortly before the school opened, a student named Jack Mello visited it and wrote an article for the *Hilltop*, the student newspaper.

"I went to the new high school with the expectation of being totally won over by this monstrous complex," he wrote, "but came back with quite the opposite opinion. . . . All the hallways and classrooms look the same (to me anyway), giving it a very impersonal feeling. Believe me, you'll appreciate the old Durfee building once you get up there."

The school was cursed from the beginning. Virtually from the day it opened the roof leaked, and fifteen years later, there are buckets strategically placed throughout the building to catch the falling water. The center of the school is a circle, with different wings radiating off it, divided into subject areas, all defined by different-colored carpeting and lockers. Now the carpet is scarred and worn, pieces of old gum are beaten down into the fabric so that it all looks seedy, the carpet of some fleabag motel on the wrong side of town.

"I still get lost in this building and I've been here for fifteen years," said Mike Walsh in his small office in the guidance wing. He grew up "below the hill" on Columbia Street, which runs south from Main Street toward the water and is now the heart of the Portuguese community. He graduated from Durfee in the early sixties, went to Providence College, returned four years later to teach in Fall River. Now he is a guidance counselor, dealing primarily with problem kids.

"It's not a friendly school. It's not personal. It's not manageable. There is a real shopping mall mentality, too many kids milling around."

Walsh can also see Fall River changing.

"In 1971 there were a few Hari Krishnas around, and the city almost came to a halt. There were major editorials in the paper. The city didn't know what to do. Back in 1971 Fall River had its own problems and those problems were not the world's problems. Durfee is still a school without the real problems of the inner city, but a few years ago the school began changing. Cambodian kids. Black kids. Kids that were essentially new to Durfee. And with it came the tensions, the stereotypes. The Cambodians fight the stereotype that people think they steal cats and dogs, the cats eventually ending up on the dinner table. There are some white girls who are fascinated with black boys, yet there are others who will see them together and say, 'What's she doing with that nigger?' The city's never dealt with blacks before. When I was growing up, the only blacks here were the offspring of Navy personnel in Newport, and most of them lived in Sunset Hill. I've heard that there's only one black teacher in the Fall River School Department. I don't know. But I go to meetings with twelve hundred teachers, and I don't see one black.

"Generally speaking, the kids in the South End take a backseat to the kids in the North End. There was a major controversy where to put the new high school, and they probably put it in the wrong place. Kids in the South End have to take two buses to get to school. To get to school by eight in the morning they have to leave at seven. Kids in the North End can get up at seven-thirty and still make it on time. The kids from the North End, the kids who went to Morton Middle School are the cheerleaders, the class officers, the basketball players. There is a general feeling that Morton kids do more things. Look out on the fields after school. They are the twenty percent who play sports, are the class officers, who are the best students.

"This is an old faculty. I'm going to be fifty and I'm the second youngest on this corridor. The administration has not adjusted to today. Everyone is yearning for a time when you spoke and kids listened. They want this to be the Durfee they remember. Teaching today is tough. It used to be that the average kid played by the rules. Now the middle kids gravitate toward the tough kids. Teachers today have to be entertainers. We have a lot of great kids, and a lot of good kids, and a few troublemakers. We also have a huge number of kids who don't know what we're talking about when we talk about the Durfee tradition. A huge number of kids here get lost in the shuffle. We have kids who probably don't even know we have a basketball team. They just come here, put in their time, and leave and no one even knows they were here. There is incredible tardiness and absenteeism, twelve to fourteen percent absent every day. Being on time means nothing. The kids in the level three and four courses—the two bottom levels—are just putting in their time. Ninety-nine percent of the kids I deal with have incredible stories, incredible problems. It's never just one simple thing. It's always complicated. The exception is the kid who has the same biological father and mother living in the same house."

Behind him was a window that looked down on the roof of the field house, glistening now in the morning sunshine.

"Think of it this way," Walsh continued. "The teachers are at war with the administration. The administration is afraid of the school committee. The school committee is afraid of the parents. The parents are afraid of the kids. And the kids are afraid of nothing."

As big and sprawling as Durfee was, as much as it sometimes resembled a shopping mall, there was a provincial quality to it too, in that so many of the teachers had grown up in Fall River. Many still lived in the city, buying houses in the Highlands in the seventies that were great deals at the time. Or else they lived in the surrounding suburbs, their emotional connections still to Fall River.

From Frank Sylvia, who had spent much of his childhood living in Maplecroft, the home in the Highlands that Lizzie Borden had moved into; to Bill Mullally, whose grandmother's brother had grown up on Third Street, one street behind the Bordens, and can remember Lizzie giving him and his friends pears from a tree in back of the Borden house on Second Street; to principal Al Attar, the roots of the faculty ran deep.

"I believe in discipline and structure," said Attar one morning in his office.

It was his first year as principal and it was generally assumed he'd been given the job in an attempt to bring some order to Durfee. Attar is a large man, six-foot-four, who grew up in the Flint a couple of streets over from Karam, in the same structured Lebanese world. It was not the only similarity between him and Karam. Karam's father had been one of his youth coaches and in a sense he had grown up looking up to Skippy, who was three years ahead of him at Durfee. Attar also had used basketball for identity, and the passport away from the poverty of his youth, for he was one of eleven children and sometimes there was not enough food to eat and he went to school with cardboard in his shoes. To this day Karam says Attar was one of the poorest kids he's ever seen.

Attar was the mainstay of the '56 team that won the state title and even now, so many years later, is one of the true icons of Durfee basketball, right there with Andy Farrissey and Ernie Fleming and Michael Herren, the four who seem to be on everyone's all-time Durfee starting five.

He parlayed his Durfee success into a scholarship to Holy Cross, then came back home to Fall River and got a job in the school department. His son Matt had been one of the mainstays on the '88 state championship team, was now a senior at Drexel, where he was starting on the basketball team, after having transferred from the Naval Academy. Attar was a product of both a different Fall River and a different Durfee, someone for whom both had worked. He saw that as one of his strengths, the fact that he had come from a poor mill family and seen the American dream come true for him. He hoped that students might be able to see that it could work for them too.

Like Karam, Attar is without pretense. One of the first things he did as principal was to ban all hats from school, a rule that made him instantly unpopular with many of the students. In fact, when Bishop Sean O'Malley, the head of the Catholic church in Fall River, spoke to the Durfee students during multicultural week wearing the seven-hundred-year-old habit of the Franciscan friars—brown robe, sandals, knotted rope belt—he said, "On these occasions Catholic bishops usually wear a little purple skullcap, but I understand hats are banned at Durfee and I want to be invited back." The remark had met with enthusiastic applause from the student body.

In the spring Attar would be involved in a mini-controversy over a skit in the Senior Follies, the annual satirical look at life inside Durfee. It was a skit that had someone playing Attar walking into a classroom, slapping kids on the back in a form of greeting, a personal trademark, and the kids falling down as if they'd just been cold-cocked. Attar reacted by telling the kids to tone down the skit for the second night, a decision that brought a negative reaction in the spring issue of *Durfee Hilltop*, the school newspaper.

"It seems to me that since he came to this building, our high school administration has become a dictatorship, with Attar taking the reins," wrote student Robert Accettullo in a letter that dominated a page. "He seems to think he can control everything in and out of this building. It started with the assignment of lockers and restrictions of hats. Neither of these add to the quality of education in this building or aid in the welfare of students. . . . Why not just shape up the disciplinary system so that rather than a mere suspension for breaching the rules, we can have ceremonial whippings in the courtyard? Students can salute the principal as he passes in the halls, and teachers can bow and kiss his ring as he enters a classroom. The sky is the limit. It seems that the power of the principal in this building has been raised to the power of prison warden. If someone doesn't put a stop to what's happening, Durfee will become a type of educational concentration camp."

Being a high school principal isn't easy in this day and age.

Another controversy would arise during the summer. It started when *USA Today*, in an article on violence in the nation's high schools, called Durfee the most violent school in the country. The gist of an article was an interview with a student named Robert Medeiros who claimed he saw drugs being sold openly in the bathrooms and that many kids carried weapons to school. The article was met with indignation by Attar, who said he'd never talked to any reporter from *USA Today*. Later, it was discovered that Medeiros never had gone to Durfee, but had gotten his information from "other students." *USA Today* apologized. It was one more indication that the job of principal has now become a minefield, with potential problems everywhere you step.

Attar faced a bigger challenge: the theory held by many residents that education wasn't all that important in Fall River, for reasons that transcended the school system, reasons embedded in the ethnic makeup of the city.

Many of the Portuguese in Fall River trace their roots to the Azores, where land was scarce and most people didn't have any. So when they came to America, to Fall River, the accumulation of land, of something that was your own, was something to be treasured. Property became the Grail, something to be obtained through work, not education. Work was respected, not necessarily education. Virtually all teachers in Durfee have stories about Portuguese kids who are pulled out of school when they turn sixteen and made to go to work, especially girls. There are even greater numbers who seem to move through Durfee as though on some large conveyer belt, faceless, merely putting in their time, alienated from the school and the culture it was trying to provide.

"It's a manifestation of the way the city evolved," said Phil Silvia. "Eighty percent of the people went to the mills every day, without a lot of benefits, without social security, without a lot of the safety nets people nowadays have. They worked all day, and they were still below the poverty line. Their children were their social security. So if one or two of their children got a job, that could be the difference between breaking even economically and not being able to make it. So what was the value of an education? In that kind of environment it was a little unrealistic to think that some kid says to his father, 'Dad, I want to go to Durfee and take Latin.' The G.I. Bill changed that somewhat. It gave people a chance to go to college who had never had it before, and that brought more people into the middle class."

Silvia has a unique perspective on Fall River, in that he's both a native and a historian who teaches labor history and American immigration and ethnicity at Bridgewater State, about twenty miles north of Fall River. He has written three excellent books on Fall River called *Victorian Vistas* that concentrate on the late nineteenth and early twentieth centuries.

"I grew up in the Highlands in the fifties, in an area that was mostly Jewish, in the most affluent part of the city, and all of those kids I grew up with left the city. They went through Durfee, got a good education, then went off and didn't come back. So the group that had the most interest in education essentially left. What you have left are the children of a lot of people who became middle class, and that's all they aspire to. The big idea for college is to commute to Bridgwater and UMass-Dartmouth. The big thing is to buy a car for their kids so they can commute, so that they go off to college, but they don't really leave the city to do it."

The statistics seem to bear that out:

Over one-third of the class of 1993 that entered as freshmen had dropped out before they reached their senior year, maybe not all that surprising in a city where less than 50 percent of the population had completed high school.

Out of the 505 who graduated, only 31 percent went on to four-year colleges, with another 24 percent going to two-year schools. Roughly one-third of the graduates who wanted to further their education were planning to do it at Bristol Community College, the two-year commuter school only a couple of hundred yards from Durfee. Of the graduates going to four-year schools, forty-four were enrolled in UMass-Dartmouth, only a few miles away, and twenty-one in Bridgewater State, about a half hour away. Only four were going to the University of Massachusetts' main campus at Amherst, and only twenty in the entire class were attending colleges outside of New England.

Then again, the surprising thing might have been that they were going at all, for according to the 1990 census only 8 percent of the Fall River population had completed four years of college.

It's not a secret that the Portuguese used to be seen as second-class citizens, referred to as "greenhorns," a derisive term for Portuguese immigrants who don't speak the language, whose customs are Old World. It's a term that exists to this day. As does the old Fall River folklore that the statue of Lafayette on Eastern Avenue, in what once was the heart of the French-Canadian neighborhood, has the horse's ass facing the South End.

"When I was a kid, Portuguese people were stepped on," said Richard "Dynamite" Estrella, now fifty-five, who grew up "below the hill" on Columbia Street in the fifties. "It was 'Little Portugal' and every block had a barroom and a bakery on it. The Irish controlled the city and everyone in the city hated us because we were the last ones in. They used to call us 'Black Portuguese.' It was instilled by our parents that we had to stick together. And playing ball was something they didn't understand. The only sport they understood was soccer, and there wasn't any soccer in the schools then. They only understood work. My grandfather would look at me, and say in Portuguese, 'Look at me. I worked all my life and what do I got?' There was a real sense that you didn't want to end up in the mills or at Firestone, where people would come home with rubber under their noses. Where I came from in Fall River, everyone had a family like that.

"When I went to Durfee there were two groups: the 'Collegians,' who wore sweaters and had short hair; and the 'Boogies,' who wore pegged pants and had 'DA' haircuts. Below the hill were the 'Boogies.' "

"In the school system you were just another 'write-off,' " said Tony Medeiros, who grew up "below the hill" in the sixties. "You were labeled, just like 'rich Jew,' and 'drunken Irishman.' You were a 'dumb Portagee.' My whole counseling at Durfee probably took ten minutes. The message was you didn't count."

A lot of this has changed, of course, as Fall River has become, in many ways, a Portuguese city, complete with a radio station that broadcasts exclusively in Fall River, though it's owned by Skippy's brother "Boo Boo." John Arruda became the first Portuguese mayor in the 1960s, the first time the Portuguese community realized that they could turn their numbers into political clout. Then in 1977 Carlton Viveiros became mayor, a tenure that lasted thirteen years.

But perceptions die hard.

"I hear it all the time that the Portuguese get screwed at Durfee," said Eric Santos, who grew up in the Milliken League, on all-star teams with Herren, Caron, Pavao, Mikolazyk, Callahan. He is another whose roots run deep in Fall River, his uncle being one of the detectives investigating the so-called satanic murders in the late seventies. Santos lives deep in the South End near the Tiverton, Rhode Island, line, near Sunset Hill, one of the first housing projects that had blacks, but now is mainly Cambodian.

"I hear all the time that this guy could play for Durfee, that guy could play for Durfee. But it's not really true. They're more street ballplayers in the South End. They don't want to play organized basketball. They want to play one-on-one. I don't think there's any prejudice against Portuguese kids, but a lot of them think there is, so they have an attitude, a kind of grudge against the world."

One who did play for Durfee was Tommy Arruda, who grew up "below the hill" and went on to become one of the greatest athletes in Fall River history. He was a talented guard on the '56 state championship team, the one that had Al Attar at center, and he was trailed by scouts in baseball.

It was the late fifties and the world was a different place. It was a time of bonus babies, a time of tryouts for kids from towns all over America. He worked out at Ebbetts Field, the Polo Grounds, Yankee Stadium, pitching on the sidelines. Eight teams offered him contracts and he went over to Margoni's Restaurant, across the bridge in Somerset, and signed with the Giants for $4,000, big money in those days for a kid from "below the hill."

The first year he was sent to Michigan City, Indiana, then it was Fresno, then Tacoma. Later it was Oklahoma City and Springfield and Buffalo and Rochester and God knows where else. Once he rode a bus for forty-two hours between Texas and Vera Cruz, Mexico. One exhibition game in Tacoma, in Triple A, he struck out eleven Giants in five innings, then Willie Mays came up and hit one halfway up the mountain.

He played with the Giants' organization for eight years, then Houston, then Baltimore. Along the way he was teammates with Juan Marichal and Gaylord Perry. He roomed with Jim Palmer. He played for Earl Weaver when the Earl managed Triple A in Rochester, often going to the racetrack with him. And he came close to getting to the big leagues. Oh, he came close.

Even to this day he's not real sure why he didn't make it. Politics? Image? Wrong place, wrong time? The fact he always wore jeans and a T-shirt, had the Fall River attitude that says you do it your way and damn the consequences? Who really knows? But in 1971 he was with the Twins' organization and he knew he was never going to get to the bigs. He had a family by then, and there had been too many summers spent chasing the dream, a dream that had started to recede into the distance. So he came home, back to the magnet that is Fall River, where he works for the city's Housing Authority and manages an American Legion baseball team called Spindle City.

"I don't know," he said. "There's something about this city, you go away and you always come back."

Born in Fall River; die in Fall River.

One who left long ago and rarely comes back is Barry Machado, one of the stars of Karam's first team. He too grew up "below the hill," just a few blocks west of Main Street going toward the Taunton River, a neighborhood that was later demolished and became the Milliken apartments.

"Things were uncomplicated then," he said. "There was such purity about everything. You wanted to be a Durfee athlete. You couldn't wait to get to Durfee. There was a whole group of volunteers in Fall River then, ones that made the culture. There were a lot of Irish bachelors, or else guys whose marriages got sacrificed on the altar of youth leagues. They were the Little League coaches. They coached the youth teams. They were the cement of the whole community. They determined what was important and as a kid you picked up on it right away. Then there were the Irish priests, the Father Flanagan types, with a selfless willingness to promote kids."

Machado's father was Portuguese, worked in Anderson-Little as a floorman because he was bilingual. His mother was Irish. She believed education was the ticket to a better life, a lesson she ingrained in him. He became an outstanding student, the president of his class, skilled in both basketball and baseball, the epitome of what Fall River envisioned for its sons and daughters.

"Durfee really was two cultures back then," he said. "There were about fifteen or twenty of us that got the best teachers, and I would stack that group up against anyone. We were tracking to some of the best colleges in the country and the rest of the kids were tracking to Anderson-Little. I was the exception, the only athlete in the group."

When he graduated in 1962, he received a lot of scholarship money from the city and went to Dartmouth, an Ivy League world in the New Hampshire hills only four hours away from Fall River, but halfway to the moon away in lifestyle. He played baseball there, some basketball, and in a sense he never returned. He completed graduate school at Northwestern, concentrating in history, then went to teach at Washington and Lee University in Lynchburg, Virginia. He's been there ever since.

Machado's parents still live in Fall River and he usually gets back at least once a year to visit and drive down the familiar streets of his childhood, enough to keep up with some of the changes in the city and with the way Durfee basketball has evolved. But he's been gone from Fall River for a long time now, has come to see it with ambivalence.

On one hand he has fond memories of growing up in Fall River. He considers it as a true "melting pot" then and points out his own team as an example: Manny Papoula, the Lebanese center; Gary Drewniak, the Polish guard; Woody Berube, the French forward, whose brother Ronny now works in Al Herren's small office on North Main Street; Donald Carey, Chris Herren's uncle, the Irish forward; and himself, the guard with a Portuguese surname.

He believes the city worked then, a dance of the ethnics where everyone was in step, believes there was a sense of community, a self-contained little city where it was safe to walk the streets, a city in which there certainly wasn't much money, but there was a sense of pride, the glue being Durfee basketball, the one thing that seemed to transcend both ethnicity and neighborhood allegiances, the one thing that brought people together even if it was only two nights a week at the old Bank Street Armory. He sees it now deteriorating, a slow decay that's the inevitable result of a poor economy and a changing America.

"When I was there, it was Camelot," he said. "Kennedy was in the White House and there was the feeling that we could do anything, that we were the greatest country in the world. Then a fourth-rate country in Indochina beat us up, we found out Nixon was a crook, and everything changed. I know that's simplistic, but the point is when I was growing up in Fall River it was the best of times to be a kid and now it's the worst of times."

Machado has also come to understand that there always was a layer of potential violence that seemed to hover over everything. People yelling at each other. People threatening each other. Then two minutes later all was forgotten, the slate wiped clean. He said that was how he grew up, and he didn't realize until he left Fall River that not everyone lived that way.

"Fall River's a peasant culture, with all its vices and all its virtues," he said "People like to drink, eat, yell, fight, argue, and do it all with great passion. There is an entire 'Fall River rap,' a language they've been speaking for thirty years. 'Fuck' is a verb, a noun, an adjective, an adverb, the all-purpose word. I've spent my entire adult life in an academic culture where people are effete and genteel. And often very boring. The complete opposite of Fall River, where people are never boring.

"There's a feistiness about Fall River and its people, the kind you see in all blue-collar, working-class places. It comes from growing up knowing that you don't call the shots, but you're not going to take any shit either. The plus side is that there's a great deal of loyalty, of taking care of your own. I never knew Al Herren, because he was just that much younger, but my brother tells me how he used to hang out in the same playground when he was a kid where there always were fights, people just whaling away at each other, but Al Herren would always protect him because I once had played for Durfee, and to Al that meant that I was one of the family and my brother was too."

And yet, when he left Fall River, first to college and later to live and work, Machado came to realize that Fall River often determined its worth by how the basketball team did, placing tremendous pressure on its children.

"I was one of those kids who had the ability to play for basketball, but I wasn't good enough to think I could ever use it for anything," he said. "And when I come back for reunions it's a little tough. Most of the people seemed to peak in high school. They've been on the downward slope ever since. And I know that resources are being squandered big-time in that city. And I know that a lot of kids are being seduced by the glitter of Durfee basketball."

Caron was sitting in the cafeteria, a wide, expansive room with yellow and brown walls. In the front sat two long tables of Cambodian kids, nearby a table of black kids. In early March there would be "Multicultural Week," when various speakers came in and discussed cultural differences and how kids must learn to respect them. There were discussions of such topics as ageism, sexual harassment, sexism, phrases that didn't even exist when these kids were born. There would be "Law Enforcement Day," in which four hundred kids attended workshops on women and minority officers, drugs and prostitution, and hazards of police work, and the police chief talked about the cultural problems between the police and the growing Cambodian population, all under the theme that "cops are not the enemy." There were the SAY NO TO DRUGS signs in the school and the large STAY IN SCHOOL sign that greets kids when they come to the second floor. Durfee was a large, multi-ethnic school, and these programs were designed to bring kids together, give them some common ground.

But now, to Caron at least, this was part of a Durfee about which he knew little and cared less.

A kid in a baggy blue shirt walked by.

"See that kid?" he said. "I've never seen him before in my life. I swear."

"What are the different groups in the school?" I asked.

He shrugged.

"The Boogies? Funky Beats? I don't know. They're just losers to me. I have no idea what they do. I guess they go to the Car Palace in Somerset, a teenage club. Or ride up and down the Ave," a reference to Plymouth Avenue, one of the main streets in the city where kids cruised on weekend nights, a nineties version of *American Graffiti*. The "preps" and the "jocks" are virtually interchangeable. The "funkies" are largely the products of rap culture, in their yellow jeans.

Caron had not found Durfee particularly overwhelming when he first arrived there in September 1990, his freshman year. After the dreariness of Morton, the middle school in the North End at the bottom of President Avenue about a mile from Durfee, he had found Durfee new and exciting. The first day he and Herren had been in a class, two older cheerleaders had come into the room to check them out, having already heard they were two of the new freshman basketball players. He had thought they were gorgeous, couldn't believe his good fortune. This was the Durfee he had dreamed about, the Durfee that apparently came with being a basketball player, just like he'd always heard.

A couple of weeks later he personally settled any adjustment problem he had, doing it in a way that made a definite statement. He had put his books on a table in the cafeteria, then had gone to buy his lunch. When he came back, they had been moved and an older kid, a senior, was sitting in his place.

"Put my books back," he said to the kid.

"I don't think so, freshman," the kid said.

"He had a chicken sandwich in front of him, so I took his milk container and dumped it on the floor and said, 'How are you going to eat your sandwich without any milk?' " Caron said. "He didn't say anything, so I picked up his sandwich, threw it on the floor, and said, 'How are you going to finish your sandwich without a sandwich?' He got up and walked away, and I never had any trouble adjusting after that."

He is in the top 15 percent of his class, but does little work, believing he could easily get by without going to class, if he just showed up the day before a test and studied for about ten to fifteen minutes. There was the sense among the players that if you did your work and studied a little bit, school was a joke, a free ride.

"There's no academic pressure on anyone at Durfee," Caron said. "If you don't care, the teachers don't care."

John Correiro would see it as much more complicated.

He has been the superintendent of schools for thirteen years, one of only four or five superintendents in Fall River in the past seventy-five years, three of whom grew up in a four-block area near St. Mary's Cathedral in the center of the city. He too grew up in Fall River, played football and baseball at Durfee, was in the same class with Skip Karam. He too has many of the same fond memories of growing up in Fall River that Karam has, a close city where he and his friends seemed to live out some *Happy Days* script, hanging out at the ice-cream shop in porkpie hats and wide pants, in the middle of a downtown that had several movie theaters, a city where you knew all the cops and they all knew you.

"We used to call it the largest town in America," he said.

He was the first kid in his family to go to college, worked for a while as a newspaper reporter, then a teacher, then in school administration.

There was a 50 percent dropout rate in the school system when Correiro became the superintendent. This year it's only 26 percent, the lowest rate in modern times for a senior class. It didn't happen by accident. Correiro instituted summer school and night school, work-study and magnet schools. He began a teenage pregnancy program, crisis intervention, a multicultural program. He constantly preached "stay in school" to kids. All these efforts were geared to deal with the realities of kids in the nineties.

"Even when I was a kid, southeastern Massachusetts had chronic unemployment," he said. "The past twenty-five years the kids who came back from college to Fall River either taught or worked in a government-related job. This area needs some major, major operation to perk it up. The economy needs a major turnaround just to get back to normal, never mind anything else. The teachers haven't had a raise in two years. They are the lowest-paid teachers in the area, as much as ten thousand dollars lower than some of the surrounding suburbs. The police and fire are in the same boat. We should have built three schools. We built one. The furniture in the schools is falling apart. We have asbestos in the schools that has to be removed. We need new signs, new windows. The playgrounds are falling apart."

He paused.

"And that's before you even talk about educating kids."

Correiro saw the demographics in Fall River start changing within the past five years.

"A lot of the public housing in the city was remodeled, and one of the requirements for federal money is that you have to advertise for people in major cities. It's changing the city. Fall River used to be full of Irish, Portuguese, French, and Polish. Now it's Southeast Asian, Hispanic, Colombian. The fear is the new people coming in will change the city. That people of color are not committed to the city the same way we were. Whether that's true or not, that is the fear."

These words were said with care and precision. Corriero is not the new breed of superintendent, in from somewhere else, like hired academic guns who spend their career going from place to place, creatures of politics and the nature of the education business. His roots are in Fall River, as is his heart.

He too is well aware of the role Durfee basketball plays in

the city, as well as the inevitable backlash. He grew up with Durfee basketball. He's been friendly with Karam since they went to high school together forty years ago. His two sons played for Skippy, his son Jason starting on the 1988 state championship team. He knows that some people in the city resent the fact Skippy got a car for winning the state title and the players won a trip to Disney World, that some see both as an example of distorted priorities and misplaced values.

"People think I have a jock mentality," he said. "They point to the banquets the state championship basketball teams got. But all of our students who achieve get recognition for it. We have banquets for the top ten students. We have banquets for the honor society, the student council.

"For all our problems, this is still a city with a lot of pride. There is still a tough, working-class ethic. Hard-nosed. The feeling that we go to work and we do it for forty hours a week. And nowhere has that been on more public display down through the years than Durfee basketball."

Yet there was a dark side to the attention too. It's the one that Mikolazyk discovered two years ago when he'd been a sophomore, had a party at his house over a weekend and Karam knew about it Monday morning. It was the realization that the spotlight didn't stop when the game ended.

Caron learned it early too. One night in his sophomore year he had gone to Lizzie's, which at the time had a disco upstairs over the bar and restaurant on the first floor. He hadn't seen anyone he knew there, but when he went to school on Monday morning, one of his teachers said he'd heard Jeff was in a drinking establishment. Ever since then he never went out on weekends with his Durfee basketball jacket on or a sweatshirt that said DURFEE on it. He tried to avoid situations where he was in a car and alcohol was there too, for he knew that the notoriety that came with being a Durfee player could blow up in his face.

"The biggest losers in the school can get drunk and no-body cares," he said. "If we do it, everyone knows."

Maybe no one had come to know that any better than Michael Herren, who had seen both extremes, the lionization and the negative notoriety. He expressed the problem in a guest column to the *Herald News* under a headline that said DURFEE ATHLETES NOT RESPONSIBLE FOR PUBLICITY THEY DON'T SEEK. He wrote it following an editorial criticizing Durfee basketball players for a fight following a game in December 1991 headlined, WHAT PRICE GLORY?, the gist being that Durfee basketball was out of perspective. Herren chided the *Herald News* for an article about an ex-player four years out of high school, who had been involved in an automobile tragedy; the paper's headline read FORMER DURFEE STAR CONVICTED. Michael said high school athletes neither ask for the publicity they receive, nor do they court it.

"No one more than myself knows the fine line a Durfee basketball player walks between positive and negative publicity," he wrote. "I have seen, at the age of 18 years old, both extremes. Growing up as a teenager, you are prone to make errors in judgment. You tend to lack maturity, foresight, etc. . . . Most adolescent shortcomings are held and worked out behind closed doors in the privacy of families and households. However, that is not the case if you are a Durfee basketball player. Your actions, whether good or bad, are made public by the local newspapers and the local media. The publicity is a double-edged sword, the positive is nice for the scrapbook, however, the negative, regardless of how many other adolescents may participate in the same behavior, becomes front-page news if you are a Durfee athlete."

There was no question a certain anti-basketball bias existed in the school.

It manifested itself in ways subtle and not so subtle.

Listen to Bill Malloy, one of the vice principals who grew up in the South End:

"Basketball gives this school a lift that nothing else does, and a school like this desperately needs it. Basketball has been the pulse beat of this city. But there's a lot of resentment too. I've seen people who never say anything about anything stand up at faculty meetings and explode against the basketball team getting gifts and presents and trips to Florida, while there are no raises for teachers and we're losing staff and we can't get supplies. It's very hard for people to accept that. And within the other sports at Durfee there is tremendous resentment. They think that the basketball team gets all the attention and that Skippy doesn't take a big interest in the other sports, even though he's the athletic director.

"I'm sure the nurses and clerks cut the basketball players a break because everyone knows them, but I have never known of a grade being changed for a Durfee basketball player, nor have I ever heard of any teacher being asked. In fact, some teachers are probably harder on basketball players because there is so much resentment. I taught English for sixteen years, and one of the years they won the state championship I had a paper due the Monday after the last game and I made sure the basketball players didn't get an extension. I even got questioned by some other teachers, but I thought it was important not to give the players any breaks and make everyone aware of that."

One example of the not-so-subtle would take place in the spring at the "senior skit," where a couple of the skits made references to basketball players thinking they were cool. One had a couple onstage, dressed as nerds, saying how they wished they were cool and got invited to all the basketball parties. Virtually all the players have stories about certain teachers making derogatory statements in class about either the basketball team or basketball players. Virtually all of them know which teachers don't particularly like Karam.

"I always walk into class the first day and try and prove to the teacher that I'm not the typical Durfee basketball player," said Caron. "Because a lot of the teachers think Durfee basketball players are just there for a good time, to bullshit with the girls and be cool. Not troublemakers, but not real serious about school either."

There was the definite sense that nothing really had changed since the fifties, that once you got by the different fashions and the different music and the different accoutrements of the early nineties, there was something timeless about the Durfee basketball players and the world they lived in. It was possible to stand in the 450s with the players between classes, watch them flirt with girls, talk about parties and who got drunk last weekend and which teachers were easy and which ones made you hand in your homework, and believe that such things as the Vietnam War, the counterculture, feminism, other things that have significantly changed the culture, had never happened; that Ike was still in the White House, *Leave It to Beaver* was on television, and the highest form of teenage status was to be either an athlete or a cheerleader.

In many ways these were still the dominant values, ones that determined who was cool and who was cute, the traditional adolescent Holy Grails. The most obvious example was the cheerleading squad, on the surface an anomaly in this feminist age. It was still a mark of status to be on the cheerleading squad, and spots on the squad were ardently sought after, as prized as making the basketball team.

"I didn't sleep the night before the selections," said Julie Kitchen. "I used to go to the games when Michael played and I was at Morton and looked at the cheerleaders, try and see what they did. The boys learned how to be Durfee basketball players. We learned how to be Durfee cheerleaders. It's something that's taught to you."

In the spring, cheerleading was to become a city-wide news story, with Peter Suneson's mother Mary Beth charging that her daughter and seven other girls who failed to make next year's cheerleading squad were victims of an injustice. Suneson charged that the varsity cheerleading coach changed the judge's score sheets, a charge vehemently denied by the coach. Fifteen sophomore girls had tried out for the team; seven were chosen to replace the departing seniors.

The school committee spent about two hours one night listening to the charges and countercharges, among them that some of the departing senior cheerleaders had instigated the controversy because some of their friends had not been chosen. Making it all the more sticky was the fact that two of the girls who made the team were the daughters of the assistant superintendent of schools and the junior varsity cheerleading coach, and that one of the new captains was the daughter of the cheerleading coach, selected by her mother because "she's not a liar and she's not a sneak and I can trust her." The school committee failed to resolve the problem, but in their next meeting two weeks later voted 4–3 to uphold the tryout results, thus ending the controversy, but not the bad feelings.

It was one more example of how important cheerleading was within the social fabric of Durfee.

"I feel fortunate to be a part of it," said Julie Kitchen, also the editor of the yearbook, one of those kids who have had a high school experience out of some adolescent fairy tale. "The feeling you get is so much pride. We've shared all of it together, just like we used to talk about."

One morning in the spring, after the basketball season had ended, she said how she wished she could stop time and live in this senior year forever.

"If I complain about something, one of my friends who's not a cheerleader will quickly say, 'Trade with me,'" she said. "And everyone in the school would trade places with the boys on the basketball team. Kids in school always are criticizing them for thinking they're cooler than anyone else. You hear a lot of resentment of them. But you know what? All the kids who resent them all wish they could be them."

Chapter

"JEFF," Karam said. "Stop throwing those alley-oop passes to that asshole."

Herren, who had been slumped on a bench in the Somerset High School locker room, suddenly sat straight up, a startled look on his face.

"Who's an asshole?" he asked.

"You are," Karam said.

"I'm not an asshole," Herren said defiantly.

"Yes, you are," said Karam. "Trust me."

It was halftime, Durfee was stomping Somerset, the neighboring town to the west, just across the Taunton River from Fall River, and Karam should have been happy. He should have been happy because he does not like Somerset, constantly referring to it sarcastically as "Camelot," a town that's full of people who grew up in Fall River and in the spirit of upward mobility moved across the river, and here was Durfee with a big halftime lead. But once again Karam was perturbed at Herren, this time for what he considered Herren's increasing tendency to act like he was different than the other players, even though everyone knew he was. The specific incident was Karam's discovery that once again

Herren had shown up for the bus without a traveling bag, having no idea where his uniform was, simply expecting it to appear in the Somerset locker room.

"Whoever has Herren's bag is a bigger asshole than he is," he had announced on the bus, before telling Herren that if he didn't start to bring his own uniform to away games, he wasn't going to play.

As soon as the game started, the gym small and crowded and pulsating with energy, someone three rows behind Karam had yelled, "Sit down Karam" the first time he had jumped up. "Oh, shut up," Karam had yelled back, waving his hand at the guy in disgust. He didn't like coaching in Somerset, where he felt he had nothing to gain if he beat them and everything to lose if he didn't. It was the worst possible situation for a coach who long ago realized that the real pressure comes from having to win the games you should win, not the ones you have a chance to win.

There also was a history of acrimony between the two schools, resulting in a major brawl following a football game a few seasons back. A sense of class warfare hovered over the games, the blue-collar kids versus the suburban ones, more so perhaps in football than in basketball where, as Caron put it, "They know they can't play with us, so it's not that big a deal." That realization came from playground games in Somerset at a blacktop called Pottersville, where the Durfee kids often played in the summer, the pecking order long established.

Yet if the players didn't feel pressure coming to Somerset, Karam did. It put him in a bad mood, one more hurdle to get over, for he knew that losing to Somerset was one of those defeats that could haunt him for years. The Somerset coach was Lennie Alves, who once had been Karam's first assistant coach, and he didn't want to lose to him. He also knew that this was the biggest game of the season for Somerset, the reason why there was a crowd outside the gym trying to get into the game, why the mood inside felt like an electric current was running through it. The gym was old and small, with only a few rows of bleachers on each side and bleachers behind each basket, a little bandbox where the noise was deafening. Just the kind of place where upsets are born.

So in the first half Caron had tried two alley-oop attempts to Herren, both times failing, two passes that offended Karam's basketball sensibilities. He had seen enough, even if he had a comfortable lead. Sloppy basketball always upset him, regardless of what the scoreboard said.

"Hey, Jeff," Karam said at halftime. "This is not an ESPN highlight film. Make the simple pass."

He paced back and forth, one hand on the side of his head, trying to think of something else to say, then stopped.

"Okay, let's go out and finish them off. Play well the second half and you get the weekend off and so do I."

"That's good," said Mikolazyk. "It's Super Bowl weekend."

"Every weekend is Super Bowl weekend for you, Gore," Karam said.

Herren was particularly interested in playing well because his new girlfriend was a Somerset cheerleader, a dark-haired girl Caron referred to as "wicked cute, a real looker." Chris had known her since the sixth grade, when he'd met her at a basketball tournament in Somerset, and they had been dating on and off for years. Now they were back again.

With a few minutes left in the game, Durfee holding a huge lead, Herren sat on the end of the Durfee bench, which was the first row of the bleachers. He was surrounded by fans. He took the water bottle and squirted himself on the top of his head, letting the water roll down his face. He had scored thirty-two points, twenty-two of them in the first half when he and Caron had personally taken away any of the pregame suspense. Herren's points moved him into third on the all-time Durfee scoring list behind his brother Michael and Kevin Whiting, who had starred on the '77 state title team. He sat back on the bench, the water glistening on his face, and smiled the smile of a high school junior perfectly content with himself.

A few minutes later the game ended and he went into the locker room, into the casual good feeling of a winning locker room. Jones and Mikolazyk were horsing around, throwing old clumps of tape at each other. Cioe snapped a towel as Jones went by, a timeless locker room scene.

"Let's go, let's get out of here," Karam said, coming into the room. "Come on, hurry up."

The players filed out of the lobby, through the hordes of people still waiting outside, and into the waiting bus. Karam was right behind them, his dark overcoat pulled up around his neck. He stepped into the bus and looked toward the back.

"Where's Herren, signing autographs?" he said. "Where's his majesty? Talking to the girls?"

Two nights earlier Durfee had played at Dartmouth, a suburban town that borders New Bedford to the west and hugs Massachusetts' southeastern coast, and things had subtly changed. It was the start of a ten-day "recruiting window," a chance for college coaches to go to games and practices to look at kids they're interested in. There had been assistant coaches from four New England schools—Larry Shyatt from Providence, James "Bruiser" Flint from the University of Massachusetts, David Leitao from the University of Connecticut, and Bill Coen from the University of Rhode Island. All had seen Herren play before, were there primarily to be seen by Herren, not so much to evaluate his talent.

Recruiting in the early nineties had become increasingly sophisticated, a cottage industry full of talent evaluators, services that rated high school kids as though they were contestants at the Miss America pageant.

Thirty years ago recruiting was a minor job in college basketball. Most coaches only had one assistant, and he was either part-time or coached the freshman team. Coaches relied on a loose network of contacts, alumni, and unofficial scouts, anyone who alerted them about high school talent. Much of it was happenstance. This began changing in the early seventies. Most schools now had two full-time assistant coaches. Freshman teams no longer existed, so the assistants virtually had no other responsibilities than to just recruit. Popping up were showcase summer camps, places where many of the top high school players in the country were paraded in front of assistant coaches for a week at a time. A proliferation of scouting services rated high school players. It became extremely specialized, a cottage industry, complete with horror stories of assistant coaches who would virtually do anything to land a recruit. Now, twenty years later, there are more rules on what assistant coaches can and cannot do, but the bizarre world of recruiting is still very much a game unto itself, a cutthroat, sometimes ruthless meat market where the stakes are high for both the athlete and the school that's recruiting him.

The recruiting of Chris Herren had begun when he was in the ninth grade, maybe even before that. In the summer following his eighth grade year he had gone to basketball camp at Villanova and on the last morning he found a pair of sneakers outside his room, his first real perk as a prospect. But in the ninth grade the first letters had started, exploratory ones, the ones that say we know you're out there and we hear you're a prospect. It all had been exciting in the beginning, these letters that would periodically arrive with the logos. The University of Florida had been one of the first schools to express interest in him and Ron Stewart, one of the assistant coaches, had made two trips to Massachusetts last year to see him play.

It had now intensified, thanks primarily to Chris's involvement with Leo Papile's BABC, and to a glowing tribute in *Eastern Basketball* a couple of months ago. It was in a section on high school players called MIDDLE ATLANTIC PREP

REPORT written by Tom Strickler. Strickler commented on each of the players, particularly Jamal Jackson and Shannon Bowman, the two acknowledged leaders of the team, then wrote, "last, but certainly not least there is my favorite player, 'Popeye.' That would be 6-foot-2 Jr. Chris Herren from Durfee High near Boston. 'Popeye,' as Papile aptly named him, could play the lead in the Bowery Boys, Boys Town, or any other flick that depicts troubled lads or hard-nosed street kids. Let me emphasize Chris is *neither*. He's just a flat-out feisty dude who plays with a scowl and temperament that could scare Jason on Halloween. The more you watch Chris, the more you like everything about his game. I chuckled at first when I first heard of Big East interest, but after five games I believed. He punctuated his three-day performance with an alley-oop dunk . . . I was surprised, then realized it was 'Popeye.' Nothing he will do could surprise me anymore. Keep up that spinach diet, kid. Welcome Big East teams, ACC teams, Big Ten teams. Here's 'robo-guard II.' "

Now the letters came to Karam's mailbox every day, letters from schools all over the country, some from places Herren had never heard of. There were clips of Virginia's victory over Duke, supplied by Virginia, of course. There were notes from coaches. There were brochures and pamphlets, a deluge of mail that never stopped. Every Big East team. UCLA. UNLV.

"There must be twenty pieces every day and maybe two of them for me," Karam told the *Standard Times* of New Bedford. "The secretaries in the office say they're going to switch the name on the box from Karam to Herren. Kentucky, North Carolina, and Duke haven't contacted him, but just about everyone else has."

Herren told the *Standard Times* he was thinking about maybe visiting such schools as Virginia, Florida, Notre Dame, UCLA, and Florida State. Maybe Maryland. But his mind changed every day. Some days he could envision himself off in some faraway place, at one of those schools he only knew from television; the next he couldn't see himself too far away from Fall River, from the cocoon that was his world.

"When the tournaments over the summer were ending, I'd sit in my hotel room and say, 'Let me get back to the city.' For the first three days on the road I'd be happy, but then I'd say, 'Get me back to the rotary,' " Chris's personal euphemism for going home, the reference to the rotary that was just off Route 24, the entrance back to Fall River from Boston.

Most of the time, though, he ignored the entire recruiting process. He often didn't even open the letters, merely looked at where they came from and put them back on Karam's desk, as though they had come addressed to someone else.

"None of the recruiting attention means anything yet," he said one afternoon. "I had more pressure on me in my freshman year when everyone was watching me to see if I was a player. People were already on my case. So they can say what they want to say now."

One reason it didn't mean anything was that in his frame of reference it was so far away, off in some hazy distant future, in some future tense that only existed as an abstraction. Karam would tell him that he wasn't going to be able to survive in college unless he changed his ways, but they were just words to him, words with no currency.

"I'm using basketball to get to college," he said, "but right now I'm not worrying about anything but this year."

Dartmouth High School is red-brick, seems to come right out of *Fast Times at Ridgemont High*, with a wide expanse of fields out behind it. It is an unlikely place to be a setting for one of the horrors of contemporary urban America, but on a morning in April 1993, three students went into a classroom at Dartmouth High School and stabbed another sixteen-year-student to death as his terrified classmates looked on. The case received national attention, not so much for the crime but for where it had been committed. Suburban kids were not supposed to be walking around high schools with knives. Suburban kids were not supposed to be getting stabbed while sitting in a high school classroom.

But on a night late in the January that preceded this event, all was serene at Dartmouth High School. It was even relatively warm, the harshness of a grim winter relieved somewhat by a few days of a false spring.

The gym was old, worn, with wooden bleachers on only one side, some green banners on the walls the only thing that brightened the drab. Durfee was here to play Dartmouth on a Wednesday night, another game Durfee figured to win.

The four college coaches did not sit together. Instead they sat unobtrusively in the wooden bleachers, there to watch what turned out to be a one-sided game. Durfee jumped out early, clearly superior to the suburban team, ignited by Herren, who continually grabbed a defensive rebound and took off down the court, maneuvering around people until he got into the lane and found a teammate for an assist. He did this over and over until it became like an endless replay. Did it so often and so well that URI assistant coach Bill Coen knew that with each sortie down the court, the chances of Rhode Island prying Herren away from the bigger schools became slimmer.

"I don't even know why I'm here," he said finally. "We can't get this kid. This kid can play anywhere he wants."

By the end of the game the Durfee reserves were in, Santos, Boardman, Campbell, Eagan, Cioe, a few minutes of playing time, the carrot for all the practices, all the hard work that goes unnoticed. It is not easy sitting on the bench on any team and different kids handled it differently. For Pavao it meant another year of frustration, another year when the dreams he'd entered Durfee with were not being realized. Cioe too wanted to play more, had gotten a lot of playing time in December when Jones had been out, so that now when he didn't receive as much, it upset him. The others accepted it, for they knew their teammates were better.

One was Matt Boardman, and maybe no one on the team had worked any harder to get to where he was. He once had been like so many of the other kids, playing in the Milliken League, shoveling the snow off Suneson's court across the street from his house on New Boston Road so he could work on his game, going to see the Michael Herren teams play at Durfee, dreaming his own Fall River dreams. He had known early that the game did not come particularly easy for him, not like it did for Chris and Jeff and some of the others, so he had worked hard to keep up. He remembered clearly the time he'd been about twelve, shooting by himself after a snowstorm on a court he'd shoveled off himself and Michael Herren coming by and saying, "Keep that up, and one day you'll be playing for Durfee."

When he was eight or nine he first had gone to Karam's summer basketball camp. The camp started every morning at 8:30, but one day Karam had announced the doors to the field house would open at 7:15, so every day after that Boardman had arrived at 7:15 to get in practice time before camp began. He used to take a basketball everywhere he went.

Yet, almost from the beginning, he'd been a step behind the best kids his age in the city, Herren, Caron, Pavao, Callahan. He'd been good enough to make the Milliken League all-star team, but not good enough to play much. Good enough to make the freshman team, but not good enough to start. Good enough to make the jayvee team, but again not good enough to play consistently. Now he was good enough to be on the varsity, but rarely played. He was only five-foot-eight, with thick legs, another guard on a team that had too many of them. His fate was to sit on the bench and only get into the game during garbage time, in the dying minutes of games that long had been decided. Still, just wearing the uniform was, for him, like being covered in glory.

"The day I made the freshman team, me and Eagan went

over Suneson's house wearing our Durfee shirts and parading around him," he said. "We felt like such big shots."

That feeling, that sense of awe at just being a part of playing for Durfee, has never left him.

"I was so high the first day of varsity practice this year, thinking that this was finally it, everything I'd ever worked for," he said. "Playing for Durfee is not like playing for any other school. Everyone knows that. You know you're playing for a winner. You know you're a part of the tradition. It's easily the best program in the state, maybe in the Northeast. It's the ultimate. I feel proud to be on the team. I'd rather be the last man on the bench at Durfee than starting for Somerset. Nothing can match that respect you get in the school because you play for Durfee. 'Cause you got to understand, there might be a thousand kids who start out playing in the Milliken League, or CYO, and they all want to one day play for Durfee. And only a handful make it. Sometimes as few as five in each class. When you walk around school, everyone knows you're on the basketball team. Being on the team is the most exciting thing that's ever happened to me. So I can accept the fact I don't play, and just be content to go along for the ride and be a part of it."

As much as Boardman grew up around Durfee basketball, he wasn't ready for Karam's coaching style. Yet he's come to understand and appreciate it, believing that to be successful in Fall River a coach must be tough, otherwise the players will take advantage of him.

"You're dealing with a lot of kids who don't get discipline at home," he said. "Either it's parents whacking them or the kids staying out of the house all day. Mr. Karam has to be the authority figure. He's the one who has to get on kids about smoking. He's the one who has to get on kids about drinking. It's too bad. He shouldn't have to worry about kids drinking the night before games."

"How much drinking is there?" he was asked.

"Too much. Every weekend. There are a lot of kids who

222 ......

think it's the only way they can have a good time. I'm the only kid I know who doesn't drink. The other guys all know I don't, so it's no big deal with them."

In fact, Boardman's dedication to basketball is respected by his teammates. He'd played on the summer league team that had been coached by Michael Herren. Michael had come to believe that several of the kids were smoking, so he decided to smell their hands before he allowed them to play. One night, he smelled Mikolazyk's fingers and started yelling at him that he was going to kick his ass after the game.

"We all thought he was kidding," Boardman said. "Just a figure of speech. But afterward Michael came into the locker room and slapped Mikolazyk. Then he slapped Pavao and Suneson. He started telling them that they were the ones who were going to determine whether we won a state championship or not, that Chris and Jeff couldn't do it all by themselves. He said that they did too much drinking and smoking; that his team had drank too, but they knew when to stop and get serious about basketball. Then he pointed to me and said, 'Matt Boardman has never put on a Durfee uniform and yet he's at the Boys Club every day working on his game while the rest of you guys take it for granted.' I had tears in my eyes, because I always had thought the same thing, but no one ever had said it before."

The two easy wins against Somerset and Dartmouth had made everyone feel better again. The reserves had gotten some playing time, Karam seemed more relaxed, Caron was playing better, the tension that had existed after the Brockton game was gone. For the first time all year Caron wasn't thinking about his ankle, told himself to just go out and play and forget everything else, convinced he'd been thinking too much. The difference was noticeable. He had scored twenty-six points against Somerset, most all of them from the perimeter in a great display of outside shooting, twenty-one more against Dartmouth.

The next afternoon there were three assistant coaches at practice, Tom Sullivan from Seton Hall, Paul Biancardi from Boston College, and Stan Van Gundy from the University of Wisconsin. Under NCAA rules they were able to be at practice and talk to Karam and Dempsey, but not allowed to talk to Herren. So they sat over by the bleachers in the center of the field house, about twenty feet from the floor. All were wearing some sort of warm-up suit with their respective school names emblazoned on them, walking billboards. They talked among themselves, shop talk, recruiting talk, where they had been and whom they had seen, this player and that one, though they did not talk about Herren, the reason they were here, as if talking about him with each other would somehow divulge state secrets. Yet they also changed the dynamics of a Durfee practice. Karam was torn. He was happy that Herren was getting this kind of recognition, but he also felt the presence of the recruiters cramped his own coaching. He knew they were not there to see him, but he still felt as if he were coaching with reins on.

In all his years of coaching, he'd only gone through an intense recruiting experience once before. The kid had been Ernie Fleming, one of the first black Durfee players, certainly the first black star. He had grown up in Harbor Terrace, a housing project a few blocks down the hill toward the Braga Bridge from the old Durfee on Rock Street, a shy, withdrawn kid with whom Karam would work in gym class. In 1965, his sophomore year, he'd been so scared during the old Tech Tournament at the Boston Garden that he didn't want to play. The next year he was the tourney MVP. Dempsey had been a senior then, and the two of them had given Karam his first state championship. At the end of the next year Fleming had been invited to an all-star game in Allentown, Pennsylvania. Karam had gone with him. The team from New England had been coached by Rollie Massimino, then a Massachusetts high school coach. Fleming had a decent game and afterward the coach of Gardner Webb, a North Carolina junior college, approached him.

So Karam and Fleming flew down to Boiling Springs, North Carolina.

"Here we were, two hicks from Fall River," Karam recalled. "There was another recruit there too. Artis Gilmore. His father was with him. He had a straw hat and a little cigarette in his teeth, looked real poor. The father went in to see the coach first and when he came out he had a ten-dollar cigar and a new suit. Fleming took one look at him and said, 'I'm coming.' Two years later he and Gilmore went to Jacksonville. Gilmore used to come up here summers to visit him; they used to play ball in Harbor Terrace. By the time he got to Jacksonville, Fleming was six-foot-seven. He later got drafted by the Pistons and the Kentucky Colonels. He was a nice kid. He's in Texas now. He went the farthest of any kid I ever had."

Herren rarely looked at the scouts at practice, yet always was conscious of their presence, could almost feel their eyes boring into him. When they were around, there was more of a self-consciousness about Herren, the sense that he was an actor playing someone else. During a break he went inside the locker room for a drink.

"I don't know why," he said, "but I don't like them here."

He shrugged.

"When they're here, it means I have to play hard and sometimes in practice I don't want to play hard."

There was still a sense of unreality about the entire recruiting process. He couldn't envision himself off at any college yet. He never thought much about the future anyway, never mind where he wanted to go to college. When he did think about it, he often saw himself at the University of Massachusetts, the state university a couple of hours away, in the western part of the state. UMass had a young, energetic coach in John Calipari, someone firmly ensconced on college basketball's fast track, who in just a few short years had taken a program that had only existed on memories and neglect and transformed it into the top program in New England, winning the Atlantic 10 conference and advancing to the NCAA's Eastern Regionals in 1992. Chris especially liked assistant coach Bill Bano, whom he had met while playing for BABC.

UMass was interested in Herren, for Calipari considered him a warrior, someone who played with unique passion and intensity. But Calipari had told Karam he didn't have any scholarships left and maybe he could convince Herren to go to a prep school for a year after he graduated from high school. Karam had told him Chris would never do it, secretly wondered just how interested Calipari really was to even suggest it, believing that if Calipari truly wanted Chris, he would find a scholarship for him one way or the other.

If he didn't see himself at UMass, Chris imagined Boston College, the Big East school where his brother had gone, because he liked coach Jim O'Brien. He wasn't alone. Both his parents also liked O'Brien, who had been supportive of Michael when he had been there. The Herrens had not forgotten that.

The closest school was Providence College, only about a half hour away, also a Big East school. The Friars played their games in the Providence Civic Center, and the coaches would leave tickets for Chris whenever he requested them, something allowed under NCAA rules. It had backfired, though. He had been to a few games but hadn't particularly enjoyed them, thinking the Civic Center was too dead, the crowd too old, a definite lack of a student presence. One night he, Caron, Cioe, and Mikolazyk had gone to the PC-Boston College and when asked the next day whether he enjoyed it, Caron said, "No, the game sucked, but we had a great time. We parked on the top floor of the new parking garage and Igor and Cioe started throwing snowballs at people when they were coming out after the game and one guy started chasing us. It was awesome."

So much for the recruiting process.

It was apparent, though, that Herren's reputation was growing. I had done a large Sunday feature in the Providence *Journal* on him, saying that in over thirty years of watching high school basketball in Rhode Island and southeastern Massachusetts I had never seen a high school junior any better than Chris Herren, that he had the potential to one day transcend the small gyms of southeastern Massachusetts. Soon after, a Providence television station had produced a feature on him, as had the local cable television station. It was not considered abnormal to come to practice and see either a coach sitting on the sidelines watching or someone waiting to interview Herren. One afternoon it was Pittsburgh coach Paul Evans and his assistant Joe DeSantis.

"Chrissie," Karam said one afternoon after the coaches had left. "My nose is growing. I keep telling all these coaches what a good kid you are. I have to lie like a bastard."

It was after practice; the college coaches were long gone. The team was shooting free throws in little groups, both on the main court and the side baskets, and Karam had caught Herren fooling around on one of the side baskets, doing trick shots instead of concentrating on free throws.

"Mr. Dempsey, wouldn't you think that if you were having trouble at the line you might work a little harder at it?" Karam said loudly, making sure Herren could hear him. "If you could get to the foul line in a game any time you wanted and could get all those free points, wouldn't you practice them once in a while? Wouldn't you think you might do that?"

"You would, Skippy." Dempsey laughed. "I would."

"That's the difference between me and you, Mr. Karam,"

said Herren. "I don't have to. Because I make them all the time now. I've got a streak of seven going now."

"Are you proud of that? Seven?" Karam said disparagingly. "I could make seven in a row blindfolded."

Skippy took pride in the fact that he once had been a very good shooter, and for years he's often beaten most of his players in HORSE, the shooting game where you match shots. In fact, when Herren had been a freshman, Karam had beaten him, then said, "I beat your father, I beat your brother, and now I just beat you. So screw."

Now Karam grabbed a ball, took a free throw. It went in. He got the ball back and as he went to shoot it again, Herren came from his blind side and blocked it, the ball bouncing harmlessly away.

"That's why you couldn't make seven in a row, Mr. Karam," Herren said. "Because I'd block them."

"Okay," Karam said louder, calling the team around him. "If Chrissie can make two fouls shots in a row, practice is over. If he misses, you run."

"How about if Jeff shoots?" Santos said.

"Not Jeff," Karam said. "Chrissie. Mr. I-don't-have-to-practice-anymore-because-I've-made-seven-in-a-row."

"Give me the ball," Herren said, running over to Karam and taking the ball out of his hands. "Just give me the ball and turn on the showers."

He bounced the ball hard three times, then brought it to his right shoulder, his right hand underneath the ball, his left hand on top of it, and shot it. It went right through the center of the basket as his teammates cheered.

"Save the cheering, fellas," Karam said. "If he doesn't make the next one, you're running."

"Now this is pressure," Herren said, bouncing the ball. He peered intently at the rim, then shot it. "Yes," he yelled, as the ball went cleanly through. His teammates erupted in cheers and started running to the locker room as though they had just won a big game. Herren pointed at Karam and ran after them.

Karam turned to Dempsey and laughed.

"Is this kid a pisser or what?"

Chapter 9

THEY WERE AT Bishop Feehan, a Catholic school in Attleboro about forty-five minutes away. It was another small gym, another game Durfee was expected to win fairly easily. There was a small section of bleachers behind one of the baskets and last year the Feehan students there had thrown tiny rubber balls at the Durfee players. A few of them already were sitting there before the jayvee game started and Herren and Santos and Cioe walked in front of them, then turned around and did it again. Once again Herren dressed in a loose sweatshirt and baggy jeans worn so low you wondered how they stayed up. On his head was a white cap with COCKS written on the front in big red letters. Underneath, in very small letters, it said SOUTH CAROLINA GAMECOCKS.

"Stop parading around," Karam said. "Sit."

He was sitting in the first row of the bleachers, a few yards down from the end of the jayvee bench. He always watched the jayvee games closely, but tonight he had an added interest. Dempsey was going to start Steve Breese—the big six-foot-six sophomore who had wanted to quit back in December—for the first time, and Karam is curious about how he will do.

Breese's status has become a running joke between them. Karam wants all the jayvee kids to play in all the games, regardless of the score; Dempsey is looking to win. Karam especially wants Breese to play more; Dempsey keeps saying he doesn't deserve to play more.

"How's he supposed to get better if he doesn't play, Bobby?" Karam invariably asks.

"He plays, Skippy," Dempsey retorts.

"He doesn't play enough," Karam counters. "How many six-six kids are walking around this school? They're not exactly growing on trees, you know."

Dempsey would laugh, turn to anyone who was listening and lament that Karam had been yelling at him for thirty years, so why should anyone expect it to stop now?

Breese scored the first time he got the ball. Dempsey turned and looked at Karam and gave a shrug. Then Breese blocked a shot. Dempsey turned and gave a bigger shrug. Then Breese got a rebound, turned and ran the floor, and seconds later scored another basket.

"Way to go, Breezie," Herren yelled.

"Where have you been hiding him, coach?" Karam yelled.

Dempsey turned and laughed.

A couple of minutes later, Breeze, visibly puffing, came out of the game. He had scored three baskets. He had gotten some rebounds. He had shown some promise. For the first time you could seriously imagine him playing on the varsity and making a contribution. Also, for the first time, he came out of a game and was both mobbed by his jayvee teammates and given encouragement by the varsity ones who were sprawled on the bleachers behind the bench. You could almost see his chest swell with pride, see his confidence visibly grow. For the first time in his life Steve Breese had glimpsed the possibilities of being a Durfee basketball player.

"He's going to start for you someday, Skip," said Ronnie

Fahey, who once again was at a road game, seated a couple of rows behind the bench.

Karam laughed. "Tell that to Bobby."

About an hour later Herren quickly began the varsity game with two drives to the basket. Then he made two free throws, gave Caron a great pass for an easy score, then another drive followed by a three-pointer, followed by two jump shots and another drive and the score was 19–2. By halftime Herren already had twenty-three points and Durfee was leading by twenty-two.

The locker room was in the basement, one flight down from the court, another small room with too many lockers in it, and as the players sat in front of him, Karam didn't like the look on Pavao's face.

"Peter, you're walking around like there's a death in the family because you didn't start," he said. "This is a team."

"I know it," Pavao said.

"Then act like it. You've contributed all year."

"I haven't said anything," said Pavao.

"It's the way you look out there," Karam snapped back. "Moping around. No emotion. Because you didn't start."

Pavao thought the criticism was unfair, thought that he'd handled his loss of a starting job ever since the Lowell Tournament a month ago very well. He didn't necessarily like it, but it was Mikolazyk playing in front of him, one of his best friends, so that made it easier. He also had gotten a letter recently from his father, Jerry. In the letter his father had told him how it always had been his own dream to play for Durfee and how he never could, and now that Peter was playing, he just wanted Peter to know how proud he was of him.

Early in the second half Karam put Pavao in the game, his way of telling Pavao there were no more bad feelings, that he had said his piece and now it was over. Pavao played well, and when he eventually came out of the game, Karam made a point of shaking his hand.

Durfee was well in front at the time, but you never would have known it by watching the bench. Karam still coached intently, urging on his players, barking at the referees, again concerned with trying to attain perfection, not with the scoreboard. At one point referee Dave Gibeau, tired of Karam's incessant voice, stopped the game and gave Karam a technical foul. Karam immediately jumped to his feet in disbelief.

"I can't believe you gave me that, David," he said as Gibeau ran by, before adding sarcastically, "I really deserved that."

Herren had yet to miss a foul shot in the game, making ten in a row, then thirteen, running his two-game total to twenty, only five short of the all-time Durfee record. Every time he made another one, he would turn to the bench and smile. He knew the irony, how just a month ago he couldn't make two in a row. Now they all seemed to go in. He finished the game with thirty-nine points, sixteen of sixteen from the foul line, now having made twenty-two straight free throws. Caron added twenty-five points, again shooting very well, his third strong game in a row.

The players showered quickly, went outside to the bus. Karam already was on the bus in his customary first seat, waiting to go. The game was over and he wanted to get back to Fall River, back to Lizzie's, anywhere but sitting on another school bus waiting for kids to get out of the locker room. The cheerleaders were back in the darkness in the rear of the bus. One by one the players came in with their traveling bags, walking past Karam: Jones, Cioe, Santos, Eagan, Campbell, Boardman, Herren with his white hat turned backward.

"Where's Callahan?" Karam finally asked.

"He can't find his uniform," said Santos.

"What do you mean he can't find his uniform?" said Karam, perplexed. "He just wore it."

"He went in the lobby to see somebody and when he went back to the locker room, his bag was gone."

"You got to be kidding me," said Karam. He turned to Dempsey. "Do you fucking believe this? This is like taking the fifth grade on a field trip."

He went off to look for Callahan. He was gone for several minutes when Callahan came out a different door and climbed into the bus.

"Cal," said Santos. "Mr. Karam went to look for you. He's pissed."

"Oh, shit," Callahan said.

None felt Karam's sharp-edged tongue more than Callahan. Ironically, Callahan was Karam's brother "Boo-Boo's" nephew, Callahan's mother and "Boo Boo" Karam's wife being sisters. He had grown up knowing Skip Karam. His family and Karam's family had socialized together. He liked Karam, loved the way he coached, although felt that Karam sometimes overdid it with the yelling and the sarcasm. He knew Karam thought he drank too much, that he was making "packy runs" every weekend. He knew Mr. Karam often said "Callahan weighs a hundred and forty pounds and a hundred of it is beer." Still, he believed Mr. Karam's style definitely worked, that it motivated people.

Especially himself.

He too had begun playing when he was just a young kid, on all-star teams with Herren, Caron, Pavao, Mikolazyk, and Santos. He too had begun going to Durfee games when he was young, remembers the '84 state championship team that had been led by Brian O'Neil and Paul Hart. His father grew up in the city, is now a lawyer with an office downtown. His mother also grew up in Fall River and went to Durfee.

Last year he'd been one of the best players on the jayvee team, but had hurt his knee halfway through the year and spiraled into a lost year. By his own admission he partied too much, drank too much. He didn't do any homework. His grades slumped. He had been an honors student, a class officer. But the partying had changed that.

"After my freshman year everyone thought I was going to be a serious ballplayer," he once said. "I went to the Boys Club all the time. But I also began partying. I walked home so many nights shit-faced. Then the next morning I'd want to get up early and go work out, but I'd roll over and go back to sleep and tell myself 'I'll go next week.' " He paused, then added, "I screw around, but I have goals too."

He was thinking of going to prep school for a year in the fall of 1994, then maybe a Division II college. He had sent away for some coaching drills. Basketball was very important to him, even if his persona was often to play the clown, Danny the party boy.

He knew he'd improved considerably since the beginning of the year. In one of the first games Herren had yelled at him to prove himself, and though it had pissed him off, it had made him play harder too. He was six-four, a decent shooter from fifteen feet, and probably would have been better playing on the wing, but because of his size he was a low-post player, a position where his lack of strength and athleticism was a disadvantage. Still, he kept getting more assertive, was becoming more of a scoring threat underneath. He knew that in the beginning of the season it had been Chris and Jeff's team, but he could feel himself becoming more a part of it.

Now, though, as he saw Karam get back on the bus, he knew he was a target. Karam's yelling no longer bothered him. In fact, he often thought it was funny and sometimes he had to stop himself from laughing when Karam got off a good one-liner. Except when it was directed at him, of course. Then it wasn't so funny.

"Way to go, Danny," Karam said. "You don't get any rebounds and then you lose your uniform and keep everyone waiting. A great night. You're a pisser, Danny. A real pisser."

"Mr. Karam," said Herren. "You know there's no such word as *pisser*. It's not in the dictionary."

"Sure it is, Chrissie," Karam said. "You look it up and your picture's there."

He turned to the bus driver. "Let's go," he said. "I've spent enough time with these idiots tonight."

The courtship of Chris Herren continued the next afternoon. This time it was an assistant from Marquette. But this time the underlying tension that had been present whenever a coach watched practice boiled over. Maybe there had been too many practices in which Karam and Herren had gotten along, too much pent-up tension. Maybe there had been too many days when Herren had felt as if he were in some display case. Whatever the reason, he came to practice with all the energy of a ten-year-old who has just overdosed on chocolate. He began working out with unleashed fury, running over some of the smaller jayvee players, bordering on being out of control.

"Calm down, Chrissie," Karam warned.

"What?" Herren said.

"You're real close to being out of here," Karam said softly. "Calm down."

He didn't calm down. He came over to the sideline during a break and Dempsey leaned over and whispered to him, "Knock it off, Chrissie, you're driving him crazy."

"Why shouldn't I drive him crazy? He's driving me crazy."

Dempsey walked away, sensing that Herren wasn't going to last the day. He knew it had become one of those days when Herren and Karam seemed to exist in different realities, and there would be a confrontation. A half hour into practice, the assistant from Marquette still watching, it came.

Herren drove to the basket, was fouled by Breese, then gave Breese a long look.

"That's it, Chrissie," said Karam. "Enough. Go home."

Herren slammed the ball to the floor and walked toward the door that led to the locker room. He stared straight ahead, not looking at the Marquette assistant.

Watching him go, Caron just shook his head. *Here we go again*, he thought. Another crisis, just when everything seemed to be getting better. He looked at Karam and wondered why Karam always seemed so obsessed with Chris's behavior.

Herren went into the trainer's room, his anger boiling over.

"What came on him today? What's his problem? He's such a bitch. Why does he have to be such a bitch?"

He sat on the training table, still fuming about Karam, when he was reminded that an assistant coach had been there to see him.

"Think about it, Chris," I said to him. "that guy just flew halfway across the country to see you, rents the car in Boston, drives down here, gets lost, to see you get thrown out of practice in a half hour. What do you think he's going to say when he goes back? Coaching is all one big network, you know. So what do you think he's going to say when someone asks him about Chris Herren?"

"Fuck it," said Herren. "I'm not going to go there anyway."

It was a Friday in early February. A blanket of snow covered Fall River, one of the first storms in what so far had been a mild winter. The next day tennis great Arthur Ashe would die of AIDS-related pneumonia at forty-nine years old.

Inside the field house another large Friday night crowd had gathered, and about forty-five minutes before the game, while the jayvee game was in the second half, the lobby was full.

It was easy to take this for granted, but this was a rarity in the Northeast, where high school athletic contests had become victims of television, apathy, and neglect, a slide

238 ......

that had begun thirty years ago. The typical high school game in the Northeast now took place in a small gym before a smattering of other students and parents, amid the feeling that no one else cared. There were several reasons for this, the most obvious being that television changed a country's entertainment habits.

But there were others too. In a sense, intense interest in high school sports belonged to another America, a simpler one, one based more on community and roots. In towns that had a strong sense of community, high school sports still flourished. The high school team was an extension of the town itself, its foray into battle against other towns. Football in small Texas towns. Basketball in small Indiana towns. These were places of legend, places where a town's identity became intermingled with the high school's athletic team, and usually the intense interest started eroding as soon as smaller schools merged, or towns got big enough to have two schools. This is why city schools rarely captured the same phenomenon, for as soon as there was more than one high school it became diluted, the civic identification gone.

If Fall River had built two high schools back in the mid seventies instead of the new Durfee, interest in high school basketball might have started to dwindle.

It hadn't. The one high school kept it alive. The good teams kept it alive. The red banners on the walls kept it alive, the tradition palpable and omnipresent. The Greek chorus kept it alive, the caretakers of the tradition, the ones who remembered all the teams. And, of course, Karam kept it alive, the living embodiment of the tradition, the one who had played for Lukey, who had been coaching since Kennedy was in the White House, who had coached fathers and sons, generations of this city's kids. He was the link between the past and the future, the reason why most of the players on the team could name the great players in Durfee's past, even going back to Andy Farrissey, who had played over a quarter of a century before they were born.

Durfee basketball was a time capsule, a slice of an earlier America that had been preserved and was on display two nights a week in the field house. It was possible to go to a game and forget what year it was, put out of your mind for a while the scourge of AIDS and the faltering economy and the unraveling of society like some old carpet that had become unhinged. You saw the cheerleaders who seemed to wear their youth like a merit badge. The passion of the players. The old men who sat in the front row beside the Durfee bench, some of whom had been watching Durfee basketball for over fifty years. The women who sold hot dogs and candy from two long tables in the lobby. The trophy case, old and dusty, the trophies too crowded together. The little kids who wore red HERREN shirts and tried to get close to the players in the pregame warm-ups.

But not even Fall River was immune to other realities that were changing high school sports in America. There were so many more sports at Durfee than there had been a generation ago. Once, in the winter, there only had been basketball. There had been no girls' sports of any significance. The Fall River *Herald News* would run big stories on the day of a game, advancing the game, hyping it. Now there were seven sports at Durfee in the winter alone. Boys' basketball. Girls' basketball. Hockey. Track. Wrestling. Boys' swimming. Girls' swimming. Now they all competed for newspaper space. And not only in Fall River. Because of the realities of the city—older, less literate fewer people—the *Herald News* had dropped the "Fall River" from its masthead, was now trying to appeal more and more to the surrounding towns, Somerset and Swansea to the west, Westport to the east, Freetown to the north, Tiverton, Rhode Island, to the south. All these places had high schools and high school teams, both boys' and girls'. All were covered in the *Herald News*, all took space from Durfee basketball. In the paper, at least, all the sports in all the towns seemed the same, reducing the perception that Durfee basketball was important.

Durfee's identity relied on its roots in the old Fall River community. There was the sense that when Karam retired, Durfee basketball would start to change, especially if someone other than Dempsey became the coach. Some observers felt that as the city changed, more black kids coming from somewhere else, more kids whose roots didn't run deep in the city, then Durfee basketball would become like high school basketball in other places throughout the Northeast, nothing more. Already there were signs: Carlos Smith, a black kid on the jayvees, had not grown up in Fall River, knew little about the tradition, only knew that he wanted to play basketball. Shawn Thames had not grown up going to Durfee games.

Still, there was something magical about a Durfee home game. It was homecoming every game, a chance to see people you'd gone to school with, people you never saw anywhere else anymore. Each Durfee home game was part of one big continuum, linking the past with the present. You could get an alumni team together from the people in the stands and play the current Durfee team, even: people like Kevin Whiting from the '77 state championship team, and Brian O'Neil from the '84 one, even Tommy Arruda from the '56 squad. They were the past, and in Fall River the past didn't just exist in the banners on the walls.

Then there was Randy Morin, a symbol of the future.

Already he was being called a future great Durfee player, even though he was only nine.

He was just a wisp of a kid, with dirty blond hair, but he wore a small red Durfee shirt with Herren's name on the back, number 24. He and a couple of his friends sat in the first row of the bleachers, just to one side of the Durfee players. Before games he ran over and touched Herren's hand. During games he exploded out of his seat every time Durfee scored.

When the games ended, he and group of other little kids surrounded Herren as though he were a rock star, wanting to

...... 241

shake his hand, wanting autographs, wanting to just touch him, little kids who stared at him, their faces luminous with wonder.

Durfee was into the easy stretch in its schedule now, playing several neighboring schools that were no match for them. They already had blasted Bishop Connolly, but Karam hadn't liked the way his team had played, thinking they had been flat and uninspired, that the only teams his players seemed able to get up for anymore were New Bedford and Brockton. So he was looking for a big effort against Attleboro, had even put a tape of an Attleboro game on the television set in the locker room.

Not that anyone was watching it.

In fact, the big topic of conversation before the game was a love letter Herren had received. It was passed around the room, the most popular line being "I want you in bed."

Herren had received fan letters before. This one was different, though, as evidenced by the players' passing it around, complete with giggles and snickers, as if it were from some other planet.

"It's from a guy," Santos said. "Chris got a letter from a guy. Do you believe it?"

"Yeah, some faggot," said Callahan.

"I've heard there are even some gays at Durfee," Boardman said, amazement in his voice.

Suddenly Karam strode into the room in dark green slacks and a blue shirt with a red plaid tie.

"Where's the tape?" he asked, looking at the blank TV screen.

"We just turned it off," Caron said.

"Did you watch it?"

"Yes," he said.

He turned to Callahan. "Can you get the tap?"

Callahan smiled.

"What are you laughing at?" Karam said. "You've gotten like one all year. Can you get the tap tonight?"

"Yes," Callahan said.

"Okay, we're going to start in thirty-three defense." He glanced over at Mikolazyk, who looked confused.

"What's the matter, Gore, never heard of it? We've only been using it since November."

He looked pained.

"Come on, you guys. Concentrate. I know you didn't come to play against Connolly. I could tell right out of the chute. Shit, we couldn't even play them man-to-man. Are you shitting me? Great teams come to play every night and if we're going to have a chance to be as good as we all want to be, we have to get up for everyone. So let's start tonight."

There were times when Karam and his team seemed to be operating in two different realities. This was one of them. It was minutes before the game and he assumed they were as focused on it as he was, had spent the afternoon thinking about it, worrying about it, consumed by it, the reasons he could never eat before a game. He had come into the locker room as though he were going into battle, as he always did, all his competitive juices evident to all, a visceral, primal man stripped to his core. It was this burning competitiveness that kept Karam coaching, let him forgive all the nonsense and all the difficulties of dealing with high school kids in the nineties. This was the moment that made it all worthwhile, the game stripped of all its trappings, just your team and the other guy's.

This was coaching at its bare bones, yet his team was in nowhere near the same emotional state as he was. His players hadn't watched the tape that had soundlessly played in the background. They had been preoccupied with Herren's love letter. They knew they were playing an easy team and they approached it that way, casual, laid back, going through the motions, feeling as though they could beat Attleboro merely by stepping on the court and playing like it was some pickup game at the Boys Club.

Durfee jumped out quick, yet it didn't deter Karam. When Caron threw an errant alley-oop pass to Herrem, Karam quickly jumped up. "Jeffrey, this isn't ESPN highlights," he yelled. "Make the simple pass." When Herren came down on a break and threw the ball away, Karam yelled, "Keep it."

"I thought you said give it," Herren yelled back.

"Don't start blaming me for your lousy pass," Karam answered.

Shortly before the first half ended, they were in front 45–7, but at halftime Karam was still intense. He walked into the room, saw an overturned wastebasket in a corner, and said, "You guys must have some nice-looking rooms at home."

He paced in front of them.

"Don't get careless out there because we're way ahead," he said. "Keep working on things. Keep working hard."

He turned to Callahan, saw that his legs were scraped.

"Danny, how did you get those bruises on you? Who's beating you up? Your mother? Your girlfriend? And Danny, why don't you get a rebound and break your record."

He paced some more.

"By the way. As you know, we're playing Sunday afternoon, so I'm going to have Mitch call everyone at ten o'clock Saturday night. Anyone who's not home doesn't play."

"I won't be home," said Herren. "I got a church meeting."

Karam gave him a hard look.

"I'm kidding, Mr. Karam," Herren said.

Callahan started the second half by getting the ball on the right side of the basket, and instead of putting in the easy basket, he took one dribble and came up on the other side and missed the shot.

"Isn't he a pisser?" Karam said to the crowd behind him. "Isn't he a pisser?"

Durfee continued to roll over Attleboro and with about

four minutes left, leading by almost sixty. Herren, Pavao, Mikolazyk, Jones, Caron, and Callahan were all on the bench. On one level they were cheering on their teammates, the reserves who were getting the last minutes of garbage time. What they really were doing was looking for two girls from Duxbury who had called Herren and invited themselves down for a date. The only problem was that he didn't know what they looked like. So they sat on the bench scanning the crowd, looking for two girls they never had seen before, two suburban girls who might look a little out of place in Fall River.

"How about those two over there?" asked Pavao, pointing across the court to the far left corner of the bleachers.

"If that's them, I'm going out the back door," Herren said.

"It's not them," Mikolazyk said. "It's the two behind us, up in the back. I spotted them earlier. It has to be them."

"Don't let them see you, Gore," Pavao said. "You're going to scare them with that forehead of yours. One look at you and they'll be running for the door."

"You've been scaring girls all your life, Beanie," Mikolazyk countered, "Beanie" being Pavao's nickname, also a derogatory slur against Portuguese immigrants in Fall River.

"They look like they have big-time money," said Herren.

"Just keep your hat on, Gore." Pavao laughed.

"Fuck you, Beanie."

When the game ended, Herren stayed on the court, briefly talked to his mother and aunt, then started signing autographs as a group of young kids clustered around him. One, about eight years old, wore a red basketball jersey with HERREN on it. Herren made small talk with the kids, signed for them, patted them on the head, made sure he accommodated all of them. He already was aware of his role as hero to the young kids and took it seriously. He never shunned them, never "big-timed" them, as if he intuitively knew that even in the height of all this Fall River fame he was just part of a larger story.

When they had left, the gym nearly deserted now, he went through the door that led to the locker room. Once inside, his mood instantly changed.

"We're going out with some rich bitches," Herren said, still in his uniform. "Girls from Duxbury. Rich girls are going to take us to a fancy restaurant."

"They came all the way from Duxbury?" Karam asked. "It's over an hour away."

"I know," continued Herren. "They came all the way down here to take us out. Rich girls from Duxbury. Rich bitches."

"Calm down, Chrissie," Karam said. "Give it a break, will you?"

Karam walked back into the empty gym. The lights were off, and sitting in the darkness were the two girls, one with blond hair, one with dark. Karam walked over and stood in front of them, a questioning look on his face.

"We're waiting for Chris Herren," the blond one said.

"You really drove all the way from Duxbury?" Karam asked.

"Chris Herren is like a legend in our school," she said somewhat shyly. "Everyone talks about him."

Karam stepped back, his head turned, as though processing the information.

"You came all the way down here to go out with Chris Herren?" he said, shaking his head, beginning to walk away. "You've got to be kidding me."

Durfee was back playing in less than forty-eight hours.

The opponent was Bishop Stang, a Catholic school in Dartmouth, on the outskirts of New Bedford. It was a rare Sunday afternoon game, a makeup from a game that had gotten canceled by a freak snowstorm. Stang figured to be no match for Durfee, but to Karam it didn't make any difference. He didn't like the way his team seemed so nonchalant, turning on the intensity only in spurts. He knew that part of it was the result of the schedule, that there were too many easy games, but there was nothing he could do about that, the result of geography and tradition. He knew that a team doesn't get better by playing too many easy games, that it falls into bad habits that can be costly when the competition is better.

His team was better than they'd been in the beginning of the year, but it was not a particularly talented group, still relying too much on Herren and Caron, and it was a lousy defensive team. That was surprising, for his teams always had been good defensively, with their halfcourt press and their different zones, defense the one constant as the players changed and the years fell off the calendar. Defense had been his trademark as a coach, for he knew, as virtually all coaches know, that it can keep you in games on those nights when shooting touch is a guest that left early. But now Durfee couldn't seem to stop anybody, no matter what defense they played. They were not a very athletic team. Mikolazyk was only five-seven, not particularly quick, in the starting lineup because he could make open shots and handle the ball. Neither Callahan or Jones played consistently. And Herren often loafed on defense, resting in the back of the zone whenever he got the chance. So Karam would watch his team and feel the anger start to well up inside him, for he knew that somewhere down the road Durfee would pay for its defensive sins.

It was one of the reasons he could get so perturbed at Herren. He wanted Chris to work harder on defense, to get himself in better shape. Most of all, he wanted him to be more of a leader, to set an example in practice every day, not turn it off and on according to some personal timetable. He looked at him now, in February, and saw the same kid he'd seen when the season started, a marvelous talent with worlds of potential, who too often seemed to be starring in his own movie, oblivious to the larger picture around him.

So when he walked into the locker room shortly before the game to talk to the team and Herren was standing up, it was as though nothing had ever changed.

"Sit down, Herren," he snapped.

Chris gave Karam a stare. This was just the kind of thing Karam did that bothered him so, the feeling that Karam was singling him out, showing him up in front of everyone.

"Do you think you're special here?" Karam asked. "Sit down when I'm talking."

Herren mumbled something inaudible as he sat down on the bench.

"What's that?" Karam said threateningly. "Do you want to play today?"

"Yes," Herren said softly.

"Then shut up."

Karam began to say something else, stopped himself, and walked out of the room in obvious disgust.

"What's his problem?" asked Herren.

"Boys," said Abe White, who was standing in the corner. "I think Mr. Karam might be a little upset. A very close friend of the family died over the weekend."

"Mr. Karam knew Arthur Ashe?" asked Mikolazyk.

"No, boys," White said. "Monsour Ferris."

Monsour "Monnie" Ferris was a legend in Fall River, referred to by the Lebanese community in the city as "the leader." He was seventy-six, and his obituary in the Providence *Journal* said he was the founder and owner of the Venus de Milo, a large banquet hall in neighboring Swansea. That was only part of it. He was the American dream in a Lebanese accent. He grew up in the Flint, went to Durfee in the mid-1930s, and worked after school at the old Empire Bowling Alley at Third and Pleasant Streets. Nearly twenty years later he bought the bowling alley, and when it was heavily damaged in a fire shortly afterward, he moved it across the river to Somerset. Later, he wanted to build another bowling alley in Swansea, the town to the west of Somerset. He was turned down for financing by every bank in Fall River. Somehow he opened, although he couldn't afford all the lanes he'd envisioned, so he was stuck with a building that was partially empty. Realizing that bowling leagues had banquets at the end of the year, he used the empty part of the building for that and got into the banquet business. Today, the Venus de Milo is one of the largest and most successful banquet halls in New England.

For over twenty-five years he was president of the Lebanon American Society, instituting scholarships for students of Lebanese descent. He also was one of the most visible citizens in Fall River, chairing fund drives, serving on committees, one of those unique people involved in innumerable charities, a civic giant. When he died, John McAvoy of the *Herald News* wrote a glowing tribute to Ferris titled THIS "FLINT BOY" LIVED LIFE TO THE FULLEST.

He also was, perhaps, the biggest power broker in the city, the head of a small group of men, mostly of Lebanese descent, whom many people in Fall River thought controlled the city. There was strong speculation that he had been the force behind Carlton Viveiros, the mayor who rode the large Portuguese vote to a thirteen-year stretch as mayor. Legend also had it that a former superintendent of schools in Fall River owed Ferris for some gambling debts, the result of some Friday night card games at the Venus de Milo, to the point that for years Ferris had a strong say in who got hired in the Fall River School Department. Whatever the truth, he had been a powerful and colorful presence in the city for a long time and now he was gone.

"Arthur Ashe?" said Caron. "Gore, you're retarded."

"How am I supposed to know who Mr. Karam knows?" Mikolazyk countered.

"That's what Mr. Karam does," piped in Herren, steering

the conversation back to Karam's mood. "He's in a bad mood and he takes it out on all of us."

"Yeh, he fights with his wife and we pay for it," Mikolazyk said.

"He must have a lot of fights with his wife," Caron said.

Chapter

10

"I'M THE ONE who is married to a legend," Betty Karam said with a laugh.

We were sitting in the sunroom of their house in the Highlands, less than a mile from Durfee, the one they bought in 1968, and she was talking about the time she saw Skip Karam's picture in the paper and told her girlfriend she'd give her right arm and part of her left to go out with him.

She was Betty DeFusco then, and it was the late 1950s. She was a senior at Sacred Heart, a Catholic high school in Fall River, very much interested in school. It was a sheltered time in Fall River, a provincial time. Everybody knew everybody. Nobody had any money. A big night out was going downtown to Main Street. There was the sense that everyone sort of lived the same, had the same dreams. Karam was four years older, a big age difference then. She met him through a girlfriend and on their first date they went to a pizza place in neighboring Somerset.

"I wore a beige knit dress and beige Capezio flats," she said, as if able to stop time and still clearly see that long-ago night: she, expectant and thrilled to be with someone older and so good-looking; Skip, outgoing, but a little shy too.

"He never put on any airs," she said. "He never pretended to be anything he wasn't. I knew he had played basketball, but I didn't know he was good. He never talked about it. That came from everybody else. And I thought he was very funny. I still do. Even now, sometimes we'll be arguing and he'll say something I think is funny and I'll go into the other room and laugh."

They were married in October 1959. She was twenty; he was twenty-four.

A year later he was the Durfee coach.

The games were played at the Bank Street Armory then, an old, dark building downtown, only a couple of blocks away from the original B. M. C. Durfee High School. It always was jammed, people shoehorned into the building, ringing the court, the noise deafening.

"Going to the games at Westport had been fun," she said, "but at the armory it was awful. People were screaming, throwing things. It was crazy. I actually used to get a headache. Everybody got nuts. His whole family got nuts. I remember thinking that someone had to stay sane. But it wasn't fun and after a while I just didn't go anymore. I didn't like anything about it. I didn't like the crowd, and I didn't like Skip's behavior."

So rather than make an issue of it, she just stopped going. She hasn't been in years, long ago made her separate peace with it. Once, asked why his wife never went to the games, Karam said, "Why would any wife want to see her husband make an asshole out of himself?"

Told that story, Betty Karam laughed.

"I've had so many people say to me over the years, 'How can you live with a maniac like that?' And I ask them, do you think I'd let that maniac you see at the games come into my house? I've heard all the stories. I think it's funny. But he's never been that way around the house. After a loss he gets very withdrawn, but that's about it. Skip's a very normal person, except for his mouth. As a kid he did exactly what his father told him to do. He's always done the right thing. I don't think he even knows what he says sometimes. He just opens his mouth and out it comes."

He was like that when he played for Durfee himself, and when he first began coaching. That was the public persona, the maniac coach, the one who admitted, "It's like someone sticks a needle in my arm when the game starts and off I go." Yet there was the other side too, the one the public rarely saw.

"I always joke that I married a legend," she continued. "But I'm very happy for him."

She might not go to the games, but she doesn't resent basketball either. She's very aware there's a price to be paid for being the Durfee coach, a certain backlash, part envy, part jealousy, part who knows what? She teaches special education at Morton Middle School and knows that when Durfee loses, some people at her school will invariably ask her what happened, though they will say nothing if Durfee wins. She's always hearing that the Karam brothers control everything in Fall River. But she also knows that being the Durfee coach has been her husband's identity, and to envision her adult life without Durfee basketball is unthinkable too, for it's always been there.

"It's been our life," she said. "My daughters used to put banners on the porch after a big win. The ticking of the clock and the ball going into the basket determined everything. People would ask me if we were going out to dinner. I'd tell them, I'll tell you after the game. When we first married, I'd tell him that the water line broke on the day of a game and he'd say, 'How can you bother me now?' "

She laughed.

"So I never did. We complement each other. I run the house, he coaches. I'm just amazed that he's kept doing it. Because I see what it does to him physically during the season. What else does he have to prove? What else does he have to win? That's the part of him I don't know. I don't know if anyone knows that part."

She hesitated. In back of her is a small lawn. It is a quiet street, with frame houses and trees, not the city, but not quite the suburbs either. Two blocks away to the west is Highland Avenue, once one of the city's most prestigious addresses, a broad street that runs like a major artery through the Highlands. One block to the south is President Avenue, which is also Route 6, a main thoroughfare that starts at the Taunton River below the hill, goes up the steep hill that crests at the Highland Avenue intersection, then slopes gently downward until it hits the rotary less than a mile away and Route 24 and the highway to Boston.

"We've had a good life here, but to tell you the truth, I'd like to see my kids leave. What are they going to do around here? Nothing. Fall River was always a great place to bring up kids. One of the things that made it good was that kids could always come back and get good jobs. But there are no opportunities anymore."

She looked out into her backyard, as if suddenly running all the years through her mind. "It sounds crazy, but we lived in another era. It's hard to see it change."

Certainly her husband has changed.

Those close to Skippy Karam knew he had mellowed, that the Skippy of legend largely belonged to the past now, all the old stories, the fiction mixed in with the truth so that nobody really was sure which was which anymore. Take the incident with a camera tripod, for example. One night in the middle of a game, a Durfee player threw the ball away just when a woman was carrying a tripod by the Durfee bench. Skippy grabbed it out of her hand and in a mock gesture threatened to throw it at the player, before handing it back to the woman. A week later the story circulating was that Skip Karam had thrown a TV camera at a player. The price of local fame.

To this day both Al and Michael Herren can recite, virtually word for word, Skippy's so-called "Catholic school" speech, the one he often gives before big games with parochial schools, one that says they think they're better than you, so you should go out and kick their ass. Class consciousness, Durfee basketball style. It was all part of the city's folklore.

Part of his mellowing was inevitable. He had come of age when a coach was larger than life almost by definition. Bear Bryant. Woody Hayes. Red Auerbach. Men cloaked in mystique, dictators with a clipboard. Weren't these the coaches America loved, one part Marine, one part Vince Lombardi, one part genius, one part bluster? Put those pampered athletes in their place, take charge; the kind of coach a father took his boy to and hoped he came back a man.

But all that was changing. Newspaper sports sections around the country were full of stories about collegiate players rebelling against tyrannical coaches. The new breed of professional coach was supposed to be able to "relate" to his players, not browbeat them. For all his success, even Bobby Knight seemed more and more like a dinosaur, clinging to standards and absolute control in an age that seemed to fly in the face of that. The old coach of legend was a dying breed, and Skippy knew it.

"Even the cheerleaders aren't afraid of me anymore," he said one night.

But just when you thought he was some Fall River version of Mr. Chips, some kindly old grandfather figure, complete with white hair and a benign smile, he would do something to remind you that he was still Skippy and the passions still burned.

One day in the preseason he had been remarkably low key for most of the practice, to the point that Nicky Salmon, who had played on the '84 state championship team and was there to watch practice for a while, said, "I can't believe how mellow Mr. Karam is. In the old days he'd be all over them."

We were near the door that led to the locker room. In my hand was a half-full can of Diet Pepsi. We were talking about this and that when all of a sudden Callahan shuffled his feet while making an up-fake underneath the basket.

"Jesus Christ, Danny," Karam yelled, his face grimacing, his lips pursed tightly together. "You're going to drive me crazy."

He stalked over to where we were, grabbed the soda can out of my hand, and in one motion hurled it against the wall. The can went clanging to the floor, the last remains of the soda staining the wood.

"Scratch what I said about mellowing," Salmon said under his breath.

But those close to Skippy also knew he was misunderstood, that the public side was only one side.

One who saw the other was Jack Campbell, who had been his jayvee coach in the early seventies.

"I liked him personally right from in the beginning. I had played against him in high school in the sixties and I knew the reputation. I had heard all the stories. Even then he was a legend. But he was always very funny and he was that way coaching too. I think the people who don't really know Skippy don't know how funny he is. My high school coach had been a screamer too, so that part didn't bother me. I knew it intimidated some kids, especially the ones who weren't used to it. But Skippy never had a bad word to say about a kid. Never. When it was over, it was over.

"Most of the kids didn't take it personally. And there was the sense that since he once called my father an asshole, I guess it's all right that he calls me an asshole too. But there was no question the kids respected him. I never saw anyone give him any backtalk. With me and him it was like good cop, bad cop. I think that's what Skippy looks for in an assistant coach. He knows he's tough and sometimes can hurt kids' feelings, and the assistant coach's job is to soothe them. In '84 Brian O'Neil, who was a great player for us, was a lousy practice player. Skippy was forever throwing him out of practice, then he'd give me the look and I'd go into the locker room and bring him back. When he came back, all was forgiven. That was just Skippy.

"But there's no such thing as an off year at Durfee. No such thing as rebuilding. One year Skippy went something like eleven-and-nine and it was like someone else going oh-and-twenty. There's always pressure because it means so much here. Durfee basketball takes people out of reality for a while."

Campbell thought Karam was going to retire after the '84 state championship season. He was almost fifty then, had been coaching for nearly a quarter of a century, and he could have gone out with a winner. His son Skippy, Jr.—sometimes just shortened to "Junior"—was about to start playing for Durfee and Skippy had a certain ambivalence about coaching him. In retrospect, it was an unfortunate experience for both of them. To Karam, the pressure of coaching his son was great, and he was tougher on him than anyone else, to the extent that he didn't start his son until midway through Skippy, Jr.'s junior year, though everyone in the city had been telling him his son deserved to start months before that. To Skippy, Jr., who now works as a substitute teacher at Durfee while he searches for what to do with his life, playing for his father was difficult. Being the son of a famous father is always difficult, and few fathers are more famous in Fall River than Skip Karam. Playing for him simply added to the difficulty.

Once, Skippy grabbed Skippy, Jr., by the throat, and when Junior complained, his father said, "Go home and complain to your mother." When Skippy got home, nobody would talk to him, his son, his wife, his daughters.

"Even the cat," he said ruefully.

Skippy, Jr., got his retribution, however. It was a game at Bishop Connolly, the Catholic school across the street from Durfee, and when Skippy got thrown out of the game after arguing too vehemently with an official and a policeman was escorting him out of the gym, his son yelled to the cop, "Lock him up."

But Skippy had survived coaching his son, and then had come the Michael Herren era and the back-to-back state championships. On the surface that would have been a perfect time to go out on top, riding off into the coaching sunset with a forty-six-game winning streak, but he didn't. Maybe he wanted to prove that he could keep winning without Michael Herren. Maybe he just wanted to keep coaching, for private reason that not even he could articulate. Who knows?

That's the part of him I don't know. I don't know if anyone knows that part.

It was virtually impossible to visualize Durfee basketball without him, and even the players who sometimes cringed at his one-liners or complained about his tough practices seemed to know that. Skip Karam was Durfee basketball, had been for decades. Most of the players had a deep affection for Karam, as if they intuitively understood that, despite his temper, he was no different than they were, just older; that he too had grown up with the same Fall River dreams.

"I know Mr. Karam will take care of us," said Eric Santos. "I understood that I wasn't going to play much, but Mr. Karam's always been there if I needed anything, and how many high school coaches can you say that about?"

"Skippy never forgets you," said Barry Machado, who played on Karam's first team back in 1961. "I never thought he'd last this long. I thought he'd use his success at Durfee to go to a good small college somewhere. The unfortunate thing is he's ending his career at a time when kids are the least coachable."

It was the last home game of the season, against Brockton.

The seniors were introduced, Pavoa, Mikolazyk, Jones, Cioe, Santos, Boardman, Campbell, Eagan. They walked out to the center of the court bathed in cheers. The senior cheer-leaders were introduced and presented with flowers.

Karam already had given the team a pep talk, reminding them they had been blown out in Brockton, that they had been laughed at and ridiculed, that there were only four games left in the regular season and they couldn't afford any more losses. But he didn't have to say anything Big games got everyone motivated, even the crowd, and senior night only accentuated it. Durfee led by eleven at the half, off to a good start. Once again Herren was dominating the game. Still, the team had a disturbing trend of dying in the second half against good teams, a point Karam tried to stress at half-time.

"Get your asses back on defense," he said. "The guys who are dying out there are the guys who dog it in practice."

His words were to no avail. Midway through the second half Durfee had lost their lead, once again sabatoged by de-fense. With a little over three minutes to play, they were trail-ing by two and called a time-out. Karam's face was a bas-relief of dissatisfaction.

"We're not losing in this gym," Herren screamed to his teammates. He had squirted water over his head, and it rolled down his face, enhancing his intensity. *"We are not losing."*

But he fouled out with 1:26 left to play, Durfee still down by two. Caron already had fouled out. For the first time all year, Durfee was being forced to play meaningful minutes with neither Herren nor Caron in the lineup.

Santos replaced Herren, Karam opting for the experience of a senior, even though Santos had played little all year. With thirty seconds left in the game and Durfee down three, it appeared hopeless. But Mikolazyk was fouled and went to the line for two shots. He made the first, cutting the Brock-ton lead to two, before missing the second shot. But Jones scored off the rebound, tying the game and sending it into overtime. When the ball went in, Jones threw his fist into the air as the field house exploded in a hurricane of noise. It was the biggest basket of his high school career, and he shouted with joy.

Durfee quickly fell behind again in overtime. Down one, Mikolazyk was fouled and missed the front end of a one-and-one. Seconds later he was fouled again, again missed the front end of another one-and-one. Seeing the ball hit the rim and bounce away, Karam muttered, almost to himself, "He couldn't be a hero. The poor little bugger couldn't be a hero."

They were down three in the closing seconds when, incredibly, Mikolazyk was fouled again, this time in the act of shooting. He would have three foul shots. He would have a chance to redeem himself.

He went to the foul line as the field house quieted. He bounced the ball, tried to settle himself, telling himself he had a chance to make amends for the two previous misses. It was the most pressurized moment he'd ever been in as a basketball player, here in his last home game as a Durfee player, the game hanging in the balance. This was one of the things he'd fantasized about as a young kid with Fall River dreams, practicing alone on the playgrounds, but now that it was finally here he felt nervous, as though everything was happening too quickly. He took a deep breath and shot. The ball went in as the cheers exploded around him. Down two now, with two shots left. He bounced the ball again, took another deep breath, and let fire. It hit the rim and bounced away. Karam quickly called time-out.

Mikolazyk came to the bench in tears. Herren hugged him.

It was one more indication that beneath all the attention that swirled around Chris, beneath the teenage machismo and the defenses he'd created to ward off the world that too often seemed to be zeroing in on him, there was a sensitivity to him that often went unnoticed. He was never so good as when little kids were around him. Moments before the game had started, a group of them had come over to him as he stood in front of the bench. He had made sure he touched every one of them, even though he'd been preoccupied with the upcoming game, the fact that it was his last home game of the season. It had been a small moment, but a telling one too, for I often had the sense that Chris's true character was revealed more in what he did, than what he said; was revealed more in small gestures like these, ones he made instinctively, then in public ones that were more studied; was revealed more in the small kindnesses he continually offered his friends, than in the personna of being Chris Herren, high school basketball star.

Now, in the midst of all the drama of the last home game, one he so desperately wanted to win, he sensed Mikolazyk's pain and reached out to him. All around him was noise and the swirl of tension, but he seemed to be in some private place, just Chris and Kevin Mikolazyk, his friend since childhood. He put his arms around Mikolazyk and told him it was all right, giving him consolation.

Karam too came over to Mikolazyk.

"Hey," he said, putting his hands on Mikolazyk's shoulders. "You didn't lose this game for us."

Mikolazyk sat down on the bench, the tears still rolling down his face. All he knew was that in the biggest moment of his Durfee career, he had failed; that after all the years and all the practices and all the hours he had spent shooting a basketball, when it came to the one free throw he had to make, he had missed. A couple of months later he would admit that he hadn't been in the best of shape, that he hadn't really done what he should have done as a player to get himself ready for moments such as these, that all those things Michael Herren had warned him about in the summer had been true, but now he sat slumped on the bench, disconsolate, as the game went on in front of him.

Durfee was still down two with seven seconds remaining. Karam's strategy was to foul immediately, hoping for a last-second miracle. So after Mikolazyk made his last free throw to cut the Brockton lead to one, Durfee quickly fouled, and when Brockton only made one of their free throws, then quickly fouled, mirabile dictu, Durfee was down two with two seconds remaining and a chance to shoot one-and-one from the foul line. Karam's strategy had worked.

At the line was the most improbable of potential heroes, little-used senior Chris Campbell, who once upon a time had been one of the Durfee ball boys. He was the son of Jack Campbell, a Durfee physical education teacher who had been the jayvee coach. One night, when Chris had been about nine, he and his father were driving home after a game in which Karam had been particularly demonstrative on the sidelines.

"Chris asked me about Skippy's swearing," Campbell said, "and how that wasn't good, was it, Dad? And I said no, that wasn't good, and someday Mr. Karam would be punished for it. So Chris looks at me and says, 'Dad, if you get punished for swearing, how come he won the state championship last year?' I just turned the radio up."

The Campbells live in Somerset and Chris undoubtedly would have been a starter if he had stayed home and attended Somerset High School. But he had wanted to go to Durfee, and now had no regrets, even though he rarely got off the bench. He had made great friends, being particularly close to Caron, and was ranked sixteenth in his class. In a couple of months he would receive the annual Tanous Karam Scholarship, which the Karam brothers give every year to one of the outstanding senior student-athletes in the school. But now he was at the free throw line in the last few seconds of his last home game, the biggest moment of his high school career.

He bounced the ball a couple of times, paused, bounced it again, and let it fly.

It hit the rim and bounded away. Durfee had lost in overtime, 77–75. They were now 13–4 on the season, but 0–3 in the Big Three which included New Bedford and Brockton.

There were no tears this time, and little remorse. Everyone knew this had been an unbelievable finish, something that would have strained the talents of a scriptwriter. It also was the first time all year that the team had accomplished anything with Herren and Caron both on the bench, a fact Karam emphasized to George Darmody of the *Herald News* after the game. He was proud of his team, that they had fought back, had shown great character in the closing minutes.

Karam came in to the locker room. He was calm, soothing, once again at his best with his team after they had lost a difficult game.

"Forget it," he said. "We got some bad bounces. This one's history already."

It had started out as snow, turned to sleet, and now was a hard, driving rain coming out of a fog that seemed to bring the world in closer, a miserable February day in New England. There were still a few inches of snow on the ground turning into slush when Herren came walking up the driveway that led from Elsbree Street to the field house. The yellow school bus was nearby, getting ready to go to New Bedford, as he walked into the field house and headed for the locker room. He was wearing jeans, a tan jacket, his white hat with COCKS on the front and black Reebok sneakers. He had just walked the few blocks from home and his clothes were wet.

"Mr. Karam's making me bring my own stuff," he said. "He said I couldn't get on the bus unless he saw me carrying my own stuff."

At the bottom of his locker was his red road uniform, all crumpled up. He grabbed it and began walking out of the locker room.

"Where's your sneakers?" I asked.

"I'm wearing them," he said.

"The ones that you just walked over here in?"

"I only got one pair, bro," he said. "I wear them in school, I play in them. They're molded to my feet."

"How about socks? Don't you have any socks?"

"I don't wear them."

"How about a jock?"

"I don't use one. I've never used one."

"How about a towel?"

He thought for a second.

"Someone will have one," he said, walking out of the locker room, holding his crumpled uniform in one hand.

Chris Herren was ready to play against New Bedford.

The bus pulled out onto Elsbree Street, took a left on President Avenue, and then quickly entered into the rotary that led to Route 24. It went south on Route 24 a couple of miles, past North Watuppa pond and the old Fall River Water Works on the left, then on to Interstate 195, the highway from Providence to Cape Cod. Off to the right was Westport and the road to Horseneck Beach. To the left was miles of scrub pine. The bus went through Westport, then Dartmouth, then took a right on an access road that led to route six and the road into New Bedford.

It is a city steeped in history, one that began in the mid-seventeenth century when thirty-six settlers, among them Miles Standish, John Alden, William Bradford, and others instrumental in the Plymouth Colony which was only about twenty miles away, bought some land from an Indian chief named Massasoit, a large parcel of land that now includes New Bedford, Dartmouth, Fairhaven, Achushnet, and Westport. They were independent settlers, looking for more autonomy than the Plymouth Colony allowed.

By the middle of the eighteenth century there was shipbuilding in New Bedford, and whaling began as early as 1765. The American Revolution put a stop to that as the British burned Bedford village to the ground, and it would be 1785 before another whaling boat set sail. By then the village was called New Bedford, to distinguish it from another town north of Boston, and by 1820 whaling in New Bedford had entered its golden age. By the middle of the century it was the largest whaling city in the world with ten thousand men employed and 329 ships.

It was a prosperous time, and New Bedford then was one of the richest cities per capita in the world. Its city seal said *Lucem Diffundo*—"We Light the World"—a tribute to whale oil that was making the city rich and many of the Quaker shipowners millionaires. The city centered exclusively along the waterfront. In fact, the city had evolved along the Acushnet River that flowed from the Atlantic Ocean on the south toward the north. The leading families were Quakers and many lived on County Street at the top of the hill that overlooked the harbor. During the first half of the nineteenth century New Bedford was a key stop on the Underground Railroad, the odyssey that took runaway slaves from the south to freedom in Canada. One of them was Frederick Douglass, who ultimately would become one of the great African-American leaders of his generation. It was in New Bedford that he found his first freedom, arriving in 1837 with his new wife Anna and working for four years on one of the wharves. It was also in New Bedford that Douglass first met the famed abolitionist William Lloyd Garrison and began to speak out against the evils of slavery.

It was a boisterous time in New Bedford, a carnival of humanity, complete with sailors who came and went, shipowners, shipbuilders, prostitutes, socialities who lived at the top of the hill overlooking the entire spectacle, and everyone in between. A whaling voyage could take as long as three or four years, travelling virtually around the world, so New Bedford became a hodgepodge of different architectural styles and ethnic influences, many of which had arrived from distant places.

The American classic *Moby Dick* was published in 1861. Herman Melville, who had once lived in New Bedford, described the city this way:

The town itself is perhaps the dearest place to live in New England. . . . [N]owhere in all of America will you find more patrician-like houses; parks and gardens more opulent, than in New Bedford. Whence came they? . . . All those brave houses and flowery gardens came from the Atlantic, Pacific and Indian Oceans. One and all they were harpooned and dragged up hither from the bottom of the sea.

By the 1880s whaling was an industry in decline. The scarcity of whales made for longer and more dangerous voyages, as far away as the Indian Ocean. The discovery of petroleum in Pennsylvania in 1859 had hurt the market for whale oil. By the end of the century the city had made the transformation from whaling to textiles, with as many as fifty brick mills dotting the skyline.

For New Bedford and neighboring Fall River, the time between the late 1880s and World War I was an economic boom for the textile industry, but the problems that plagued Fall River's textile economy—poor management, outdated physical plants, the reluctance to put profits back into the mills—were a death knell in New Bedford too. When the Depression arrived with a vengeance, many of the mills already were out of business, both formerly wealthy cities facing the same social problems.

In many ways New Bedford never recovered. Its dropout rate is one of the worst in the state, under 50 percent of its residents having complete high school. It suffers from high unemployment, over 13 percent, with over a thousand jobs lost in the greater New Bedford area in 1992 alone.

A week after the basketball game, there would be a riot in the 165-year-old Bristol County House of Corrections, located in a residential neighborhood on the west side of the city, the jail being one of the oldest in the country still in use. The inmates, protesting the jail's conditions, armed with homemade shanks, needles, and syringes, set fire to the jail and tossed food into the courtyard, screaming for their rights. It took more than a hundred police, some armed with shotguns, to bring the disturbance under control.

Then there is the legacy of Big Dan's.

In the early 1980s six men were accused of gang-raping a woman in Big Dan's, a New Bedford bar in the north section of the city, complete with allegations that men had been cheering while the woman was being raped. The case attracted national attention and was eventually the basis for the Jodie Foster movie, *The Accused*. The fact that the six men were Portuguese only made the case more incendiary, for it resurrected a lot of anti-Portuguese sentiment.

In March 1984 over sixteen thousand marchers filled the streets of New Bedford with a candlelight vigil one night and Fall River the next, in protest against the guilty verdicts given to two of the defendants. The overwhelming majority of the marchers were Portuguese, who claimed the verdicts reflected prejudice against Portuguese immigrants. No matter that the victim, the district attorney, and many of the police investigators and jurors also were of Portuguese descent. The case was a lightning rod for repressed hostility and ethnic anger. The march in Fall River was accompanied by helicopters and police in riot gear. Two of the acquitted defendants joined the procession and were met with scattered applause along the parade route.

There was widespread sentiment in the Portuguese community in both cities that the media gave the case so much attention simply because the accused were Portuguese. There also was sentiment that this publicity expanded the charges against the six men into an indictment of the entire Portuguese community; that it resurrected prejudice against them both for their unfamiliarity with the language and their different culture; that they had to endure ethnic slurs and scores of Big Dan's jokes, their values and way of life under siege.

The trial was held in Fall River in March 1984 and received more national attention than any other local trial since Lizzie Borden's 102 years earlier. In fact, the site of the trial eventually became a negative for Fall River, in that the dateline on all the newspaper stories said Fall River, giving the impression that the rape had happened there. Some civic leaders thought that the combination of the Big Dan's trial and the Lizzie Borden case had made Fall River seem like a city of "just millworkers who have no culture or leisure pursuits."

The Big Dan's case was followed by a string of mysterious murders of young women, whose bodies were found in the woods of southeastern Massachusetts, another story that made the national news.

But New Bedford had a bright side too. In the seventies, thanks to a combination of civic pride and government money, the run-down waterfront area was restored and revitalized. Buildings were moved. Restaurants opened. There is an air of gentrification now, but not an inauthentic, plastic one. The Whaling Museum and the Seamen's Bethel sit on Johnnycake Hill, just as they always have. Downtown New Bedford now is the sound of sea gulls and the smell of ocean, narrow streets that summon the past. The historic district along County Street is an architectural textbook, with houses done in several styles of the different eras in the city's history: Federal, Greek Revival, Victorian, Gothic.

There's still an active fishing industry, as there has been for over two hundred years, though it's recently fallen on hard times. For years the high school was downtown, an old yellow brick building with a view of the harbor, next door to the courthouse where Lizzie Borden had been acquitted.

New Bedford High School is now in the western end of the city, a large, red-brick, sprawling structure that looks suburban. The gym is in the middle of the complex with a separate entrance. It is large, with the two grandstands pushed far back from the court, creating the impression of space. There are red banners on the walls, with three for state championship teams in 1940, 1946, and 1961. In the thirty-two years since New Bedford has won its last state title, Durfee and Skip Karam have won five.

Dempsey's jayvee team was getting pasted, going down to their worst defeat of the year. The New Bedford jayvees were younger imitations of the varsity, a lot of quick, thin black kids who pressed throughout the game, controlled the game's tempo. To Karam, this jayvee game seemed to represent everything he always feared about New Bedford as the years changed and the players' names changed, their quickness and their defensive pressure. The Durfee varsity players seemed oblivious. They saw no portents in jayvee games. To them, the jayvee game was just something to sit through before their game started. They sprawled on the bleachers across the court from the two benches, then left midway through the second half and went into the locker room.

As Herren came through the door, he was hit by a beach ball.

"Igor, you little bugger," he yelled, as Mikolazyk ducked behind one of the dressing stalls.

Herren grabbed the ball and chased him in the shower room as Mikolazyk cowered in the corner. Herren threw the ball at him, then got hit himself again by Pavao, who had retrieved the ball. The three started chasing each other through the various stalls, into the shower room, then back again. For a moment they seemed like young kids, lost in the exuberance of play, oblivious that they were minutes away from playing one of their biggest games of the year, a game in which reputations have been made and broken in Fall River.

Minutes later Herren stood in the middle of the room wearing only red-plaid boxer shorts. He pulled his red uniform trunks over them, slicked back his hair with some water. He felt ready. He had spent his entire life hearing about big New Bedford games, about how until you do it against New Bedford it's merely the equivalent of a pregame layup drill. So it didn't make any difference that New Bedford already had clinched the Big Three title, or that there really was no significance to this game. It was Durfee–New Bedford and that was more than enough. The Whalers were 15–2 on the season, losing only to St. Anthony's of Jersey City, New Jersey, and an Andover team they defeated by twenty in a rematch. They had won nine straight.

Herren also had a personal score to settle. After the first New Bedford game at Durfee, the one in which he'd had the great first half and had tired in the second, Coach Eddie Rodrigues had said afterward that Jeff Correia had shut Herren down, a remark that got played up in the *Herald News*. Herren knew better, knew he had tired, that the excitement and exertion of the first half had robbed him of the little something extra he usually possessed. He had picked up the paper the next day and couldn't *believe* what Rodrigues had said. *Shit*, he thought, *Correia couldn't stop me if he had a gun.* He vowed to make amends tonight, to prove to Rodrigues and all of New Bedford that all of this talk about Correia was just New Bedford bullshit.

He wasted little time.

In the first half alone he hit five three-pointers, three of them coming from NBA range, as he showed that his long-distance shooting, thought to be the weakest part of his game, had gotten much better as the season had progressed. He scored from the outside, he scored on powerful drives to the basket, he even scored when he caught a pass over his head that was going out of bounds and, contorting his body in the air, somehow managed to get the ball into the basket before his momentum carried him off the court. Once again he was off in some personal zone, someplace where time seemed to slow down, the private place he entered when everything was going right and he felt invincible, able to make every shot, unstoppable. At these times he was completely focused, oblivious to everything else, completely absorbed in the game and its unique rhythms. It was an incredible performance, made all the more dramatic by the fact that he was doing it in a sold-out New Bedford gym.

Caron also started off strong and, unbelievably, the two of them scored thirty-three of Durfee's first thirty-five points.

Durfee led by six at the half, and this time they didn't tire in the second half, never losing the lead and winning 87–78.

Herren finished with forty points, nineteen rebounds, and seven assists, his best game of the season, and afterward he stood in the middle of the court in his rumpled red uniform being interviewed by a local cable television network, saying that he felt great, that anytime you beat New Bedford you feel great. Caron ended with nineteen, most of which came in the first half, when Durfee had taken control of the game. Maybe just as important, Callahan and Jones also had great games, dominating the backboards, maybe their best game collectively of the year. The next day a column would be written on them in the *Herald News*, next to two large action shots of Herren and Caron, referring to Callahan and Jones as unsung heroes, lost in the shuffle of all the attention focused on Herren and Caron.

"You've made my year," Karam told the team in the locker room. "Thank you."

He went over to Herren and gave him a hug.

"Hey, Chrissie," he said. "Want me to carry your bag for you? Tonight I will."

The locker room was ebullient, as celebratory as it had been all year. Herren came out of the showers, toweled off, put on the same red-plaid underwear that he had just worn in the game, covered them with his baggy jeans, and slicked back his hair.

Mitch Lown, a former player in the mid-1980s who had begun helping out every day in practice, watched him.

"Let me tell you," he said, with a knowing smile, "when

you get forty against New Bedford, you can have a good time in Fall River. A *real* good time. You get forty against New Bedford, and you're immortal in Fall River forever."

The team walked out of the locker room together into the still-jammed lobby. More people were lined outside, some with their faces pressed against the glass. Two policemen walked up to Herren, began to escort him out to the bus.

"Stand next to me," he said to them.

He walked out between the two policemen in the rain, through the gauntlet of people, and onto the bus, where Whitney Houston's version of "I Will Always Love You" reverberated.

The bus pulled out of the parking lot, the rain streaking the windows, shadowing everything inside. Karam leaned back in his seat and closed his eyes as the motor droned and the young voices in the back mingled into unintelligible noise. He had beaten New Bedford, and for the first time all day he started to relax, could feel his stomach loosen. There was maybe nothing he liked better in coaching than beating New Bedford, for he knew that there were many people in Fall River who still believed that this game was the only important measuring stick of a successful season, outside of winning a state title. The bus was on Route 195, almost to Fall River, sheets of rain still slapping against the side, when three cars came up alongside it and stayed.

"Mr. Karam," called out Santos. "There's some cars out here that are acting strange."

"Good guys or bad guys?" Karam yelled back.

"Bad guys," said Santos.

Karam knew enough to take the idea of three unfamiliar cars seriously, for the threat of violence always hovered over a Durfee–New Bedford game like thunderheads on a July afternoon. The cars stayed alongside the bus.

"You got a radio on this thing?" Karam said to the driver. "Call ahead and tell them to have the police meet us at the school."

There was concern on his face. *It never can be easy*, he thought. *It's always got to be something.* The highway was dark; the rain continued to splash against the windshield.

The bus took a right onto Route 24, the cars still surrounding it, but as the bus took a right turn onto President Avenue and the rotary toward Durfee, the three cars continued north on Route 24.

Karam let out a deep breath.

"Do you believe I only get about four thousand dollars a year for this shit?" he said. "I must be crazy."

He had decided to quit after one more year, had already told Dempsey and a few close friends. He was fifty-eight years old, in his thirty-third year of coaching, and he'd had enough. Enough of the bus rides with the bad music, enough of the practices, enough of the battles with kids that never seemed to get any better, only worse. Most of all, he'd had enough of the pressure, the unrelenting pressure that only seemed to increase the older he got. So he would retire after next season, go out with Chris Herren, along with Abe White, who also planned to retire.

Most people close to him thought it was a good decision. What else was there to prove? What else was there to win? He didn't seem to enjoy it as much as he once did, and the consensus around the city was that Skippy had mellowed, that he wasn't as tough as he once had been. Part of that undoubtedly was age. But part of it too was that coaching was more difficult now. Kids chafed at any kind of discipline, resented it, questioned it. He saw it every day in so many ways. The clothes they wore to school. The way they talked back to teachers. The lack of structure in the school itself, an erosion of the values that he had grown up with and that once had been so much a part of his life as a teacher.

"The parents can't control them and the school can't control them," he liked to say. "What's the coach supposed to do?"

Still, he tried, for he knew no other way, even if he knew that he was a dinosaur, that he belonged to another era, one that already had ended. He had been shaped by Lukey, had begun coaching in a time when the coach's word was law, inviolate, a court with no appeals. *A coach without discipline has nothing.* It was one of his personal mantras, one of the codes upon which his entire career had been based. Yet discipline now was tougher to maintain, because everything else in society seemed to refute it, and there was the sense that Skippy Karam's basketball court might just be the only place where these kids got any discipline at all.

Most high school coaches dealt with the new reality by acquiescing to the players, letting them do what they wanted to, realizing that to try to discipline them certainly wasn't worth the aggravation and probably wouldn't work anyway. Either that or they tried to be the players' friends, hoping to influence them with subtle pressure. Skippy did neither.

There was little question in Skippy's mind that his coaching style wouldn't have worked in a lot of communities, probably wouldn't work in Fall River if he were some young hotshot coach hired from another town. Parents wouldn't let it work. School administrators wouldn't let it work. He would have sworn at some kid, the parents would have complained, and that would have been it. He survived for one reason only: He was Skippy Karam in Fall River.

So when Callahan made the mistake of talking to his father on the side of the court during halftime of the Brockton game, Karam was all over him the next day at practice. "Danny, there's no use asking your old man for advice; he couldn't play either."

Dempsey had winced at that one. He got nervous when Skippy made references to parents, for he knew that was potential trouble. One time Skippy had told freshman Colin Crist that he was stupid, then stopped himself and added, "Now, don't you go running home and tell your parents I called you stupid."

Dempsey also felt the pressure of Karam's retirement decision. On one hand he wanted to be a head coach, be his own boss. He once had been, at Bristol Community College in the city, before that school had dropped the sport. Yet he knew that following Skippy was not going to be easy, no matter who did it. Coaches who followed legends invariably got carried out on their shields, victims of too many comparisons, too many expectations.

He wondered how he would deal with the inevitable second-guessing, for he had been around Skippy long enough to know that there was a downside that came with coaching Durfee. There were the parents of the kids you had to cut, or the ones who didn't play enough, or didn't get enough shots. And unless you won a state title, or at least got to the Boston Garden for the semifinals, there was the feeling you had somehow failed. A couple of years ago he figured it might be best to coach somewhere else, maybe in one of the suburban towns that ring Fall River, because being a jayvee coach was essentially frustrating; but deep down he knew that if he one day had the opportunity to coach Durfee and didn't do it, he would always regret it.

Durfee came back to win a four-team tournament in Sharon, a suburb of Boston, to conclude their regular season record at 16–4.

Once again Herren was great, picking up another MVP trophy, one more example that he'd gotten better as the season had progressed. He also moved into second place on the all-time Durfee scoring list with 1,357 points, passing Kevin Whiting and trailing only his brother Michael. In the second game of the tournament, against the host team, which included the son of former NBA player Gerald Henderson, some of the Sharon students behind one of the benches began yelling at him as soon as the game started. It was the price of his growing notoriety, something his brother had gone through his entire senior year. So every time he scored for the rest of the game he pointed to them, which only made them yell all the more. At one point he and Germaine Henderson started jawing at each each other, and during a free throw at the other end of the floor Herren went over and put his face into Henderson's.

"What was that all about, Chrissie?" Karam had asked later.

"I told him to pawn some of his father's championship rings," he said.

Karam just shook his head.

Now it was time to prepare for the state tournament, the focus of the entire season. It was the reason Karam felt the pressure grow as the season progressed. The players lived in their present-tense world, oblivious to what lay ahead. Karam knew differently. He knew that this team, this season, would be judged solely by how it did in the state tournament. If they got upset in one of the early rounds or didn't make it to the Boston Garden, this season would be quickly forgotten, one of those that didn't deserve to be immortalized by banners on the field house wall.

Karam's early fears about his team still existed today. He knew it wasn't a great team. After a great player in Herren, and very good one in Caron, there was no one he could really depend on. Callahan had improved, was scoring more, but he still didn't rebound much, wasn't physical. Jones battled, but was limited offensively. The high point of Mikolazyk's season had been in the Lowell Tournament during Christmas week; he still started, but now his deficiencies were more noticeable. His lack of height hurt him in the press. He never had been an expert ball handler anyway, and now he wasn't shooting as well as he had earlier in the season. Karam thought about replacing him with Pavao, but it was late in the season, the team was playing better, and he was reluctant to change. He even considered replacing him with Steve

Josephs, a jayvee kid who'd been shooting very well recently, but he hadn't played in a varsity game.

After that?

Cioe's time had declined since Jones had come back, for though they were similar players, Jones was bigger. Shawn Thames still was an enigma. He had more potential than both of them, but he was still a kid, immature, with little savvy as a player. He occasionally missed practice, and always missed Sunday practices because his grandmother made him go to church. Some nights he played well with the jayvee team, some nights it was as though he wasn't there. There were times in practice when he dominated both Callahan and Jones, more athletic than either of them, but the most he'd played all year was against Duxbury in the first game of the season, when the pressure of the situation had overwhelmed him.

It was a fragile team. Karam kept waiting for Herren to emerge as a true leader, off the court as well as on it, but it hadn't happened. One day at the end of practice, the team running their customary wind sprints, Chris had been near last, obviously loafing, expending the least amount of energy possible.

"He's always got to push it," Karam muttered to Dempsey. "He's always got to test me. How much shit am I supposed to take?"

He knew Caron was frustrated, unhappy that he spent too much time in the corner waiting for a ball that rarely came. He could feel his own anxiety start to increase, for he didn't need a schedule to tell him it was tournament time. His stomach told him.

But when the pairings for the state tournament were announced, New Bedford and Brockton in one half of the South Sectional draw and Durfee in the other, with what looked like a clear run to the sectional finals, Karam got his hopes up. He had been wary of having to beat both Brockton and New Bedford again, but now, through a fortuitous schedule, he knew he could avoid at least one of them. He looked at the tournament and saw it wide open.

"I'd love to get these kids to the Garden," he said one afternoon before practice. "I'd love to get Chrissie to the Garden."

There was an eleven-day layoff before the tournament started, and Karam had given the team a few days off. Now it was back to the laboratory on this day in late February, back to the gym, at a time in the season when everyone was sick of the gym.

"Danny," he yelled at Callahan for the thousandth time. "Get a rebound. Break your record."

When Callahan again failed to get a rebound, Thames beating him to the ball, Karam covered his face with his hands. "Danny, I haven't laid anyone out in thirty years. You might be the first."

Here it is near the end of the season, thought Karam, *and I'm dealing with the same shit I've been dealing with since November.* He stood at center court, intently watching his team, and the more he watched, the angrier he got, for he knew there was no more time for mistakes, that in tournament time the line between who wins and who doesn't is a fine one. So when Callahan put a back screen on Herren's man and Herren cut to the basket wide open and Mikolazyk didn't throw him the ball, he'd seen enough.

"Gore, did you see him?" he said.

Mikolazyk nodded.

"Then why didn't you give him the ball?"

"I didn't want to," Mikolazyk said.

"You didn't want to. Who the hell are you?" Karam said, frowning. "I wanted you to."

Mikolazyk glared at him.

"Is that your tough look, Gore?" Karam snapped back. "Am I supposed to be afraid? Gore, I know you broke the all-time turnover record even though you only played a year,

278 ......

but when Chrissie's open, you give him the ball. Or else you sit down and watch someone else do it. Let's go, run it again."

They ran the same play. Callahan set a back screen on Herren's man. Herren broke to the basket. But Mikolazyk's pass was too high, threw Herren off stride, making him knock into Thames and lose his balance. Herren took the ball and slammed it angrily off the backboard.

"That's it," Karam said disgustedly. "Start running."

He walked over to Dempsey as the players ran around the court.

"They look tired, Skippy," Dempsey said.

"Bobby, if you spent every weekend drinking, you'd look tired too," he countered.

Practice ended soon after.

Karam had learned long ago to shorten the length of the practices as the season progressed. The season was too wearing, both physically and emotionally, to continue having long practices. He also had learned to vary the practices, to try to keep the players interested and focused, rather than running the same routines day after day. Some days they would have shooting games, the squad split up into teams headed by Herren and Caron, the losing team having to run laps. Anything to break up the monotony of playing against the same faces every day.

"You know what's the worst part now?" Karam said, leaning back in the first row of the bleachers as the players took foul shots. "Everyone's saying that we're already in the South Sectional final. I know we have a chance to get there, but doing it is another story. So many things can happen in a single-elimination tournament. One bad game and you're history."

Durfee, seeded fifth in the South Sectionals, had its first game of the tournament in its own field house against Plymouth.

But that was not the big news. The big news was the rumor the players had shaved their heads, their public statement that it was tournament time, time to get serious.

"I haven't seen anyone yet, but if they really did it, it's stupid," Dempsey said, sitting in the small coach's office off the locker room, about an hour and a half before the game was to start. "Because it really doesn't mean anything. It would be better if they all said they weren't going to drink throughout the tournament. That would mean something. This means nothing."

Last year's team had sworn off drinking in a last-ditch attempt to dedicate themselves. Now this year's team had shaved their heads.

On one level it was a form of adolescent solidarity. On another, it was a way of saying they were unique, for no Durfee team ever had done it before. It demonstrated the pressure all Durfee teams faced to establish their own identity, a task that got more difficult all the time. How could you be different when every script seemed to already have been played out and everyone remembered all of them? How could you stand out when Michael Herren's teams had won forty-six straight games? How could you gain your own little sliver of Durfee immortality when anything you might accomplish already had been accomplished? How? You shaved your heads, something no Durfee team ever had done.

At least that's what Herren and Caron had come up with. They had been thinking of something to do for the tournament, something to bring everyone together. Then one day in school, during something called "Career Day," they were walking around talking about the team.

"I think we should all shave our heads," Caron said.

"No fuckin' way," Herren said.

"Think about it," Caron said. "Everyone with a shaved head. We'll look like cuckoo clocks. Other teams we'll see us and think we're all crazy, like maniacs."

Herren thought about it for a second, then a gleam came into his eyes.

"Yeah," he said, his voice growing more excited. "Yeah. Yeah. I like it." Mikolazyk had been easy to convince. So had Pavao. Cioe had a crew cut anyway, so he didn't see it as any big deal.

They all had met after school and gone to Pete Fastino's barbershop on Robeson Street, a major street that ran from President Avenue south into downtown. "Pete the Tweet on Robison Street," as the shop was unofficially called. Fastino had been cutting the hair of many of them since they were young kids, and now every time Herren came into the shop for a haircut, he asked Fastino, "Who is the greatest player in Durfee history?"

"Brian O'Neil," Fastino would say—or Kevin Whiting, or Ernie Fleming, or Michael Herren. Anybody but Chris Herren.

"Yeah, right," Herren would say, laughing.

On this day Herren had jumped into the chair first.

"What do you want?" Fastino asked. "Your typical schmuck cut? Once around the block, nice and tight?"

"Everything off," Herren said. "All of it."

Then came Caron. After that, there was no turning back. They had even dropped by Callahan's house, eleven of them, shaming him into also shaving his head.

Now Herren and Caron came into the locker room, saw Dempsey, who only shook his head and laughed.

"Does Mr. Karam know?" Herren asked. "How pissed is he?"

Karam did know by this time, and he wasn't happy about it. He saw it as a distraction when they should be focused on the game, another example of the immaturity and foolishness he felt permeated the team, the lack of genuine leadership.

A few minutes earlier he had met with Dempsey and expressed his surprise with the shaved heads.

"I heard they were going to do it," Dempsey said, trying to downplay it.

"I guess everyone heard they were going to do it, except Skippy," Karam said.

He walked next door into the trainer's room and looked at several of the players who were getting taped.

"This is a first," he said.

The players were silent.

He turned to Suneson, the closest player to him.

"Peter, do you know what an asshole you look like?" he said disgustedly.

He came farther into the room, walked over to Callahan, and pulled a red bandanna off his head, revealing a skinned head. "You know something, Danny, you were ugly before. Now you're ridiculous."

He shook his head and walked out of the room. *It never stops*, he thought. *The shit never stops.*

A half hour later he went into the players' locker room, the large cage at the end of the area across from the shower room. In front of him were twelve kids, all with shaved heads, some still raw, their heads covered with small cuts.

"You better back up what you did," he said. "Because you're turning this into a circus. Ringling Brothers. You better back up what you did."

He paused, went over to the blackboard at the front of the room, thought better of it, then came back. The players sat on two benches on both sides of him. He knew he had to forget about the shaved heads, that to dwell any more on them would be self-defeating. He had said his piece; now it was time to move on. He wanted to tell the players what he long ago came to know, that they would ultimately be remembered for what they did in the state tournament, nothing else, and if that wasn't necessarily fair, that was the way it was.

"Some people in this city have you in the finals already," he finally said. "If you're thinking like that, you're stupid. If you're thinking like that, you're dead. Because of who you are, you're a double target. Everyone wants us badly. So be prepared. Shit, be overprepared."

He paused again, looked over at Dempsey.

"You got anything, Bobby?"

Dempsey shook his head.

Karam turned back to his players, the room still. He looked at them for a moment. When he started to speak, his voice was soft.

"Fellas, you're another in a long line of Durfee teams in the state tournament. And the people in this city support you like they do nowhere else. Don't let them down. Don't let yourselves down. It's tournament time. *Let's go.*"

The players exploded from the benches, gathered around Karam, joining their hands over their heads.

Tournament time.

Chapter

11

CARON CAME INTO the locker room at halftime shaking his head, even though Durfee was leading Plymouth by ten at the half.

"What's the matter with you?" Herren asked.

"We're playing like shit," Caron said.

"If you weren't throwing the ball away so much, we'd be playing better."

"Fuck you," Caron shot back defiantly.

"You're talking to me like that?" Herren said, walking over to Caron.

Caron stared back at him.

Herren pushed him. Caron pushed him back. It was quickly broken up before Karam came into the room. Their conflict was a reflection of both the tension that now hovered over the team and Caron's continuing frustration. For though he was averaging nineteen points a game and already had broken the all-time Durfee three-point shooting record, he hadn't particularly enjoyed the season. The ankle problems. The offense that all too often had him buried in the corner waiting for the ball that never seem to come at the right time, if it came at all. The lack of interest from any Division I schools while Herren's celebrity grew with each passing game. It all had taken its psychic toll.

There were times he seemed to overcompensate by trying to do a little too much—the spectacular pass, the clever dribble—things he hadn't done the year before when his steadiness, along with his shooting ability, had been his greatest assets. Occasionally, his attempts at creativity backfired, for the core of his game was old-school, solid, fundamentally sound. They were the qualities he admired in other players. He liked the way Larry Bird had played, the old Celtics, a style based on teamwork and solid basketball, not the flash and dash of the way the game was now played.

Now here was another game in which he was frustrated and feeling left out. Not that he was mad at Chris. He wasn't. Secretly, he was mad at Karam for allowing it to happen. But he wasn't going to back down from Chris either, wasn't going to let Chris intimidate him the way he thought Chris intimidated the others.

But as quickly as the incident happened, it subsided.

As they left the locker room, Herren came over to Caron. "Sorry about that," he said. "It was my fault."

Shortly into the second half Herren gave Caron a pass and he quickly buried a jump shot. They slapped palms as they came back up the floor.

Just before the end of the game, Durfee holding a comfortable lead, Herren dunked on a fast break and threw his fist into the air as the crowd roared, the exclamation point on Durfee's first victory in the state tournament, 81–61. He had finished with thirty. Caron had added sixteen and Callahan and Mikolazyk had chipped in with eleven apiece.

But the big news was their skinned heads.

"I didn't know who I was passing to." Caron quipped. "Everyone looked the same. Imagine if we had lost tonight and had to look at each other for the next couple weeks. If we had lost, people would have said we were too ugly to win."

Durfee's second tournament game, the quarterfinals of the South Sections, was at Brockton. The opponent was Braintree, a town to the south of Boston, best known for its large mall that sits at the corner of routes 3 and 128. Karam had told the players that Braintree was a good team, that they had upset Newton North by twenty in a controlled game, but when Braintree came out on the court about an hour and a half before the game to casually shoot around and get used to the gym, they seemed less than physically imposing, one player having what looked like a towel wrapped around his head. Skippy was nervous. It was still over an hour before the game, and already the players had shot around, had changed into their red road uniforms. He knew they had left Fall River too early; he didn't like to spend too much time in the locker room, seeing the tension build. He had learned over the years that all it did was make everyone more nervous, including himself. He liked to arrive, change, play. He also didn't like the fact that this was another game Durfee was supposed to win rather comfortably, the pressure all on him and his team.

"I don't know anything about this team other than it's a 'mall team'—a town that has a big mall—and that mall teams always suck," Caron said. "Taunton. Dartmouth. Swansea. They all have good malls and their teams all suck. Maybe that's why we're good. Because our mall sucks."

He sat on a bench in his red uniform. Vic Ortiz, the Brockton coach, came into the room to say hello. A few minutes later Karam stood at the blackboard. He went over the scouting report, then gave them a long look.

"No one's going to give us anything, fellas," he said. "This guy does a good job coaching them. They play like a team."

He paused, gathering his thoughts.

"All right, if things don't go right, we've had a great season. And I want to thank the seniors. If there's anything I can do for you guys in the future, come and see me. If I can help you with a job, or anything. Don't forget to come back."

He meant this. He thought of Durfee basketball as one big extended family, a tree that stretched back through the decades. You were not just a Durfee player when you were in high school. You were a Durfee player forever, part of the tradition.

He looked at this watch, said it was time. The team came together, their hands over their heads. There was a moment of silence, then a loud *"Durfee"* and the huddle broke up. They went out of the locker room, turned right down the corridor, then started going up the stairs to the gym. Mikolazyk bounced a ball on the stairs.

"Gore, knock it off," said Karam. "You'll have a turnover before the game starts."

There were four thousand people crammed into every nook and corner of the gym, five and six deep behind each basket, and by halftime it seemed as if there was an upset in the making. Karam was beside himself. His sport jacket had been off since the start of the game, his blue shirt stained with sweat. His face was ashen, the tension etched into it. He urged his team on. He pleaded with them during time-outs. He screamed at the two officials. He paced back and forth in front of the bench, all his worst fears being realized. His team could not stop Braintree on one end. On the other it wasn't shooting particularly well. All the practices, all the bus rides, all the pressures and expectations that had begun in early December appeared to be ending right here, against a team they should be beating.

At halftime he threw the chalk and kicked over the wastebasket. Nothing seemed to work. He pleaded again for his team to rebound, to get back on defense, to work harder in the halfcourt trap. But Durfee fell behind by eleven in the second half, and it appeared that the season was going to end right here, at Brockton, in the same gym they had played so poorly in back in January when Brockton had given them their worst defeat of the season. With roughly three and a half minutes left to play, Durfee was still down eight.

Karam couldn't stand it anymore. It had all become too much, a personal torture chamber.

He grabbed Dempsey.

"This is it," he said. "I'm never coaching another game again. This is it. I can't go through this anymore."

There was a sense of apprehension among the Durfee fans. Nothing seemed to be going right. Just when Durfee had started a comeback, a Braintree kid would bury a shot and quell it, over and over. Herren had picked up his fourth foul with four and a half minutes left in the game, a bad omen, reminiscent of the Brockton game at home when Herren had fouled out and Durfee went on to lose.

Michael Herren stood along the baseline near where the end of the court met the end of the Durfee bench, and it was as though he were playing himself. He bit his fingernails. He shook his head. He looked pale. He had left Belmont Abbey in North Carolina early for spring break, driving straight through, twelve hours, because there was no way he was going to miss Durfee in the state tournament.

"I don't fuckin' believe this," he said, biting on one of his fingers. "Ending the season to this team. I don't believe it."

On the court Chris Herren also is thinking that it's over, wondering what's going to happen when they lose and have to go back to Fall River, and how he doesn't want to go to school tomorrow.

Neither does Caron. He's gotten scared, for he too senses it's over, that they aren't going to be able to pull this out, that the entire season is going to end here against a team with a kid who is playing with a towel wrapped around his head. *We're supposed to be shitting down this team's throat,* he told himself. *We're supposed to win the state title, and here we are going to lose to this shit team in the state tournament.* He feels depression start to wash over him.

Then the comeback started.

Fast and furious, with only slightly more than three minutes to play, Durfee refused to lose.

Herren made two free throws. Then two more. Then the Durfee press, more frenetic now, playing with the kind of passion Karam was always exhorting them to reach, forced a Braintree turnover, Mike Cioe coming up with the big steal. Mikolazyk canned a three-pointer. Suddenly the game was tied as the Durfee crowd exploded, the gym one loud, pounding, pulsating noise. But the game was far from over. Tournament games, in whatever state they're played, are famous for upsets, for unheralded players who make big shots, unheralded teams that grab on to destiny's coattails and get swept along for the ride, teams that do things no one ever thought they'd be able to do.

Wasn't that the history of Durfee basketball? Hadn't a kid named Peter Collius made a shot at the buzzer in the Eastern Massachusetts finals in the Boston Garden to give the Hilltoppers the championship? Hadn't a kid named Ron Golz won a game at the buzzer in the '51 tournament, back when Karam had been a sophomore? Hadn't the 'Toppers won four straight games in the '56 tournament in the final seconds, each by two points?

Now it was Braintree's turn. Since halftime they had been building the incredible upset, their confidence growing as the game progressed, and they weren't ready to fold merely because Durfee had come back to tie the game.

Braintree scored underneath to go ahead by two, a shot that silenced the large Durfee crowd. But Caron drained a jumper from the corner and the game was again tied, with 2:30 to play.

The gym was in pandemonium, the tension thick as summer haze. The Durfee bench was standing, the reserves cheering, exhorting their teammates. A precious minute went off the clock as both teams squandered opportunities. Who was going to fold first?

Herren made a foul shot with forty-one seconds remaining, giving Durfee its first lead since the first half. Braintree quickly answered with free throws, taking a one-point lead with just twenty-nine seconds left.

Durfee then came down the court, seconds ticking off the clock, and Herren, who already had scored thirty-four points, missed a drive to the basket. But Jones got the rebound and threw the ball outside, giving Durfee one more chance. Herren began to penetrate, saw there was no place to go, and passed to Caron on the perimeter, the game now in its final seconds, the noise defeaning.

Caron took the shot, and when he saw it was going to miss, he followed it. As fate would have it, no one boxed him out and the ball bounced directly to him, and as the bigger bodies tangled and collided with each other, he snared the rebound and in one motion put the ball right back into the basket, giving Durfee a 68–67 lead with just two seconds remaining. It was the kind of basket that all little kids dream about, shooting baskets by themselves in the dying twilight, the biggest basket of his life, and as it dropped through, he threw his fist high into the air, overcome with emotion.

Almost as quickly as the ball went through the basket, the Durfee reserves were on the court in celebration, falling to the floor in joy. Caron was tackled by Chris Campbell.

The season had been saved.

As players and fans and students all celebrated together wildly, Karam just stood there. He was completely drained, both physically and emotionally. *Why does it have to be this difficult?* he thought. *Why?*

The celebration continued in the locker room.

"That was our wake-up call," Herren told a reporter. "Because we were done. But there's no turning back now."

The players knew they had escaped, that they should have lost, that they were one miracle shot way from slinking back to Fall River, the unfortunate victims of a huge upset. It made the victory all the sweeter. Karam's blue shirt was stained with sweat. He knew how lucky they were, and he felt almost embarrassed to have won. A couple of reporters stood around him.

"They ripped us apart and outplayed us eighty-five percent of the time," he told them. "They probably deserved to win. But we'll take it."

The next day the headline screamed across the top of the *Herald News*, DURFEE SURVIVES WAMPS, 68–67. There was a large color picture of Caron going up for a shot, and a smaller one of Karam, Santos, and Boardman standing on the sideline, Karam's left hand on Santos's chest, as if restraining him from charging out on the floor. The game story ran on the left side of the paper and a George Darmody column on the right, titled JEFF CARON'S SHOT LANDS IN THE ARCHIVES.

"Caron's basket will now become one of the most talked about field goals in Durfee basketball history," Darmody wrote.

The pressure was building, was there in the practice before the next game with Bridgewater-Raynham. For Karam, the euphoria of the Braintree game was over. What remained was the reminder of how badly they had played for most of the game, how much work was still left to do if the season was going to continue, the realization that if they struggled so much against Braintree, what was going to happen when they played a better team?

So when Pavao informed Karam that he couldn't practice, that he was limping with a sore hip, Karam's mood started to sour.

"How'd you do it, Peter?" Karam asked.

"I don't know," he said. "I just woke up with it."

Karam shook his head in disgust. He didn't yet know that Pavao and several others had been in Santos's jeep when he had dropped Herren off at his house, then purposely skidded his jeep on some ice at the end of the street, a motion that jarred Pavao in the backseat. But Karam sensed the injury was something more than Pavao waking up on the wrong side of bed.

When Callahan dropped a pass, Karam picked up the ball, went rushing toward Callahan, and threw it as hard as he could from about fifteen feet away.

"Catch it," he yelled.

He got the ball back and threw it again.

"Catch it. Catch it."

Over and over it went, Karam throwing the ball at Callahan.

"Who taught you to catch like that, Danny, your father? Your father at halftime. Your father at halftime of the Brockton game?"

Midway through the practice, Michael Herren walked in, wearing dungarees, a gray sport jacket, and a black baseball cap. He stood along the sideline and watched for a while; eventually the words started to tumble out of him.

"I still can't believe they almost lost to Braintree. They wouldn't have been allowed back into the city. Losing to Braintree. That's like losing to Somerset. These kids still don't know the dedication it takes to win a state tournament. They don't understand that it takes a total commitment. They watched us do it, and they think it's easy. That all you do is show up and win because you're Durfee."

On the court Karam was prodding his team, telling them that they hadn't won anything yet, that they had to start playing smarter or their season was going to end quickly.

"That's good," Michael said, motioning toward the court. "These kids need that. Almost losing to Braintree. That would have been one of the worst losses in Durfee history. They got to realize that they can win a state title. That it's theirs to take."

Three nights later it was another Massachusetts state tournament doubleheader in the South Sectionals, this time at Taunton High School, another spacious gym that can seat over four thousand, about fifteen minutes north of Fall River on Route 24. The first game was Durfee versus Bridgewater-Raynham, a large regional high school to the north of Taunton, the second game New Bedford against Silver Lake. New Bedford had won their first game easily against Barnstable, a team from Cape Cod, then defeated Catholic Memorial from Boston.

It was a cold night with snow in the forecast and the cars filed into the large parking lot in the twilight, some with their lights already on. Once again, the gym was jammed, people standing in packs behind the baskets. It also was another "recruiting window," so assistant coaches Dave Leito from Connecticut, Stan Van Gundy from Wisconsin, Tom Sullivan from Seton Hall, and Boston College head coach Jim O'Brien were all there to watch Herren.

O'Brien stood in one of the groups behind the basket, feeling a bit of ironic déjà vu. Five years ago he had first come to Fall River to recruit Michael Herren, then a Durfee junior.

"I loved his competitiveness," O'Brien said. "He was an in-between size and he had scored a lot of his points in high school by going inside and overpowering people, but I understood that. I always thought he could have been a good role player for us by his junior and senior year, someone you wanted to have on your team because he was a winning type of kid. There's no underestimating that. I also was attracted to his personality. And when I went to Fall River to recruit him, Christopher was always around. He was the kid who was always running out on the court to shoot during a time-out. He was just a little kid then, and everyone there was saying he was going to be good someday, but you have a tendency to shrug that off because it's so far away.

"Then one day, probably a year or two later, they had this big three-on-three outdoor tournament at the City Hall Plaza in Boston. I was there because my daughter Erin was playing, and Christopher was on a team with a couple of his friends. You could see then he was going to be a good player someday, agressive, hard-nosed. So I spent the day with the Herrens. I watched Christopher play with them and then they came over with me and watched my daughter play. So last year when my two assistants told me that we had to start recruiting Christopher, I wasn't surprised."

But this is the first time O'Brien had seen him play since that long-ago three-on-three tournament in City Hall Plaza in downtown Boston.

Bridgewater-Raynham was a big team, featuring a six-foot-nine center. They had defeated Newton South by five in their quarterfinal game, and they wasted no time taking control of this game too. They hurt Durfee underneath with their size, and went up nine at the half.

Once again the Durfee players found themselves in trouble, their limitations all too apparent: not good defensively, not athletic enough. Karam tried to fire them up them at halftime, calling for them to get tougher, do better on the boards, for he could see the Braintree game unfolding all over again, Durfee getting too far down.

Only this time Durfee wasted no time in taking control of the game after the half. Herren's brilliance seemed to carry the entire team. Time and time again he swept through to the basket, an individual highlight film, scoring twenty-seven in the second half alone. Time and time again he used his quickness to get into the lane and then his body control to slither around defenders, often shifting the ball from his right hand to his left while in the air, then scoring the basket. He played with the growing confidence that no one could guard him, no one could stop his quick, explosive first step to the basket, one that seemed to freeze defenders until until it was too late. He finished with forty points, maybe his most impressive game of the year next to New Bedford, and as he came over to the bench near the end of the game, he threw his hands over his head in triumph, like a prizefighter who had just gone the distance and knew the decision was his.

The final score was 85–78, Durfee scoring fifty-seven points in the second half, and BC coach Jim O'Brien knew that Chris Herren had just become his number one recruiting priority.

"When I first saw him tonight, I was surprised at how big he had gotten, how physical," he said. "He's no longer the little kid I remembered. And to tell you the truth, he's better than I thought he'd be. I'm surprised at how good he is. Paul Biancardi and David Spiller, my assistants, have been telling me how good he is, but I don't think I really believed them until now. He's a great player."

Karam stood in the small hallway outside the locker room. He told three reporters who circled around him that Herren was the best player in the state. He kibbitzed with the three college assistant coaches. His face was pale and drawn, the tension still etched around his eyes. These play-off games took a toll physically, draining him, making his voice hoarse, seemingly aging him in just a couple of hours. The games were a trip through an inventory of his emotions, running the spectrum from rage to anguish to satisfaction to fulfillment and, finally, catharsis. But as soon as one game ended, as the players rejoiced in the moment, the specter of the next game was right there in front of him again, robbing him of the joy, ultimately ruining the moment. Once again, all winning was, was not losing, merely a temporary relief before it all started again.

Outside in the gym, New Bedford was rolling over Silver Lake, setting up a Durfee–New Bedford final in the South Sectionals at UMass-Boston, the winner to go to the Boston Garden for the state semifinals. Karam came out under the far basket where the Durfee players were watching the game, looked at the scoreboard, and winced. *New Bedford*, he thought. *Always, New Bedford.*

The bus waited on the other side of the building, so Karam and the team trudged alongside the darkened building. It had started snowing, the ground already covered, and

Karam pulled his coat up against the cold. The bus went south on Route 24 in the thickening snow. Inside the bus it was loose and happy in the way all winning buses are, part muffled laughter, part fragments of conversation, all amid the heavy noise of the engine. Eventually, Herren came up to the front of the bus and sat next to Dempsey, one seat behind Karam.

"Mr. Karam," he said. "Are we practicing tomorrow?"

"What do you think, Chrissie?" Karam said. "You don't think we need it?"

"Maybe we could use a day off, Mr. Karam."

"That's the trouble, Chrissie," Karam said. "That's why we're struggling. You guys practice like every day's a day off. Like you can turn it on in the games. It doesn't work like that. That's what I've been trying to tell you bananas all year."

"I listen, Mr. Karam," Herren said with a smile. "I just don't believe it."

The snow was turning to sleet now, making the streets slushy as Karam drove through Fall River, past the darkened mills, the remnants of the past that were everywhere, hulking shadows in the darkness, the mills that once had defined this city and most of the people in it, including himself. There was little traffic by now, and when he met Dempsey in the parking lot outside Lizzie's, it had turned into a nasty evening, a stiff wind blowing the sleet sideways.

"Did you win, Skip?" someone yelled from the bar.

"Barely," he said. "I almost coached us into the ground."

He and Dempsey sat at a table, running through the game again as they always do, win, lose, or draw. They both knew that Herren had carried them, that in the past couple of weeks he seemed to have taken his game to a new plateau.

"Chrissie was so good tonight in the second half, it was scary," Karam said.

"He keeps getting better and better," Dempsey said.

Karam had come to admit that Chris was the most talented player he'd ever had. He hadn't yet told the media that, still clinging to his party line that he never had had anyone any better than Herren, as if that slight distinction would prevent him from any backlash from those people who still embraced the heroes of the past. But he and Dempsey often speculated about Chris's future, about where he should go to college and how high a level he could play. For the recruiting of Chris Herren had become one of the themes that ran through the season, impossible to ignore.

They both agreed he should not go to Boston College, for no other reason than Michael had gone there, that Chris had lived in Michael's large and imposing shadow for too long and that it would be better if he went somewhere else. There was sentiment for the University of Massachusetts for a couple of reasons: Dempsey had played there, liked it, and thought it would be a good place for Chris because John Calipari had significantly upgraded the program and there was a new ten-thousand–seat arena on campus. The school was only about two hours from Fall River, close enough so everyone could follow his career.

"Could he play at Kentucky?" Karam asked. "Is he that good?"

Dempsey smiled.

There was no overestimating the lure of Kentucky to both Karam and Dempsey, and it existed for one reason: Kentucky coach Rick Pitino. Both knew him personally, Dempsey because he had played at UMass with Pitino, Karam because Pitino had spent two years coaching at Providence College in the mid-eighties. They both considered Pitino as good as any coach in the country, Kentucky the absolute pinnacle of college basketball.

But Kentucky wasn't recruiting Herren. Nor was Duke, North Carolina, Indiana, or Kansas, making up the five schools considered perhaps the best basketball schools in the country. Virtually everyone else seemed to be after him, but not the true elite. Could he play at Kentucky? Was he that good? Neither Karam nor Dempsey really knew. That world seemed far away, far removed from the bus rides and the small gyms of southeastern Massachusetts, as though basketball were a different game at Kentucky than in Fall River.

Dempsey finally left to go home. Karam and I continued to sit there, nursing our beers, the night winding down.

I had come to like Skippy very much, for the same reasons as Dempsey and Campbell, two men who both had spent years as his assistant coach: He never blamed his players for anything, he was always self-deprecating and fun to be around, and beneath the surface he had a big heart. Karam cared about the kids he coached, and tried, in his own, sometimes flawed way, to help them navigate the often rocky road from adolescence to adulthood, one that seemed to get more perilous all the time as America and its youth moved into the nineties. I had begun the season not really knowing what to expect, and had quickly come to learn what Dempsey and most other Durfee players know: Karam's bark was infinitely worse than his bite, and there was nothing mean-spirited about him, ever.

You could see that in the way he handled Herren. Chris could drive him crazy, could be moody and petulant and all the things a seventeen-year-old having a bad day can be, and Skippy always forgave him the way a parent forgives a child, with equal parts anguish and love and hope that next time it will be different.

Now he sat there and talked about his long career, how none of it was ever planned, how in the beginning he just wanted to prove himself, prove that the Skippy Karam who had grown up in the Flint was worthy of being the Durfee coach.

"If you could go back and start all over again, would you do anything differently?" I asked.

He paused for a minute, running all the years through his mind, all the kids and all the games, thirty years that changed America, not just himself.

"I'd probably play more kids," he said finally. "But back when I started, that was the way everyone coached and I just got used to it."

He paused again. "But there's only one thing I really regret."

"What's that?"

"I regret the swearing," he said. "I wish I didn't swear at the kids. But I can't help it. I open my mouth and out it comes. I was like that as a kid. I've always been like that. If you saw me at the country club, you'd think I hated everyone I played with. That's all we do is swear and pound each other. And nothing's sacred. Certainly not someone's ethnic background. That's just the way it is. It's not malicious. There's nothing malicious about it. I know most of the kids know that. I don't even remember half the things I say and I don't mean any of it."

He took a drink from his beer, swallowed, then started again.

"I worry about these kids. Take the drinking. People always are telling me about the parties and the drinking. Not that we didn't drink back in my era, or that kids haven't always drank in high school. But there always was the fear of being caught. Now there's no fear.

"It's the liberalism that's taken place throughout the country. Things that were not accepted are now accepted. By parents. By the schools. By everybody. So I keep on them about the drinking. Warn them. Talk about it. Because I already buried one of them because of it. Todd Majkut. And that was the worst thing that ever happened to me in coaching. So I yell at them about it and try and make them aware of it. Put some fear into them. Because they don't have any."

Back when he first got the Durfee job, he didn't realize there would be any downside to being the coach. He was naive enough then to think that everyone in the city was on his side, supported him. The realization that it was more complicated than that would come later, the painful knowledge that everyone in the city wasn't on his side.

There had never been any game plan. He didn't set out to win state championships or six hundred games, to be the dean of Massachusetts high school basketball coaches, to become synonymous with Durfee basketball, synonymous with Fall River.

"So you didn't set out to be a legend?" I asked with a smile.

"God, no," he said with a laugh. "I just didn't want to fail."

Chapter 12

IT HAD ALL COME DOWN TO one game against New Bedford. One game for the South Sectionals championship and a trip to the Boston Garden.

"Is Durfee High a team of destiny?" asked George Darmody in the *Herald News*. "Sunday will tell."

It was Saturday morning, the day before the game. The team was going to practice at noon in the field house, but already there were people in the lobby buying tickets that would shortly be sold out.

Al and Cindy Herren were sitting in their family room a couple of blocks away. Al worked the phone in a futile search for tickets.

"I can't get enough tickets," he said.

He would put the phone down and in a few seconds it would ring again. Over and over. Every once in a while the front door would open and someone would come into the living room through the small, narrow kitchen, then down into the family room. It seemed everyone in Fall River needed more tickets.

Chris trudged down the stairs into the kitchen in gray sweatpants and no shirt, his eyes still heavy with sleep. He opened up the refrigerator and took out some orange juice. He seemed oblivious to what was going on around him, people coming and going, his father on the phone frantically searching for tickets. This morning, he was just a junior in high school who was hungry. The big game could wait.

About an hour later he was at practice. Uncharacteristically, it was an easy one. They worked against the press for a while, for everyone knew New Bedford was going to come with full-court pressure, just like they always did. Karam stood on the sideline in his red and black warm-up suit, but he was subdued. In a sense it had all been said. He'd been flirting with the idea of playing Pavao in place of Mikolazyk, who'd been struggling, and playing a box-and-one defense, with Pavao on New Bedford scoring ace Marcus Wills. He knew that would surprise Coach Rodrigues and force New Bedford to adjust, maybe get them out of their game plan a little. So now he tried it in practice, with Steve Joseph, a good-shooting jayvee player, in the role of Wills.

"What do you think?" Dempsey asked.

"Pavao can't guard Joseph, never mind Wills," said Karam.

"It might confuse them," Dempsey said. "A different look."

"Right now we look confused," Karam said.

The team continued to scrimmage, the practice winding down, when Herren drove to the basket on a fast break and a jayvee player named Eric Couto stepped in to pick up the charge. Herren crashed into him and the two went sprawling on the floor.

"What are you doing, Couto?" Karam yelled as Herren got up, obviously unhurt.

"Skippy." Dempsey laughed. "You should be happy he stepped in. All year you've been saying no one's got the balls to step in on him, that when he drives to the basket, it's like seas part."

"Yeah," said Karam. "What's your point, Bobby?"

304 ......

"So he stepped in," Dempsey said, still laughing.

"What are you, crazy?" Karam said excitedly. "All we need now is for Chrissie to get hurt and we all can go jump off the Braga Bridge."

Sunday was a beautiful day in New England for early March, sunny with the promise of spring. In less than a week the area would be hit by the biggest blizzard since the infamous one of 1978 and winter would drag drearily on for another few weeks, but on this morning in the parking lot outside Durfee it seemed crocuses and daffodils were only days away, that the long gray winter was finally, mercifully, over.

It was ten-thirty and everyone stood in the parking lot—Karam, the players, the cheerleaders, a few students. Everyone except the bus.

"I told the guy ten-fifteen so he'd be sure to be here," muttered Karam, looking at his watch.

He went into the building to call the bus company, while everyone else mingled outside, sitting on cars, milling around, rap music blasting from car windows, as though ready to go off on some class outing. There didn't seem to be any tension, any sense that in just a couple of hours this team was going to play a game that would determine its season. Karam came out of the building shaking his head. He didn't know where the bus was. All he knew was that it better get here soon.

"Do you believe this shit?" he said, grimacing.

He continued to stand in the parking lot in the morning sunshine, constantly looking at his watch. He was tense enough; he didn't need this. He hadn't slept well in weeks. His stomach was bothering him. The anxiety he felt every year at this time was back again, like some old familiar nemesis who never forgot the calendar. And now there was no bus on the biggest day of the season.

He glared at the entranceway to the parking lot, as if he could will the bus to materialize.

"Okay," he said. "We're going to have to go in cars."

"Just like in *Hoosiers*," said Herren, a reference to the movie about high school basketball in Indiana in the early fifties, a caravan of cars carrying a small town's dreams all the way to the state title. He was bothered by a sore right wrist, already had it taped, but he was ready. He'd been ready since last year, when Durfee had lost in overtime to Brockton, also at UMass-Boston.

The players scrambled into cars driven by Mitch Lown and Fran Desmairas, avoiding Karam's car.

"Look at that," Karam said, as none of the players got into his car.

"Would you have ridden with Lukey?" he was asked.

He laughed.

"I would have walked first," he said.

But it hurt him a bit too. For beneath the yelling and the one-liners, beneath the sarcasm and the demands, Skippy wanted to be liked by the kids. In a more perfect world he would have loved to be closer with the players, to go out for pizza or something after the games, to be more of a friend. But he'd never done it, for he believed that to get too close to the players would erode the control, the unyielding authority he felt a coach had to have.

He got into his dark blue Mercury, the one he had received for winning the state title in 1988. With him was his uncle Tony, his late father's brother. He pulled out of the parking lot, past Papa Gino's and the small shopping center, left onto President Avenue, and around the rotary that led to Route 24 and the road to Boston. A car full of players, driven by Mitch Lown, passed him. He looked over at them.

"I just want to get them to the Garden," he said. "Because that's one of those things you never forget your whole life."

The stage was set.

Two old rivals.

Two teams playing for the right to go to the Boston Garden for the state semifinals, but also for pride and turf and reputations and tradition, all the things that are an integral part of this rivalry regardless of the state tournament.

UMass-Boston is red-brick and modern, sits out on Columbia Point, on the tip of where South Boston juts out into Boston Harbor, past the Boston *Globe* and Boston College High School. It is the same place and the same game where Durfee lost last year to Brockton in overtime. The gym is large, seating about five thousand, with colorful banners of UMass-Boston's Division III rivals hanging from the rafters.

Durfee had come far as a team since that opening night in Duxbury three months ago. Herren had achieved the kind of year that had been predicted for him coming off his summer success with BABC, had emerged as the best player in Massachusetts and one of the top juniors in the East. Caron had proven he was one of the best guards in the state, already had broken the all-time Durfee three-point shooting record. Callahan, who had been on the jayvees last year, missing much of it with an injury, had been a starter since the first game and had played better and better as the year went on. Mikolazyk had realized his childhood dream of starting for Durfee. So had Jones. Cioe had been a valuable reserve, especially early in the season when Jones had been out with his ankle injury. Maybe more importantly, he had been accepted by the other kids and had found new friends. Only Pavao had had a frustrating year, once again failing to start, but he was such a good kid, team-oriented, liked by everyone, that it didn't seem to bother him.

They were 19–4, and in many ways had overachieved, regardless of the expectations. Now they were one game away from the Boston Garden and a legitimate chance at the state title and their place in Fall River history.

"This is it, fellas," Karam said, pacing back and forth in front of the room. "You know what you have to do."

The gym was jammed with people, festive, an atmosphere fitting for a game of such importance.

Durfee started the same five that had been its starting lineup since the Lowell Tournament in late December: Herren, averaging twenty-seven a game for the season, thirty-four in the tournament; Caron, at nineteen for the season; Callahan at eleven; Mikolazyk at eight; and Jones at five. New Bedford countered with Marcus Wills, who was averaging close to nineteen a game, but had scored forty-three against Catholic Memorial; Matt Poitras at sixteen a game; Duane Ramos and Mike Rocha at nine a game; and T. J. Goodine at five. New Bedford had more firepower off the bench, with good-shooting Jason Bennett at eleven a game and Jeff Correia at nine.

Durfee had lost to Duxbury on the first night of the season, Brockton twice, and the first game to New Bedford. New Bedford was 18–3, having lost to Durfee, Andover, and St. Anthony's of Jersey City. Durfee was bigger, with both Jones and Callahan at six-foot-four, while New Bedford had only one player over six-foot-two, and he played sparingly. Yet New Bedford had better overall talent, was deeper and more athletic, and was playing better in the tournament. It was little wonder that they were favored.

New Bedford started the game as though they should have been favored. The Whalers jumped all over Durfee in the beginning minutes of the game, Durfee unable to handle the press. It was a basketball version of being mugged: Durfee didn't look prepared for New Bedford's defensive intensity, as if it had somehow taken them by surprise. Karam quickly took a time-out. He knew his team wasn't handling the New Bedford press, nor were they handling the emotion of the game. He also knew that unless they found a way to get through the New Bedford press, the game was going to be over very quickly.

"Let's get smart," he yelled. "Work the press offense and we'll be all right. Don't panic. There's no reason to panic. Make short, crisp passes and try and get rid of the ball before the double-team gets there. Come on, let's be smarter."

The time-out didn't help. When the game resumed, it was the same script, and they were quickly down 35–15. It appeared the rout was on.

Herren had started off badly. He missed a couple of drives in traffic, had a shot blocked, was called for a charge, and it seemed to set the tone for the game. He felt out of synch somehow, and could feel things starting to slip away.

Wills already had scored twenty-two points in the first eleven minutes of the game, seven more than the entire Durfee team, many coming off steals in the backcourt as Durfee failed to handle the New Bedford press. But when he picked up his second foul, Rodrigues took him out. This seemed to coincide with Durfee starting to settle down, and by halftime they were only down thirteen, 42–29. That in itself was an accomplishment.

Karam was livid. *Here we go again*, he thought. *The third game in a row. Another game where we've put ourselves in another large hole.* He couldn't understand how they had folded against the press, as if it had caught them by surprise. Hadn't they spent days practicing against it? Hadn't New Bedford been using the same press for years? Yet here was his team folding against it as if they'd never seen it before. He couldn't believe it. In the South Sectionals final, no less. Against New Bedford, no less. *It never stops*, he thought. *The shit never stops.*

"You guys are playing like assholes," he said as soon as he came into the room.

"Why are you calling me an asshole?" Herren asked, the hurt in his voice.

"I'm not calling you an asshole."

"Why are you pointing at me, then?"

"I'm not pointing at you. I'm saying you're all playing like assholes."

"But you're pointing at me," Herren said.

"I don't believe this," said Karam in disgust. "I should just quit and Mr. Dempsey can take over. Because this is ridiculous."

He walked out in the hall, trying to compose himself. He was mad at himself for losing his temper, mad at Herren for making a big deal out of nothing, mad at his team for playing as if they had never seen a press before, mad at the world.

Yet Durfee didn't quit. All season long they had come back from adversity. Today would be no exception. Handling the New Bedford defense better, they began to inch back into the game. With about eleven minutes left to play, they had narrowed the New Bedford lead to seven, then a minute later it was back to ten again. Still, they continued to scratch and claw, cutting into the lead as the minutes began to disappear off the clock. Seven points. Then five points, as the noise in the gym became deafening, the tension starting to escalate.

With three and a half minutes to play, Durfee amazingly had crept back to within three, 61–58. More importantly, the momentum was all on their side.

"DURFEE . . . DURFEE," screamed the Fall River crowd, sensing another miraculous comeback in the making, as there had been against Braintree, as there had been against Bridgewater-Raynham, those nights when Durfee had simply refused to lose. Wasn't the same thing happening now? Hadn't Durfee been down by twenty in the first half, seemingly blown out of the building?

"DURFEE . . . DURFEE," the Durfee student section screamed, stamping their feet on the bleachers, the noise reverberating through the gym. "DURFEE ROCKS THE HOUSE."

Besides, New Bedford had visibly tightened, perhaps thinking about those old perceptions that New Bedford and Rodrigues could never win the big game. This was Rodrigues's own white whale, and as Durfee slowly, inexorably kept narrowing the lead, it reappeared.

Enter Mike Rocha.

On a New Bedford team characterized by quick, athletic black kids, Rocha often was overshadowed, the little white point guard. Wills got all the attention; their defensive pressure was their trademark; Matt Poitras was their second leading scorer. Rocha? Rocha was an afterthought. Yet high school tournament games traditionally are full of unlikely heroes, kids who seem to rise out of nowhere to steal a moment that is freeze-framed forever. This was Rocha's moment. He hit a three-point shot to give the Whalers a five-point cushion, and after Jones had answered with a short jumper, Rocha threw in another three-point shot. This put New Bedford up by seven again, two shots that would prove to be the final daggers into Durfee's heart. When Rocha's second three went in, you could sense Durfee's incredible comeback was over, that they had spent much of the afternoon trying to recover from their horrible start, had fought and scratched and battled in the frenzied excitement of the gym, and now there was no more energy left.

Rocha later added four free throws as New Bedford pulled away in the final minutes. With twenty-nine seconds left and New Bedford leading 76–62, Herren fouled out. As he walked to the bench, his face expressionless, the Durfee crowd rose to give him a standing ovation.

With eight seconds left, Karam walked down the sideline, shook Rodrigues's hand, and patted him affectionately on the neck. Then he turned around and walked slowly back to his bench. He had just lost in the South Sectionals final for the second year in a row, and all he could think about was that he'd let his players down, that he had been outcoached, should have done something different, anything. When the final buzzer sounded, the New Bedford players burst onto the floor in joyous celebration. They hugged each other, and screamed, and hugged some more as the New Bedford crowd cheered, while the Fall River fans began silently filing out of the gym, mourners past a casket.

The Durfee players sat on the bench, portraits in sadness.

The season that had begun at practice back in November, had offered so many great moments along the way, and just a couple of hours earlier had been filled with the promise of going to the Boston Garden and playing on the parquet floor beneath all those storied rafter banners, had now ended in the worst way imaginable, losing to hated New Bedford and now having to sit here and watch the Whalers celebrate. Jones and Pavao were in tears. They had played their last game, their Durfee careers over. So had Mikolazyk, who had suffered a horrible first few minutes, disintegrating against the New Bedford defense. Their basketball careers were over; there would be no more seasons, no more big games, no more cheers.

Caron watched the New Bedford players celebrating, hating the sight of it. The scoreboard overheard said 80–62. It seemed to Karam to be an accuser.

Moments later he and Caron got up to accept the second-place trophy. Then they all watched as Rodrigues accepted the first place award, a larger trophy, and with it the trip to the Boston Garden. They walked across the court and out under the far basket and through the lobby to the narrow hallway that led to the small locker room.

"We have been walking a tightrope for the past three games and we finally fell off," Karam told George Darmody of the *Herald News*.

The pressure had started to take its toll on Herren in the tournament, the feeling that he had to score forty for Durfee to win, had to be Superman in sneakers. More and more he felt the demand to make the big basket, the great play, to do something to make his team win, for if he didn't, they were going to lose and the season was going to be over and they all would be seen as failures.

But he had not played well this afternoon, certainly not at the level he'd been playing at. He had missed a couple of drives early in the game, shots he usually made, and it seemed to set the tone for the entire game. It had coincided with Durfee's inability to get the ball through the New Bedford press, and it made him nearly crazy with frustration. All he could think about was he was going to lose another South Sectionals final, and he didn't know how to deal with it, didn't know what to do.

Months later, he would be able to look back and realize that it was the first time in his life he'd experienced real basketball failure and that it taken him by surprise. He had lost a little of his confidence, that edge he'd had since the beginning of the season, that feeling that nobody could stop him. It was only later, with some distance from it, that he came to learn that the game had taught him a valuable lesson, namely that so much of the game is mental toughness, the belief in your ability no matter what is happening, the belief that you can overcome a bad stretch and rectify it.

But now he sat at the end of bench, off in a corner. He was by himself, distraught, inconsolable. When the game had ended, he had run off the court in the direction of the locker room, even though both teams were supposed to stay on their respective benches, then had changed his mind and come back into the gym, only to stand on the far end, looking a little lost and bewildered, as the awards ceremony went on without him. He was still not emotionally ready to handle losing. It was all too personal, for he saw his team's failure as his failure. He wasn't supposed to lose. Hadn't his brother won two state championships? Hadn't that always been the unspoken standard? Now that goal was impossible, and the frustration engulfed him. When the game had ended, he had just wanted to run out of the gym, out of the building and keep on running, away from everything. He had finished with thirteen points, only half his average, and though he had played a good floor game and scored some key baskets when Durfee had made their run at New Bedford, it had been his worst game of the year. Why hadn't he played well? His wrist hurt, but he knew that wasn't the reason. His wrist had been hurting for a while now. He didn't really know what had gone wrong. He hadn't been particularly nervous. He had felt ready. Later, he would come to understand that it hadn't only been his failure that had caused Durfee to lose. New Bedford had shot extremely well, especially in the beginning of the game, and his teammates had wilted under the severity of the New Bedford pressure defense. There had been other factors, not just his own performance. But now he blamed himself.

In that sense he and Karam were alike; they both blamed themselves when Durfee lost, went off into some private hell. The difference was Karam had long ago learned to be gracious in defeat, to put on a public face. Herren hadn't learned how to do it yet.

So he sat with his face buried in his hands. A few minutes later his brother went over and put his arm around him.

Inside the locker room, Jones was in tears, upset not only with the loss but with the probable end of his basketball career.

"I can't believe it," he said over and over again. "I can't believe it."

The rest of the players dressed quickly and in silence. Most didn't even bother to take a shower, so eager were they to get out of the locker room, away from everything. Some had tears in their eyes.

"We sucked," said Caron. "We just sucked. All year, to play like this." He stuffed his red uniform into his gym bag in disgust.

He too felt he'd let everyone down. He had been the only Durfee player to have a good game, but he felt that he could have done more, because he knew in the second half that something was wrong with Chris. He didn't know what it was, but he knew that for whatever reason there would be no last-second heroics from Chris, that he was going to have to carry the team by himself, but he hadn't done that.

He would be one of the few players to go back on the bus, which finally had showed up in the Durfee parking lot and taken the cheerleaders. In the parking lot the New Bedford cheerleaders taunted the bus, several of the Durfee cheerleaders giving them the finger in return, and finally, Caron yelled for them to shut up. For he believed that once you had gotten beat, there was no way of saving face, no way of coming out ahead in the postgame arguments. Later, when he finally got home, he turned on the television and began watching a college basketball game, just staring mindlessly at the set, getting more depressed by the minute.

Back at UMass-Boston, about a half hour after the game had ended, Karam stood outside in the hallway talking to a handful of reporters. He said that the first few minutes of the game killed them, a hole they never could crawl out of. He praised New Bedford, especially the ferocious way they had started the game. He said Rocha's two big threes had been the killers, the two shots that ultimately ended his season. "I hope they go all the way," he said about New Bedford. "Let someone from our area win it."

He hesitated.

"I am sorry we didn't win for our fans. We have the greatest fans in the world."

A few minutes later he went out into the lobby, which was still jammed with people. He shook some hands. He made some small talk. Then, at the first opportunity, he went out the door and down the ramp that led to the small lot where his car was parked. The players were gone by now, off in the same cars that had brought them here from Fall River. The season was over and Skippy Karam just wanted to go off somewhere alone and nurse his hurt.

He drove back down Route 24 in the late-afternoon sunlight. I felt sorry for him, not so much that he had lost, but because he blamed himself. It didn't matter that his players had disintegrated against the press in the first half, or that

Chris had had his bad game at the worst possible time; he didn't blame anyone. Again he blamed himself, second-guessed himself, as though he should have been able to do something, anything, to prevent it. Again, he felt as though he had let Fall River down, as if he alone had carried the city's banner and been found wanting, as though he alone had tarnished the tradition.

"That's crazy," I said to him.

"I know," he said softly. "But that's how I feel."

After all the years, the losses still hurt.

His record now was 627–144, a winning percentage of .813, the best in New England. But there was the sense that he would have traded half of those victories for one this afternoon.

In the next day's *Herald News*, George Darmody began his column this way:

> The telephone rang.
> The caller asked: "How did Durfee do?"
> "They lost 80–62."
> "They weren't supposed to lose," he says, slamming down the telephone.

It didn't matter that they ended their season 19–5, that they had won two in-season tournaments. Or that they never lost to an inferior team all year and managed to beat Cambridge Rindge and Latin and Duxbury when they were ranked number one in the state. Or even that they had played all year with three new starters, plus very little depth. They now were just another Durfee team that didn't win—a good team, certainly, but not a memorable one. Not one that would be immortalized on the wall of the Luke Urban Field House with a red banner with the black writing on it. Not one that could lay any claim to being a great team in the endless barroom arguments, the names of its starters becoming part of Fall River lore. No, they would be soon forgotten, as would this season, just another team that gave it a good run, but didn't do enough.

They weren't supposed to lose.

Chapter

13

A FEW WEEKS after the season ended, there was a banquet
for the team at the Venus de Milo in neighboring Swansea.
Unlike the one in 1988, where there had been two thousand
people and an awards ceremony that lasted for over an hour,
complete with jackets, rings, and a trip to Disney World, this
one was just the team, Karam and Dempsey, principal Al
Attar, and superintendent John Correiro, held in a small
room. The small room was the only symbolism you needed,
for losing teams don't get honored in Fall River.

New Bedford had gone on to win the state tournament,
and everyone in the room felt that if Durfee could have gotten by the Whalers that afternoon at UMass-Boston, these
players would have had an excellent chance to win the state
title and their slice of Fall River immortality.

Both Herren and Caron had been named to the Boston
Herald's all-state team after the season, a team that also included New Bedford's Marcus Wills. Herren thus would go
into his senior year with the opportunity to become only the
third high school player in Massachusetts history to be
named all-state by the *Globe* three years in a row, alongside

his brother and Patrick Ewing. He also had been named the Massachusetts Player of the Year by the Boston *Globe*.

There was the obligatory roast beef dinner, and the mood was light and relaxed. The players' hair was starting to grow back, so they were starting to look more like themselves and less like the ones who had played in the tournament looking like, in Caron's words, "cuckoo clocks." Afterward, Karam said a few words, but he didn't like speaking in public, had never felt comfortable doing it, even after all these years. He thanked the seniors, and again stressed what he had said in the locker room before the Braintree game, that if they ever needed anything, a reference, help for a job, anything, not to hesitate.

Correiro reiterated the theme that the seniors were now part of the Durfee basketball tradition and that that was forever. It was a nice moment, for it emphasized that the players' connection with Durfee basketball did not end with graduation, that it really was like being part of an extended family, along with the subtle promise that being an ex-Durfee player could help you in Fall River. The fact that Correiro, Attar, Karam, and Dempsey all were ex-Durfee athletes was a testimony to that.

Then Dempsey spoke.

"You guys coming back have to rededicate yourselves," he said. "You got to get yourselves in better condition. Drinking beer is the worst thing you can do. I know you don't believe that, but it's true. It's all bad weight. Winning a state championship takes total dedication, and it starts now, not next December."

There it was again, the state title disguised as Oz, off in the distance through the mist.

Already there was a look forward to another season. For in Fall River the basketball season never really stopped. It just went around and around, one season surrendering to another, forever.

* * *

One day in the spring, there was an outdoor pickup game in Ruggles Park. There had been a challenge in school from some of the kids who played CYO that they could beat the basketball team. Herren and Caron had instantly accepted the challenge, so by the time everyone gathered at Ruggles Park, there were about a hundred kids there to see the big showdown.

It was a warm afternoon that promised summer, a day that even made Ruggles Park look good. Someone had written FUCK YOU in Magic Marker on one of the backboards. Old candy wrappers and paper cups lay strewn in the overgrown grass. The court was macadam; one of the rims had been bent downward. There was a grittiness about the park, the sense it had seen better days, an old dowager who'd fallen on tough times. Across the park was Seabury Street, the tenement where Herren's mother had grown up, just a few blocks away from Caron's mother. Off in the distance, down a small hill and across the rest of the park, you could see some of the factories glistening in the afternoon sun.

The other team was warming up on the far basket, full of teenage bravado. They saw this as their chance for redemption, their chance to show the Durfee players that they were just as good, that it was merely politics and bad luck that had kept them off the team, prevented them from wearing the uniform and hearing the cheers and receiving the perks that went with being a Durfee player.

Herren loved these kinds of challenges, and he wasted little time showing the kids on the other team that they had no chance. Free from the structure of an actual game, he continually drove and dunked. Fifteen minutes into the game, Caron arrived, began playing with a navy blue cap turned backward on his head, quickly made his first two shots. Then he began throwing alley-oops to Herren, where Chris would go up and catch the ball with two hands, then throw it down through the basket in one motion. Over and over he did it, then talked trash as he came back down the court. He seemed happier than he'd been in months. It was playground basketball, free of coaches and referees, and they all played it with the kind of spontaneity and exuberance that keeps the game alive in Fall River. It also was an example of the resiliency of youth, the season already tucked away, the pressure over.

Herren was back playing with BABC, and one of his first tournaments was a weekend one in North Carolina, unofficially known as Bob Gibbons's tournament, Gibbons being one of the national recruiting gurus. Chris made the all-tournament team, and his national reputation began growing. He was mentioned frequently on Gibbons's tapes, accessible by dialing a 900 number.

"Duke called, and so did Georgetown," Karam said one morning, soon after Herren had returned from North Carolina. "Can you imagine? Duke." The basketball world was discovering Fall River.

Skippy too had relaxed. The season was over. The pain of the last game against New Bedford had been stored away, the season all in the past tense now. He was back to supervising spring sports as the Durfee athletic director, playing golf on weekends at the Fall River Country Club, winding down from the season.

Yet his team and next year were never far from his mind. There was Herren's recruiting, which had become an almost daily occurrence, this coach, that coach, always something. There was his concern about trying to find a school for Caron. Plus there was the omnipresent worry of trying to keep his players out of trouble, both in school and out. One day it was Shawn Thames getting into a fight in school and being suspended. The next it was Karam seeing Callahan at a softball game, out past the outfield with a bunch of kids and a keg of beer.

"That banana," he muttered. "Sitting out there so everyone could see him. I told him if I ever saw him doing that

322 ......

again, I'd suspend him myself, he wouldn't have to worry about the school doing it."

He shook his head in disgust. "I need this shit? Here it is May and it's always something."

But his anger didn't last long. The season was over.

One morning Herren was in Karam's office, an oblong-shaped room with no windows, off the hallway that leads to the field house. He was looking at his mail. He held a stack of letters from colleges in his hand, glanced to see where they were from, then put them back on Karam's desk unopened.

"Chrissie," Karam said. "Get that stuff out of here. Every time I go to my mailbox, it's all your stuff. I can't even use my desk anymore."

Herren put a couple more letters back on Karam's desk.

"Where are you supposed to be?" Karam asked.

"Flex," said Herren, the word for a free period in which students were supposed to go to the cafeteria. Herren loved Flex, because there always was someone to hang out with, talk to.

"Then why aren't you there?"

Herren shrugged.

"I walk around the school and I see you more than I see the security guard," said Karam.

Karam was forever asking Herren's teachers how he was doing, trying to monitor his academic progress, to little avail. Herren didn't like Karam checking on his academics, felt he was meddling in his life. It was one more of the tensions that ran between them, Herren feeling that Karam was too concerned with his business. Still, Herren was forever coming into Karam's office during the day, like a politician paying homage to the ward boss.

"We had a party in the woods over the weekend," Herren said suddenly.

"Chrissie, why do you tell me that?"

"I wasn't drinking, Mr. Karam," he said. "I was just there.

But then the cops came and I ran like a rabbit. I was flying through the woods. There was no way they were going to catch me. I was running like a rabbit."

Karam just shook his head.

"Chrissie, don't you have somewhere to go?"

When Herren eventually left, Karam shook his head again.

"I had to go to one of the middle schools the other day and tell them about all the athletic opportunities at the high school," he said. "Right in the middle some kid raises his hand and asks, 'Do you know Chris Herren?' Another kid said, 'Of course he does, that's Mr. Karam. He's Chris Herren's coach.' "

Karam laughed.

"Thirty years of coaching and that's what it's come down to. I'm Chris Herren's coach."

As spring turned into summer, Michael Herren was back home. He and several of his friends had rented a beach house in Westport about a half hour away, close to Horseneck Beach. It was one-story, weather-shingled, with a deck that faced the ocean a block away. It was a beautiful spot, with a marsh out in back and ocean breezes, summer along the New England coast in all its glory. It seemed a long way from Fall River. They put a few old Durfee basketball pictures on the wall, and a sign that called the cottage WACO, and settled in for the summer.

Michael was still a couple of courses short of his degree from Belmont Abbey, was planning to finish them somewhere in southeastern Massachusetts. He looked at the future, and it was unclear. He talked about maybe going to law school, or to graduate school at UMass. Like many twenty-two-year-olds, with college behind them, he seemed to be searching for his future. By the fall he and Juddy McDonald would be planning to open a restaurant-pub in the north end of the city. For now, though, he was planning to run a city-wide summer basketball league to be held outside at Heritage Heights, the housing project in the shadow of the Braga Bridge, to be unofficially called the "Blacktop League," a league for all ages. A league that he was going to run for no payment, his way of giving something back to the city.

The summer league in Taunton had started, in the same gym where Durfee had beaten Bridgewater-Raynham in the state tournament, and next year's Durfee team was in it. They played three nights a week, only this time there was no Pavao, no Mikolazyk, no Jones, no Cioe. They already were part of that vast club of ex-players now, no different than Andy Farrissey or Al Attar or even Michael Herren himself. Now it was Chris and Jeff and Callahan, the three returning starters from last year's team. But it also was Shawn Thames and Steve Breese, and some others off last year's jayvee team, Carlos Smith, Colin Crist, Eric Couto, Steve Josephs, Brendan Gettings. Mitch Lown coached them, and on those nights when Chris was not off with BABC somewhere, they never lost, rolling over teams, already more athletic and deeper than they had been last year.

Caron was a lifeguard at a beach in Little Compton, Rhode Island, already burned brown by the sun. Holy Cross had expressed some interest in him, and there were a couple of Division II schools that kept writing him, but there was nothing substantial and that realization gnawed at him. What else did he have to do?

"I don't even care anymore," he said, although you knew he cared very much. "I'm just going to play and whatever happens, happens."

Herren did not work in the summer. After North Carolina there had been a weekend tournament in Pittsburgh, then one in Connecticut, and a big one in Jacksonville, and on and on it went, BABC on tour. Some nights he stayed at Michael's beach house. Or else he stayed at home, often sleeping late, hanging around during the day, waiting for the mail, which invariably brought something else from another school. At night he either played in a summer league game or coached a team in his brother's Blacktop League. His team was from the Fordney Street projects across New Boston Road, only a couple of hundred yards away from his house, the projects where he had lived as a child.

There were about thirty kids on his project team—boys and girls, black and white—and Chris felt an attachment to them. He had a real affinity for kids, and he encouraged them, praised them, took a genuine delight in coaching them. With kids he could let the softer side of his personality come out; with kids there was no reason to posture or hide behind the defenses he'd erected. There were no expectations to live up to, there was nothing to prove, so there was none of the self-consciousness that he often seemed to have in other situations. The kids, in turn, idolized him. One afternoon when he walked into the project, kids came running out of their houses when they saw him, standing around him as if he were the Pied Piper. Sometimes kids would come and wake him up in the mornings, walking over from the project and entering the house and going up the stairs and into his bedroom. Or else they would come over in the afternoon and shoot baskets in the backyard. One afternoon Chris and Michael had returned from lunch only to find about a dozen of the Fordney Street kids hanging out on the front porch, climbing the tree next to the driveway, one kid even standing on one of the branches and urinating into the street.

"Maybe we can have them over here during the coaches' visits," muttered Michael.

One night Boston College coach Jim O'Brien came down to the summer league in Heritage Heights, the court surrounded by several red-brick buildings that have been refurbished but still wear the look of a housing project. The sun had gone down, but the night was still languid, the day's heat still in the air. The Durfee team, coached by Michael Herren, was playing against a local team made up of guys in their late twenties and early thirties. There were about a hundred people watching, from young mothers with little kids who lived in the projects to guys who were there every night in the summer to watch games.

O'Brien was in a peculiar situation with Chris. Because he knew the family so well, he had told Chris that he wasn't going to call him all the time, wasn't going to keep sending him mail, wasn't going to court Chris as if he were a potential prom date.

Like Karam, O'Brien was the product of a different coaching era. He was not like the new breed of college coach, many of whom had made their reputations as recruiters, had come of age in the sophisticated, high-tech era of recruiting in which how you recruited had become more important than how you coached. He was forty-three, had grown up in Brooklyn, back when New York City was the soul of the "City Game" and turned out an assembly line of tough, fundamentally sound guards who had been weaned on textbook basketball. O'Brien had been one of them; a great player at Boston College on teams coached first by Bob Cousy and later by Chuck Daly, he had been named the New England Player of the Year in 1971. After graduation he had played for a while for three different teams in the old American Basketball Association, then had begun coaching. His first job was as an assistant at the University of Connecticut for five years, then he became the head coach at St. Bonaventure in upstate New York. In his first year he was named the Atlantic 10 coach of the year. He was there four years before coming back to his alma mater as coach in 1986.

It hadn't been easy. He had inherited a program from Gary Williams that had started to slide, one which had tightened its academic standards after a mini-scandal in the mid-1980s, when it was discovered that one of its key players was actually enrolled in night school and not the college's regular classes. Now he was in Big East, one of the most competitive in the country, and he couldn't recruit many of the same kids who could gain admission to other Big East schools. Not only did it make things difficult, it also had started giving him the reputation as a poor recruiter, a label that can get coaches fired in an age when recruiting is considered paramount. Boston College had not been advancing to the NCAA tournament, and O'Brien's job was rumored to be in trouble.

So Chris Herren was an important recruit for Jim O'Brien on several levels. Chris was a great player an hour away from BC, whom O'Brien had known since Chris had been a kid; O'Brien needed someone who could come right in and play in a league as physical and competitive as the Big East; and Chris was the kind of recruit who could send a message that O'Brien could recruit, a kid who could take some of the heat off O'Brien and attract other recruits for the future.

But O'Brien knew that the stakes were higher now, that as soon as high-profile schools like Duke got involved, his chances declined. So he stood and watched Chris in a summer league game, wondering about a profession that sent grown men chasing after teenagers when they ought to be home with their families or on vacation.

"It's good to see Michael doing this," O'Brien said, watching Michael enthusiastically coach the Durfee team, both admonishing and praising them at the same time, urging them on. "He seems much calmer now, more settled. I always liked Michael; he's got a lot of very positive qualities. I always thought he was very misunderstood."

O'Brien had just returned from Jacksonville, Florida, where he had watched Chris play in a national tournament for BABC, along with Mickey Curley, the kid from Duxbury, whom O'Brien also was recruiting. Later in the week he was scheduled to fly to Las Vegas for another AAU tournament that BABC was entered in. Not to convince himself whether he wanted Chris or not, but to let Chris know he was there, that he was still definitely interested.

"The whole thing's ridiculous"—he shrugged—"but what are you going to do?"

The game was close, only a couple of minutes left, when

suddenly the lights went out. Seems a city ordinance shut off all the lights at public parks at eleven o'clock. No problem. The game continued anyway, with only the glow from nearby streetlights providing any illumination. Chris was fouled in the closing seconds, his team down by one point. He stood in the dark and made both free throws to win the game.

Summer basketball in Fall River.

The following weekend, BABC went to Las Vegas for the prestigious John Farrell Memorial Tournament at UNLV. There were sixty-four teams, including the best AAU teams in the country and virtually all of the top high school players in the country, among them Felipe Lopez from New York City, readily acknowledged as the best high school player in the country, already the subject of a profile in *The New Yorker*. Most of the top Division I coaches were present, this being one of the biggest recruiting showcases in the country. The games started in the morning and often ran until midnight, the best high school players in the country in a daylong smorgasbord of dunks and jump shots.

The Boston team was small, with only Mickey Curley possessing true size. It was a team comprised of quick guards—Chris, Eggie McRae, Scoonie Penn, and Michael Edwards—and Coach Leo Papile's style was to press all over the floor, control the game's tempo. Because the team was so guard-oriented, Chris usually played the second guard position, unlike at Durfee, where he had spent the season as the point guard. Once in a while he would switch over to the point. Whichever position he played, he had become the team's "go-to guy," as he was at Durfee, and time and time again when BABC needed a basket, Chris would get it for them, just as he had done so many times for Durfee.

When it all ended, Boston had won the championship in what was considered an upset, and Chris Herren was the tourney MVP. The three previous MVPs had been Jamal

Mashburn, Chris Webber, and Scottie Thurman, three kids who already had made a serious imprint on college basketball, Webber and Mashburn having been two of the top picks in the recent NBA draft.

So where was he going to go to college?

That was the question he was endlessly asked in Vegas.

"I'm going to Durfee," he had finally said.

It was so good a line that the *Herald News* wrote an editorial about it. It praised Chris for his good sense to live in the present tense, to realize you are only a high school senior once and to seize the moment.

Ah, that it could be quite so simple.

He had gone out to Las Vegas as one of the most highly recruited high school players in the country and returned as one of the truly elite. One scouting service now had him ranked as the seventh best player in the country. Another called him the best player in the country under six-foot-five. The new school involved with him was Kentucky, Rick Pitino having fallen in love with him as a player. Pitino was in search of a point guard for the 1994–95 season, someone to come in to replace the departing Travis Ford, and he looked at Herren in Las Vegas and thought he could be the one. He quickly assigned Herren's recruiting to assistant coach Billy Donovan, the former Providence College star who also had played briefly for Pitino with the New York Knicks, because Chris was old enough to remember Donovan from his days on the 1987 Providence College team that went to the Final Four.

Donovan began sending Chris mail virtually every day. One day it would be what Kentucky graduates were doing. The next it would be a note about how Kentucky could get Chris to the "next level," the euphemism for the NBA. Virtually every day a different note. Kentucky's pitch to Chris was essentially this: We need a point guard and we think you're good enough to come in and start on a team that will very likely be good enough to compete for the national title when you will be a freshman. The pitch also came with a qualifier; Kentucky also was recruiting Allen Edwards, a point guard from Miami, and the first one of the two to decide would get the scholarship. It's been said that basketball schools the caliber of Kentucky don't recruit, they select. This was recruiting at the highest level, and it also was Pitino's way of telling a kid, yes, we want you, but you have to want Kentucky too.

Outwardly, Chris seemed oblivious. He seemed to deal with it as he dealt with many other things in his life: He didn't. It all swirled around him as he did the things he always did, hanging out with his friends, playing ball, completely immersed in the present tense. He had a new girlfriend, a twenty-three-year-old who once had gone to Durfee with his brother, who often picked him up after summer league games. Back in December he had said privately that he could play with the best high school players in the country, that his experience with BABC had convinced him of it, but no one in Fall River had really believed him, for all that seemed like a different world. Now he was being courted by Rick Pitino and Kentucky. Kentucky, the school Karam and Dempsey used to fantasize about all those nights in Lizzie's when the talk had turned to where Chrissie should go to college.

Is he good enough to play at Kentucky?

Now Rick Pitino was saying he was.

One afternoon in early August, Chris and Michael were in the house on Phillips Street, preparing for what figured to be a big day in Chris's recruiting. Michael was pacing around the room, full of energy that had no place to go. Chris was sprawled on the couch. Several coaches were scheduled to be in Fall River that night to watch Chris and next year's Durfee team play against a team made up of older guys.

"Is his team going to play your team?" Michael was asked.

"We don't need that," said Michael with a rueful smile.

"We'll play that game during the 'dead time.' Or else in the backyard where no one else can see."

Michael knew that the last thing the coaches needed was to see the two brothers playing on different teams, a scenario that always had the potential for trouble. They were almost mirror images of each other on the court, intense, passionate, consumed with winning, all heightened by the unique dynamics of a big brother–little brother relationship.

It was a cloudy, humid day. Any minute Chris was scheduled to go to the Boys Club and shoot baskets while Florida coach Lon Kruger and his assistant Ron Stewart watched, Kruger and Stewart unable to talk to him under NCAA rules. Their visit to Fall River to watch him shoot for an hour or so was supposed to be a sign to Chris, a token of their commitment to him. At the same time his parents and Karam were at Providence College, being squired around the campus by coach Rick Barnes.

That night, at an outdoor basketball game in the Heritage Heights housing project, in the shadow of the Braga Bridge, there was a scene very rare in southeastern Massachusetts. In one corner was Wisconsin coach Stu Jackson and Kentucky assistant Billy Donovan, reunited, if just for a moment, from the days when Donovan played for Providence College and Jackson had been the assistant coach under Rick Pitino. Along one baseline was Stewart and Villanova assistant John Leonard. In the other corner was BC coach Jim O'Brien. A local cable TV station was doing interviews. A photographer was taking pictures. A couple of hundred people surrounded the court, from little kids to old men to teenage girls with oh-so-tough looks on their faces.

"I've never seen anything like this around here," said Karam. "I've spoken to more coaches in the past few days than I did in thirty years."

After the game, the coaches went to T. K. O'Malley's, a sports bar in a small shopping center owned by "Boo Boo" Karam in the north end of the city. O'Malley's is spacious,

with a large bar in the middle of one room and booths in another, all looked down upon by large screens and TV sets.
The coaches sat at one end of the bar; at the other was Michael Herren and his friends. Much of the talk was of Chris,
of where he might go, of how good he might someday be, his
future analyzed as if he were some lab specimen under a microscope.

I left around midnight, headed toward my car in the parking lot. There, sitting on a bench by himself in front of the
supermarket next door, was Chris. He was wearing baggy
shorts, a loose-fitting T-shirt, and a black cap turned backward on his head. Two nights earlier he had scored sixty-
seven points against Brockton in a summer league game, but
at this moment it was hard to picture him as one of the most
highly recruited high school players in the country. Instead,
he looked like any other teenage kid on summer vacation.

"What are you doing?" I asked.

"A friend dropped me off. I'm waiting for my brother to
give me a ride home."

"How are you dealing with all this?" I asked, pointing to
the restaurant.

"I'm sick of it. I don't even open the mail anymore. I just
pick it up, see who it's from, and put it down. And I don't like
it when the coaches come to Fall River. I don't mind playing
in front of them at national tournaments, but when they
come here, it's not the same. I don't know. I guess it's good
for the city, for the younger kids to see the coaches around.
But I don't like it."

"Do you have any idea where you want to go?"

"Not really. I kind of like them all."

On one level he was the little kid in the ice-cream shop
looking at too many flavors. On another, he would have
loved to stop time, to be able to remain seventeen years old
forever in the cocoon that was his life in Fall River, his
friends, his familiar world.

Did he want to stay close to home or go away? Did he

want the biggest college basketball stage he could find or the place where he would feel the most comfortable? Was he going to sign in November or wait until the spring of '94, after his senior year in high school? Questions. Questions. Questions that now came with fuzzy, undetermined answers.

"I don't know where I want to go," he said finally. "If I did, it would be in the paper and then everyone would know."

Every once in a while someone would come out of the restaurant and Chris would look to see if it was his brother.

"Why don't you go in there and get him?"

"I can't go in there. All those coaches are in there."

So we sat there for a while, talking about this and that, in an empty parking lot at midnight, the most highly recruited high school player ever in southeastern Massachusetts waiting for his brother to give him a ride home because he didn't have his driver's license yet.

As the summer wore on, so did the recruiting.

Where was he going to go?

Was he going to leave or stay close to home?

Michael seemed to be leaning toward UMass, but he liked O'Brien personally. He did not want his brother to go to Kentucky, seemed to want Chris to stay close to home. His father leaned toward him going away, afraid that Boston College was too close, and that Chris's friends would end up sleeping on his floor at BC, as so many of Michael's friends once had done, becoming a distraction. His mother leaned more toward BC, for she both liked O'Brien and felt he would have Chris's best interests at heart. Both Skippy and Dempsey favored Kentucky, feeling that if Kentucky wanted you and you were a basketball player, how could you say no? Skippy also felt Chris should go away from home, away from Fall River and Michael's ghost, somewhere where he could make a fresh start. Everyone seemed to have an opinion, and

334 ......

as the summer wore on, they swirled around Chris like bees around honey.

And what did Chris think?

He didn't know. But as the process dragged on, it seemed that Boston College, long thought to be the front-runner, was slipping, as he more and more toyed with the possibility of going away from home, going off to a bigger program.

Chris had become Fall River's heirloom, community property, with everyone somehow having a stake in his future. The local consensus seemed to be anywhere but Boston College, anywhere except where your brother went. Everyone wanted him to go off to the big-time somewhere, to a place where the games were on television and Dick Vitale sang nightly hosannas to the players, someplace far from Durfee High School and the Luke Urban Field House and Fall River. Chris Herren had become their ticket to ride.

In late August the *Herald News* ran a three-part series called THE COURTSHIP OF CHRIS HERREN. The first day featured an interview with Karam, who said he'd never gone through anything like this before and that he didn't try to pressure Chris one way or the other, because "as a coach, if you push him to a particular school and he doesn't do well or doesn't like it you feel responsible. I don't think it's my place. It's his life, his future, and he's the one who's going to have to live with his choice."

But Skippy did publicly say Chris was the best he'd ever coached, a tribute he'd always been reluctant to make. "He's by far the best. I don't usually say those things, but if I didn't say that Chrissie was the best I'd be lying."

In the same article Leo Papile, the BABC coach, said Chris was the best high school player in the country. It was not the first time Papile had said this. He had told both the Boston *Herald* and the Boston *Globe* he considered Chris one of the top talents ever to come out of Massachusetts, someone who had the potential to have a "10 year career in the NBA."

Part two of the series centered mainly on Chris and Michael's relationship, how Michael had gone through the recruiting process himself, thus served as Chris's guide dog. Michael said that he never really felt comfortable at Boston College, then attempted to set the record straight once and for all about why he left BC.

"I left because my basketball career was in jeopardy because of the injuries I had and because the media pressure was becoming stifling," he told the *Herald News*. "Everything I did was in the paper, it seemed. I was 18, 19 years old going through that. I wasn't a senator, someone 35. I was still a baby.

"I want to set the record straight about those troubles. I do not have a police record. I lived life on the edge for a 17, 18 year old. I definitely did, but I wasn't the only one doing it. Maybe I shouldn't have been drinking as much as I was for an 18 year old, or fighting as much. I shouldn't have put myself in those tough positions, but almost every 18 year old kid was doing what I was doing. Here I was 18 and having exposés done on me, people snooping around police stations trying to get dirt. It created a monster. There were rumors about me that were crazy. . . .

"I'm not going to tell Chris not to go out and have a good time. I'm not going to tell him not to enjoy his high school experience. What I can tell him is not to test fate. If you test fate you're going to get burned. I tested fate a little too much.

"I just want him to live the life of a 17 year old kid growing up in Fall River. That might not be as conducive to a basketball environment as staying alone in the woods shooting jumpers all day, but I think it is important that he enjoy life's experiences. I truly believe that experiences enrich your life and it's a lot more than basketball. What I remember about Durfee aren't the games themselves but what we went through in the locker rooms, on the bus trips, having fun and sharing it. The friendships I have are the true treasure of Durfee basketball."

But Chris Herren knew it was all getting crazy, that there was no way he ever could be a normal seventeen-year-old growing up in Fall River.

"Fortunately I haven't been in any situations where my name would be in the headlines," he told the *Herald News*. "I've always had positive ink, but if I stub my toe, people are going to want to know about it. I had some friends at Howard Johnson's the other night who got arrested [for drinking]. I could have been with them, but I wasn't. If I were there, I'm sure it would have been in every paper in the area. I'm 17 years old. I'm a kid and kids make mistakes, but I guess I have to keep myself out of those kinds of situations."

Many an afternoon Chris and Michael would talk about colleges, or the upcoming Durfee season, tossing the two subjects back and forth like Frisbees. They both thought that Durfee would be better next year, would win the state championship. It was Michael's unspoken challenge to his brother: that he had to win a state championship, that it was the one thing left that would validate him forever in Fall River. Over and over on long sultry afternoons they would sit in their family room and talk about the future, both near and far. Who was going to start next year for Durfee? Would Mr. Karam play more people this year, unlike in the past? Where should Chris go to school? Over and over.

For Durfee basketball was never far from Michael's mind, and he guarded it and its traditions with all the fervor and tenacity of a pit bull. Once I told him my theory that we all were witnessing the end of an era, that sometime in the relatively near future, after Karam resigned and the demographics of the city continued to change, Durfee basketball would be very different. Michael didn't want to hear it.

"No way," he said forcefully. "You're crazy. Durfee basketball will never change. It will always be the same. I'll tell you why."

"Why?" I asked.

"Because in a few years when we're all married, me and

my friends and Chrissie and his friends, we're all going to impregnate our wives at the same time. Then fifteen years later there will be great players and it will continue."

At first I thought he was kidding. But wasn't this his fantasy vision of the future, he and all of his friends living forever in the Fall River they had grown up in, going to Durfee games, still getting psyched about beating New Bedford, all growing old together, as timeless as the banners that hang on the walls in the Luke Urban Field House? Forget that it was a preposterous premise, one that started with the basic assumption that everyone was going to end up living in Fall River, a premise that seemed to fly in the face of the bleak economic future. Born in Fall River, die in Fall River. It reminded me of something Leo Papile had said about Michael, how Fall River could become Chernobyl, a nuclear winter, and Michael would be the one with the gas mask on saying, "Don't leave, it's coming back, we took more tests this morning, Fall River's coming back."

Now, though, his brother's choice of a college had become the top priority.

"Where is he going to go?" Michael said one afternoon in exasperation. "I wish there was one school that would just jump out."

It seemed Chris was leaning more and more toward Kentucky. He asked more questions about Kentucky. He liked Billy Donovan, liked the idea of going to the biggest basketball stage he could find, someplace where the fans were frenetic, an entire state obsessed with a basketball team, like one big Fall River. Maybe Boston College wasn't big enough, maybe he should take his talents to the highest level he could.

"Come on," Michael said. "We'll all just jump in the car and drive to Kentucky right now. Drive straight through and take a look at it when they don't know we're coming. See for ourselves."

"How far is it?" asked Chris.

"Who cares how far it is?" Michael said. "We'll get in the car and we'll stop when we get there."

"You're crazy, bro," said Chris. "I'm not driving to Kentucky."

"Chrissie, the biggest decision of your life and you don't care enough to go find out for yourself."

"How far is it?"

"Who cares how far it is?"

"I do, Michael."

"That's your problem."

"I don't have a problem, Michael."

"Keep it up, Chrissie, and you'll have a problem."

"Not from you, bro."

Michael snorted. "Chrissie, just remember who you're talking to. You're still the little brother. Just remember that."

But there was no extemporaneous ride to Kentucky. They went out for grinders instead.

The recruiting process had taken on a life of its own, hovering over everything, invading nearly all discussions. In Fall River it had become *the* topic of conversation, outweighing the upcoming mayoral elections, the teacher negotiations, and the strong rumors that riverboat gambling was going to come to Fall River. Where was Chris Herren going to go to college?

School started shortly after Labor Day, but it didn't stop the phone calls from coaches, or the mail.

His list was down to nine schools: Florida, Wisconsin, Kentucky, Boston College, Villanova, Providence, UMass, Seton Hall, and Syracuse, which had started recruiting him after Las Vegas. The coaches of those schools had been invited to come in for the official home visits that started in mid-September.

Rick Barnes of Providence College was the first coach to visit, though he didn't think he had much of a chance. Chris had never warmed up to Providence, largely because he felt it was too close to home and when he'd gone to games in the

Providence Civic Center the crowd had been dead. Providence was viewed by him mainly as a backup school, a place close to home if for whatever reason he decided to go to school nearby and Boston College didn't work out.

Stu Jackson of Wisconsin came in the next night. It was only his second year at Wisconsin, but already he'd made his mark, with a great year that almost landed Wisconsin in the NCAA Tournament and an excellent recruiting class. He once had coached the New York Knicks, then had spent a year working in the NBA office in New York City, before knowing he wanted to coach again. He saw Wisconsin as a wonderful opportunity, a prestigious school in a competitive league where the only way to go was up. He viewed Chris as the best guard in the country, someone who could come in and start right away, and his manner was low-key. He talked a lot about the academic support system, and about Madison, Wisconsin's amenities. He sold Wisconsin as the kind of program that would help Chris develop as a player.

Most of the time Chris sat slumped in a chair, a dark cap turned backward on his head. It would be his behavior for all the home visits.

He would sit there, his face impassive, revealing little, as the various coaches talked about his future, what his mother called his "bird on a branch" pose. In front of him was a table covered with hors d'oeuvres. His father would ask questions, mostly centering on how a particular coach saw Chris fitting into the particular system. He was concerned about a school's style of play, realizing that Chris would be better in a running type of offense rather than a slower halfcourt one. His mother would periodically ask about things extraneous to basketball, her main concern being how well taken care of Chris was going to be if anything went wrong.

Karam was at most of the visits, along with Dempsey and Michael.

The third visit was by UMass coach John Calipari, and it didn't go well. Afterward, Calipari went to T. K. O'Malley's in

Fall River and called it the most difficult home visit he'd ever had in coaching. It was the result of what had happened in February, Calipari's suggestion that maybe Chris should think of a year of prep school. His recruiting of Chris Herren never really had survived that, and Calipari had sensed the tension when he'd first entered the house. When he left the house, he knew he didn't have much of a chance.

Pitino and Donovan were scheduled to come in a few days when one night the phone rang. It was Donovan telling Al Herren that Kentucky was no longer recruiting Chris, that Allen Edwards, the kid from Miami, wanted to come and that was it, the scholarship for a point guard was going to Edwards; they were not going to wait anymore for Chris Herren to make up his mind.

He had waited too long.

On the surface Chris said he didn't care, that he understood that college basketball was a business, and that he didn't take the rejection personally, but it seemed to hurt too. One minute he was being pursued as if he were the prom queen on a Saturday night. The next it was over. Just like that. All the letters and phone calls from Donovan, all the courting, no longer counted.

One night shortly afterward I gave him a ride to his English teacher's house to pick up a book he needed for the next day.

"What's going on with all this recruiting stuff?" I asked. "What are you thinking?"

He hesitated. It was a rainy night, the roads slick and covered with puddles. Chris seemed to stare at the windshield wipers as though their cadence had transported him to some private world.

"I wish there was a University of Fall River so I could go there," he finally said.

University of Fall River.

It all seemed to be wearing on him, the endless questions, the speculation about where he was going. He couldn't walk down a corridor in school without someone asking him that question. He was afraid to answer the phone, for fear it would be another coach. A couple of times when he did answer it and it was a coach, he quickly said he was Michael, that Chris wasn't home. He got a beeper so his friends would have a way to reach him. He seemed more guarded, more irritable. In school he was distracted, falling behind in a couple of his subjects, outward signs of increasing inner turmoil.

"A lot of people don't want me to go to BC," he said. "I hear it all the time. They tell me go anywhere you want, just don't go to BC."

"Is that fair?"

"I think it's fair that they hope I go somewhere else. But I don't think it's fair they demand it."

He also was hurt, a succession of nagging injuries that were preventing him from playing a lot of basketball. At the end of the summer he'd had his right wrist placed in a cast for a couple of weeks, the injury that first had started to bother him at the tail end of the season. He had sprained his ankle in a tournament in Boston, spent a couple of days on crutches, and missed a big AAU tournament in Boston, one in which Duke's Mike Krzyzewski was supposed to come watch him play. What should have been the best fall of his young life was starting to get complicated, the recruiting process a burden that seemed to get heavier and heavier.

"I want to go out with my friends," he snapped to his parents one night. "I don't want to be in here talking to coaches."

Still, the coaches continued to visit.

Lon Kruger and Ron Stewart from Florida. P. J. Carlesimo from Seton Hall. Steve Lappas and John Leonard from Villanova. They all made their pitch, Kruger low-key, Lappas more intense, Carlesimo as New York as a Scorsese movie. Chris sat and said little. He felt an allegiance to Ron Stewart, because Stewart had been the first coach to actively recruit him. He liked Villanova because he once had gone to Rollie Massimino's camp there when he was in the eighth grade and had liked the campus. He thought Carlesimo was cool, for out in Vegas he'd been drinking a cup of soda one day and Carlesimo had come over, grabbed the cup out of his hand, taken a drink, and given the cup back to him.

Then Jim Boeheim from Syracuse visited.

Syracuse had been late in recruiting Herren, and that became one of the first issues Boeheim addressed. He sat on a couch as comfortable as if it were in his own house, amiable, no pretense, direct, and admitted that since Syracuse had been on NCAA probation, their recruiting had not been as extensive as it usually was. He described how Syracuse sold twenty-six thousand season tickets, had placed players in the NBA with a collective salary of $81 million, and said that if Chris came to Syracuse, he would start in the backcourt next year alongside Lawrence Moten. His staff considered Chris to be the best point guard in the country, Syracuse was poised to have the kind of recruiting class that would again propel them to being one of the top teams in the country, and he wanted Chris to be a part of it. He said that Syracuse had the best facilities in the Big East and said that once Chris visited, he would know that—the implication being that once he saw Syracuse, there was no way he could think of going to Boston College.

After Boeheim left, Chris was noticeably excited. Finally, a school that on the surface seemed to have everything: big-time basketball, away from home, but not too far.

The last coach to visit was O'Brien. He brought a gallon of ice cream and an easy smile into the house. He certainly didn't have to sell himself. He didn't really have to sell the school. He certainly didn't have to sell Cynthia Herren, who always had believed that of all the coaches, Jim O'Brien had her son's best interests at heart. He talked about how he saw Chris as a combination guard, someone to play a little point one minute and some second guard the next.

O'Brien knew that sentiment in Fall River was against Chris's going to Boston College, and he tried to sell the fact that Chris and Boston Collge were a match for a number of reasons, not the least of which was familiarity.

Al Herren's main concern was that BC was too close to Fall River, just an hour up Route 24, and that Chris's Fall River friends would be a constant distraction. O'Brien countered by saying that if Chris came to Boston College, he wanted to impose an edict that his friends would be banned from the campus from Sunday through Thursday nights, a proposal that Chris didn't particularly like because he felt it didn't give him enough credit to be able to control his life.

"I'm not Michael," he said, the frustration in his voice. "Why does everyone think I'm going to do what he did?"

"I know you're not Michael," Al Herren said. "But these are real issues here that have to be addressed."

"Well, I don't want to hear them," said Chris.

It had been a strange visit, full of too much unresolved history, but then again, BC was the familiar school. In Chris's mind, going to BC was the equivalent of staying home, of opting for the comfortable. Unlike the other coaches, O'Brien didn't have to impress him or make him feel comfortable. He didn't even have to bring the ice cream.

By mid-October Chris had narrowed his list down to four: Florida, Wisconsin, Syracuse, Boston College. These were the four schools he would visit, although there was no reason to officially visit BC, since he'd been there so many times in the past.

And just as everything appeared to finally be going along smoothly, Chris tried out for football. No matter that he had never played football in his life. Or that it already was in the middle of the football season. Or that there was no football tradition at Durfee, few crowds, the antithesis of basketball. This year's team was the best in years, and one day he decided he wanted to play. He had friends playing; he wanted to play with them. So there he was one day, all dressed up in pads, at football practice.

"I can't wait to start hitting people," he said to me, the most animated he'd been since school had started. "I can't wait to play against New Bedford."

"But you've never played before," I said.

"So what? I'll catch passes."

"Do you understand what's at risk here?"

"I can get hurt crossing the street," he said.

He seemed adamant about it. He had made his decision and now he guarded it with the rigidity of someone who had just turned eighteen.

Enter Skippy Karam.

"Do you believe this?" he asked, shaking his head in mock exasperation. "I thought I had seen it all in thirty years. One of the best high school basketball players in the country and in the middle of October of his senior year he decides he wants to play football. Who could make this shit up?"

Karam discovered an obscure rule that said in order to play in a football game a player must have practiced at least fifteen days, and he told Chris that as athletic director, he was going to make sure it was enforced. Chris, upset at Karam, realized that by the time he'd be eligible to play, there would be only three games left in the season and it wouldn't be worth it.

"I know people are going to think I'm doing this because I want him for basketball, but that's not it," Karam said. "If he were a sophomore and he wanted to play football, fine. But not now. He has too much to lose."

Chris Herren's football career had ended.

But why had he wanted to play in the first place?

Had it been merely what he'd verbalized, the desire to play with his friends instead of sitting in the stands and watching them, a quick decision made by a high school senior who seemed to live in the moment and damn the conse-

quences? Had it been the search for some socially accept-
able outlet in his desire to hit people, a vehicle to release his
increasing irritability? Or was it simply a self-destructive decision, a symbolic statement that, for whatever reason, he
was finding it more and more difficult to live up to the role
everyone had placed him in?

Or was it all of the above?

His first visit was to Florida, the school that seriously had
recruited him first. He loved it, the campus and the weather
and the coaches and everything about it. He left seeing himself there next year, the only negative being that coach Lon
Kruger was recruiting him as a second guard, and he had envisioned himself as a point guard in college, believing that at
six-foot-two he had to be a point if he ever was going to have
a future in basketball past college.

The second visit was to Wisconsin, flying with his father
to Madison. He loved it. Loved the campus and the coaches
and everything about it. When he walked into the locker
room, the lights dimmed and a single light shone on a locker.
In the locker was a uniform with his number on it. A tape
played, one in which an announcer broadcast a game, complete with crowd noise, in which Chris Herren hit the winning shot that sent Wisconsin to the Final Four. He was
given large, blown-up press clippings of his success at Wisconsin.

He liked those things, was impressed by them. They
meant that Wisconsin was serious about him.

The only negative came when he was in Camp Randall
Stadium following a big win over Michigan in football, a
tragic day when many students were trampled during an out-
of-control celebration when the game ended. Herren was
frightened by the spectacle.

Several weeks later, only a few days before the November signing period when high school seniors can sign letters
of intent, he visited Syracuse, and at the conclusion of the

weekend he thought he was going there. He loved the Carrier Dome, the apartments the players lived in, the tradition, the nightlife along M Street, the fact that Syracuse was one of the country's glamour programs. Syracuse played every year in Boston, in Providence, in Connecticut, places where everyone in Fall River could travel to see him play. Plus it was only a six-hour ride from Fall River, an hour flight from Boston. He viewed Syracuse as a school away from home, but not too far away, certainly not like Florida or Wisconsin. Just a couple of days before the signing period was to start, Syracuse seemed to be it.

The Syracuse coaching staff believed he was coming too. Boeheim had thought Syracuse and Herren were a perfect fit; he needed a guard and Chris seemed to want a big-time school where he could start right away. The day after Chris returned from Syracuse, longtime assistant coach Bernie Fine called Karam's office, wondering why Chris hadn't called him to say he was committing to Syracuse.

But the next morning Leo Papile came down to Fall River and met with Chris, his father, and his brother. They met at a breakfast place on Meridian Street. The night before, Chris had gone to sleep thinking he was going to Syracuse; he had woken thinking about Boston College. Papile, who always had advocated BC, envisioning a sort of BABC alumni club there, knew what buttons to push. Papile talked to Chris about staying home, playing in front of his family and friends; of playing with Mickey Curley; of maybe someday also playing with BABC teammates Scoonie Penn and Wayne Turner; of the familiar. When he'd finished talking, Chris Herren was going to Boston College.

Not that anyone knew it. Ron Stewart of Florida continued to call Karam's office. So did Stan Van Gundy of Wisconsin and Bernie Fine of Syracuse. They kept asking Karam what Chris was going to do, and more specifically, why wasn't he calling them back? Karam tried to finesse them on the phone, but the truth was he didn't know either.

...... 347

"Do you think the kid might tell me what he's doing?" Karam asked.

The next day the Boston *Globe* ran a story that said Chris was going to Syracuse. The Providence *Journal* reported he was going to Boston College. Still, no one really knew for sure. He seemed to keep changing his mind by the day.

He had chosen the gym at the Talbot Middle School for the press conference because it was the home of the Milliken League, the traditional spawning ground for basketball in Fall River. His brother and Papile had arranged it. The school is between Eastern Avenue and Route 24, close by Watuppa Pond on the eastern end of the city, in the middle of a small residential neighborhood of wood-frame houses.

The press conference was scheduled for 6 o'clock and by 5:45 there already were about two hundred people in the gym, a sense of expectation in the air. Three television trucks stood in the parking lot. On the court a Milliken League game was taking place, two teams in blue and orange uniforms running up and down the court, the kids about ten years old. all Herren already was giving an interview to the local cable television station. Cynthia Herren sat in the bleachers, relieved the whole thing was finally over. In one corner was Leo Papile, down from Boston. He was talking to Karam, who gazed out over the gym at the people sitting expectantly, the guys carrying the TV cameras, everything looking like Hillary Rodham Clinton was going to walk in at any minute, and quipped, "This is a little different than in 1953 when I announced I was going to prep school."

Chris stood over in another corner with his brother, getting more and more nervous by the minute. He was wearing baggy dungarees, a jeans jacket, and a white cap.

"I don't know if I'm ready for all these cameras," he said, taking a deep breath. He looked terrified, pale and drawn. Gone was the self-assurance he so often played with. Now he was a high school senior faced with a major press conference, and realizing it was going to be more difficult than taking the ball to the hoop against some kid from Somerset.

"Just relax, Chrissie," Michael said. "You know what you want to say."

A couple of minutes later he walked out to the center of the court. In front of him were nearly a dozen TV cameras and photographers. Behind him were some of the most important people in his life: his mother and father; his brother; his grandfather; Karam and Dempsey; his teammates, Pavao, Mikolazyk, Caron, Callahan. Even Mike Cioe, home on leave from the Air Force.

As Chris stepped to the microphone, Eggie McRae, one of his teammates at BABC, gave him a maroon and white Boston College cap. He put it on and turned to face the phalanx of cameras.

So much for the suspense.

"My brother went to Boston College and I feel very comfortable with Coach O'Brien and have a good relationship with him," he said into the microphone.

He turned and hugged his brother, and was quickly whisked away to an assortment of interviews, another step in the media waltz.

"I'm relieved the whole recruiting thing is over," he said to one of the reporters. "At times I was very sick of it. I didn't realize how mentally and physically draining it would be."

Over in the corner by the door was Caron.

"I knew he'd go to BC," Caron said. "I knew he'd never leave."

Never leave.

In the end, ultimately, after all the letters and all the phone calls, after all the coaches' visits to Fall River and his visits to Florida, Wisconsin, and Syracuse, after all the endless speculation and rumors, Chris had not wanted to leave the Fall River world he was so much a product of. He had

...... 349

chosen the same school his brother had once chosen, for two reasons: He felt comfortable with Jim O'Brien, and it was close to home.

Never leave.

Boston College would not be the University of Fall River that Chris, deep in his heart, had wanted all along, but it was close enough. Close enough. An hour from home. Just up Route 24. It was all on his terms now, and that's what he had become accustomed to in the city that idolized him. Now he could leave home without leaving his cocoon, without ever having to put his glory days at Durfee behind him. Without ever having to face starting over, moving on. For, win or lose at Boston College, Chris's Durfee days would be there forever, where the little boy in him wanted them, a city-sized set of crutches he could keep in the periphery of his vision as he exploded down the lane for a basket, there to support him if he fell.

Never leave.

Chris continued to go from interview to interview. In between, little kids would come and ask him for autographs and he would sign pieces of paper, their shirts, anything. He sat in the middle of the television lights and the kids stared at him, the wonder on their faces.

"I'm very happy with my decision," said Chris Herren to one television sportscaster.

Behind him, the Milliken League game had started again, a backdrop to his interview, little boys in blue and orange uniforms. They played with all the passion and intensity of kids, diving on the floor, cheering when someone made a basket, caught up in the exuberance of the moment, running up and down the court, visions of the future dancing in their heads. All chasing their own Fall River dreams.

Epilogue

ALL THE SENIORS, with the exception of Mike Cioe, who joined the Air Force, started college in September of '93. Eric Santos went to Bridgewater (Massachusetts) State, where he made the baseball team. Chris Campbell entered the University of Miami, Matt Boardman began at Northeastern in Boston, John Eagan started at the University of Massachusetts in Amherst, and John Jones entered Castleton State, where he made the basketball team.

Peter Pavao started at Bristol Community College, virtually across the street from Durfee, but dropped out before the end of his first semester since he had fallen behind after severely hurting his ankle in a fight shortly after school started. In the summer of 1995 he was working in his aunt's gas station in nearby Swansea and was still thinking about going to school.

Kevin Mikolazyk also began at Bristol Community College, but quickly dropped out. In January of 1994 he visited the University of Massachusetts in Amherst with plans to go to school there, but came back to Fall River a few weeks later. He flirted with the idea of going to a junior college in Boston, maybe even trying to play basketball, for he'd discovered he missed the sport more than he ever thought he would, but by the summer of 1995 he was working in a diner in Fall River.

The '93–94 Durfee season began with great expectations for a state championship, but the team lost by one point in the semifinals of the South Sectional to Catholic Memorial of Boston.

Dan Callahan had a good senior year, was the third leading scorer, and was looking at a prep school for the following year. Shawn Thames started and Steve Breese made the varsity. Peter Suneson didn't play much, but he was accepted to Columbia, which recruited him to play football.

Jeff Caron went over the 1,000-point mark in his high school career in February of '94, but by the end of the season he still had not been offered any Division II scholarship. He couldn't understand it, endured a frustrating time, and in the fall of '94 entered UMass as a non-scholarship player.

Caron was on the basketball team for a while, but quickly realized he wanted a situation in which he could play, and left UMass at the end of the first semester. He came back home and started taking some courses at Bristol Community College. He also began writing letters to Division II schools in New England, letting them know of his availability. In February of 1995 Caron was offered a scholarship by Merrimack, where he planned to go in the fall.

Amidst much fanfare, Skip Karam announced in February of '95 that he was retiring as the Durfee coach at the end of the season. More than a thousand people came to his testimonial at the Venus de Milo in nearby Swansea in late June, where the guest speakers were Kentucky coach Rick Pitino and UMass coach John Calipari. By this time Bob Dempsey already had been named the new Durfee coach, and Abe White had announced his retirement as official scorer.

Chris Herren broke his brother Michael's all-time Durfee scoring record, and in his last game in the Luke Urban Field House reached the 2,000-point mark for his high school career. On February 27, 1994, at halftime of a nationally televised college basketball game, he was selected to the 1993–94 McDonald's High School All-American team. That March, Boston College surprised the basketball world by upsetting North Carolina and reaching the Final Eight of the NCAA Tournament, and Herren looked forward to playing for BC in the fall of '94.

Herren immediately liked everything about BC, and didn't go back to Fall River for the first month. He said he wanted to concentrate on school and distance himself from home. He felt comfortable with his new teammates and was targeted to be the starting point guard as the Eagles went through pre-season practice. He was one of the youngest players featured in *Sports Illustrated*'s cover story "The Big East Is Back" in the magazine's college basketball issue, complete with a full-page picture of him in his maroon BC uniform superimposed on Boston's Fanueil Hall. The caption read, "BC's Herren could become as big in Beantown as Fanueil Hall."

But it wasn't to be.

In his first game against Cal-Poly at BC's Conte Forum, in which he was starting point guard, Herren fell going to the basket late in the first half and hurt his left wrist. Although he came back and played in the second half, it was discovered afterward that he'd severely injured the ligaments and would need surgery. He was out for the entire year and became a medical red-shirt. His wrist was placed in a cast that went to his elbow, and for the first time since his childhood, Chris Herren spent a winter not playing basketball.

At first, he tried to put a positive spin on his situation. He told the Boston newspapers he was going to be at Boston College for four more years, and that he already had come to terms with being out for the year.

But it was more complicated than that.

Without basketball, Herren quickly seemed to lose his focus at BC, missing too many classes and showing little interest in his academic work. Much of what his father had feared when he'd decided to go to Boston College had come true: His friends from Fall River were visiting him at BC, his grades were declining, and he couldn't seem to put his hometown behind him. In the late spring, shortly before the school year ended at Boston College, there were stories in the Boston papers about rumors that Herren was considering transferring.

"I think I need to get away and get a fresh start," Herren said. "It's all closing in on me here."

He already had begun looking for another school. Very

soon into the process he got a call from Jerry Tarkanian, the new coach at Fresno State. The controversial Tarkanian, who had built the University of Nevada at Las Vegas into a national power and won the national title in 1990, had resigned from UNLV in June of 1992 after innumerable troubles with the NCAA.

Now Tarkanian had surfaced at Fresno State with designs of quickly turning the California school into a national basketball power. Herren visited in May, a few days after he finished the second semester at Boston College, and liked what he saw and heard from Tarkanian.

I saw Herren a couple of weeks before he left for Fresno State in June to go to summer school. I hadn't seen him in a while, and I immediately noticed that he looked older, not quite as boyish, as if the year had taken a psychological toll as well as a physical one on him. There also was the sense that for the first time in his life his behavior had jeopardized his basketball; he was becoming aware of how fragile careers can be.

He was upbeat, though, had already put his lost year at Boston College behind him, and was looking forward to going out to California. He said he understood he was getting another chance, maybe his last one, to be the kind of college basketball player everyone around him thought he could be. As a transfer, though, he would have to sit out the '95–96 season. He would have three years of college eligibility remaining.

As fate would have it, on the morning he was leaving Fall River, he ran into Karam in the parking lot of a local convenience store. The two embraced, and Karam wished Chris luck.

"Chrissie," Karam said. "There's nothing here in Fall River for you anymore."

"I know," said Herren.

Then he got into a car, heading for Logan airport in Boston and the plane that would take him to California.